The Catholic Worker after Dorothy

Practicing the Works of Mercy in a New Generation

Dan McKanan

LITURGICAL PRESS
Collegeville, Minnesota

www.litpress.org

Cover design by Steven Heymans

1   2   3   4   5   6   7   8   9

Library of Congress Cataloging-in-Publication Data
McKanan, Dan, 1967–
    The Catholic worker after Dorothy : practicing the works of mercy in a new generation / Dan McKanan.
      p.   cm.
   ISBN-13: 978-0-8146-3187-4
   1. Catholic Worker Movement.   2. Christian sociology—Catholic Church. I. Title.
BX810.C395M35   2008
267'.182—dc22

                              2007030125

Contents

Introduction

Still Going On

We cannot love God unless we love each other, and to love we must know each other. We know Him in the breaking of bread, and we know each other in the breaking of bread, and we are not alone any more. Heaven is a banquet and life is a banquet, too, even with a crust, where there is companionship.

We have all known the long loneliness and we have learned that the only solution is love and that love comes with community. It all happened while we sat there talking, and it is still going on.

—Dorothy Day[1]

Indeed, it is still going on. Three generations after its founding, and a full generation after the death of its founder, the Catholic Worker movement is as vital as ever. At hospitality houses in nearly one hundred fifty cities, and farms in more than a dozen other places, the battered survivors of addiction and urban decay talk and break bread with idealistic college students, charitable churchgoers, and full-time Workers who have given their lives to the vision articulated by Dorothy Day and Peter Maurin when they began publishing the *Catholic Worker* on May Day 1933. It

1

is a vision as old as the Gospel. In Matthew's vision of the Last Judgment, Jesus tells the righteous sheep that they will inherit the kingdom because "I was hungry and you gave me food, I was thirsty and you gave me drink, I was a stranger and you welcomed me, I was naked and you clothed me, I was sick and you visited me, I was in prison and you came to me" (Matt 25:35-36). Following this teaching, Catholic Workers have built a movement around the practice of what they call the "works of mercy"—attending directly to the physical and spiritual needs of the strangers and guests in whom they glimpse the face of Christ.

It is a rare thing for a movement of this sort to last three-quarters of a century. One influential study of communal groups in the nineteenth century classified communities as "successful" if they endured for a single twenty-five-year generation and nevertheless identified twice as many "failures" as "successes."[2] Even among the successful communities, many collapsed—sometimes in spectacular dissension—within a few years of the founder's death. Yet in the years since Dorothy Day's death in 1980, the number of hospitality houses associated with her movement has more than doubled, and the number of local communities that are themselves more than twenty-five years old has increased tenfold. Though longevity is certainly not the only measure of success, the Catholic Worker's endurance is a token of the relevance Dorothy Day's vision has had for generations other than her own.

It is a rare thing, also, for a new religious movement to preserve its original structure and vision for the better part of a century. Throughout its history, the Roman Catholic tradition has spawned intense spiritual movements that have dramatically transformed themselves by the second or third generation. The Franciscan movement, for example, began as an alternative to traditional monasticism in which lay men and women would take the whole world as their cloister, yet within a decade or two of Francis's death his followers wore habits, lived in convents, accepted priestly ordination, and followed a rhythm of daily prayer that was scarcely different from their Benedictine and Cistercian neighbors. The Waldensians, emerging around the same time, preserved their vision of lay discipleship only by severing ties to the Catholic Church, transforming themselves into a renegade heresy isolated from the mainstream of society. Yet the Catholic Worker has maintained a fierce commitment to the "lay apostolate" while preserving a life-giving, if sometimes tense and ambiguous, connection to the larger Catholic community.

It is a rare thing, finally, for a community's third and fourth generations to attract as much attention from scholars and admirers as the glorious age of the founders. On this score, perhaps, the Catholic Worker does not represent such an exceptional case. Despite the phenomenal growth of the movement since Day's death, books and articles about Day herself continue to pour from the presses at a faster rate than studies devoted to her movement. Many otherwise informed observers of religion in America continue to perceive the Catholic Worker as an expression of Depression-era radicalism; more than a few continue to wonder, "Whatever happened to the Catholic Worker?" The two most widely cited studies of the Catholic Worker—one of them published two years after her death—bring the story to a conclusion well before the end of her life, while two more recently published essay collections devote more than two-thirds of their space to Dorothy Day, Peter Maurin, and the houses of hospitality founded in the 1930s.[3]

This book represents one small attempt to respond to this puzzling situation. My purpose is twofold. I hope, first, to offer a general account of the Catholic Worker movement that takes the past few decades as seriously as the founding generation and that takes the houses and farms spread across the nation as seriously as the New York houses of hospitality. Many scholars have, understandably, concluded that such a general account of the Worker movement is impossible given the diversity of its expressions. They may well be right. Yet many people who have spent time at one Worker house have an immediate sense of familiarity when they enter another. The key to this familiarity, I contend, is that throughout the movement the works of mercy—concrete acts of care for the "least of these"—function both as a defining practice and a hermeneutical principle. One cannot claim to be a Catholic Worker unless one is practicing the works of mercy, and for most Workers the works of mercy are not merely a practice but also a way of seeing the world. The Catholic Worker's commitment to the works of mercy, moreover, is what allows it to be diverse and inclusive: simply by feeding the hungry and clothing the naked the Worker has been able to welcome not only the whole of the Catholic Church, both "conservatives" and "liberals," but also the whole of the American Left, both "secular" and "religious," "radical" and "reformist." Indeed, much of its abiding significance lies in its capacity to sustain a decades-long dialogue between the Church and the Left.

My second goal is to identify some of the key factors that have allowed the movement to survive, relatively unscathed, for such an extraordinary span of time. This story has much to do with Dorothy Day: though the movement is deeply indebted to Peter Maurin's ideas and she always insisted on his status as cofounder, it was her leadership and not his that sustained the movement for its first half century. Unlike many charismatic leaders, moreover, Day led in a manner that prevented a significant crisis after her death. Paradoxically, I contend, this was because she consistently took more interest in the people who were drawn to her movement than in the preservation of the movement itself. On those occasions when she tried to "lead" directly, by appointing subordinates or setting boundaries, her efforts almost always backfired. But as a mentor, friend, and teller of stories about her own mentors and friends, she inspired thousands of people to devote their lives to the works of mercy.

The story of the Catholic Worker's survival is thus also the story of those thousands of people. In the early years, especially, many Catholic Workers were drawn to the movement by a direct encounter with Dorothy Day's intense interest and friendship. Increasingly, though, the national web of Workers began to form friendships among themselves. By the early 1970s, in particular, a generation of Workers had emerged who were able to learn from one another what it might mean to make a lifelong commitment to the works of mercy. Dozens of these individuals are still feeding the hungry, welcoming the stranger, and comforting the afflicted as this book goes to print. The story of this generation of friends has scarcely been told, and in this short volume I will not be able to do it justice. Ultimately, though, they deserve as much credit for the endurance of the Worker as Dorothy Day herself. They are, moreover, the ones who have handed Day's legacy on to the new generation that is now adapting the Worker vision to the twenty-first century.

In the chapters to follow, I will flesh out the story of Dorothy Day and the movement she befriended in two ways. Part 1 is organized chronologically, with chapters devoted to the four major "generations" of the Catholic Worker movement. In each chapter, I begin with the character of Dorothy Day's leadership during a specific historical period, then sample the diverse ways individuals and communities responded to that leadership. The history I present is far from exhaustive; there are a great many stories that I do not know or did not have space to tell. But the examples I have chosen should illustrate the diversity and creativity that has always characterized the movement.

In part 2, I turn to a thematic analysis of three especially interesting aspects of the relationship between Dorothy Day and the Catholic Worker movement. Chapter 5 examines the Catholic Worker's unique alternative to the "rules" that govern many religious communities: Dorothy Day simultaneously encouraged her followers to create their own evolving rules and provided them with more enduring guidance through a distinctive style of hagiography. Chapter 6 challenges the widespread perception that Dorothy Day did not intend for families to be part of the Catholic Worker movement. On the contrary, I suggest, she always believed it was possible to combine family life with the works of mercy, and this conviction provided a firm foundation for the many families who participate in the movement today. Chapter 7 considers the complex relationship between the Catholic Worker and the Church, with particular emphasis on such hot-button issues as women's ordination, homosexuality, and abortion. I challenge the view that these issues were not widely debated in the movement prior to Dorothy Day's death, but more important, I suggest that the hermeneutic of the works of mercy has always allowed Catholic Workers to see these issues in a distinctive way. Finally, in my conclusion I consider the future of the Catholic Worker, arguing that the works of mercy still have the potential to transform American society.

The Works of Mercy as Practice and Hermeneutic

I have suggested that the works of mercy are the heart of the Catholic Worker movement. In this sense, Peter Maurin was surely right to say that the philosophy of the Catholic Worker was "so old that it looks like new," for the idea of the works of mercy comes straight out of the Gospel of Matthew. In the midst of a long discourse of parables, Jesus' teaching takes an apocalyptic tone. "When the Son of Man comes in his glory," he begins,

> and all the angels with him, he will sit upon his glorious throne, and all the nations will be assembled before him. And he will separate them one from another, as a shepherd separates the sheep from the goats. He will place the sheep on his right and the goats on his left. Then the king will say to those on his right, "Come, you who are blessed by my Father. Inherit the kingdom prepared for you from the foundation of the world. For I was hungry and you gave me food, I was thirsty and you gave me drink, a stranger and you welcomed me, naked and you clothed me, ill and you cared for me, in prison and you visited me." Then the righteous will answer him and say, "Lord, when did we see you hungry and feed you, or thirsty and give you drink? When did we see you a stranger and welcome you, or naked and clothe you? When did we see you ill or in prison, and visit you?" And the king will say to them in reply, "Amen, I say to you, whatever you did for one of these least brothers of mine, you did for me." (Matt 25:31-40)

A few aspects of this passage are worth noting. First, it offers a pointedly communal vision of salvation. No one is saved or damned alone; rather, the sheep (and, later, the goats) are brought forward and addressed as a group. They are commended, moreover, for their service to another group, the "least brothers" of Christ. These two groups, however, are not fully conscious of themselves as groups. The sheep are surprised to learn that they have been feeding, housing, and caring for Christ; they, apparently, did not realize who the "least brothers" were. There is no suggestion that the sheep shared a common theology or ideology. Their identity as a community stems entirely from their common care for an anonymous Christ.

The idea that care for the anonymous Christ could provide a basis for community was an important influence on the early monastic movement. Saint Benedict, for example, made hospitality central to his *Rule,* adding that "great care and concern" should be shown for the poorest guests, "because in them more particularly Christ is received."[4] By the Middle Ages, the specific examples given by Jesus became the basis for a standard list of seven "corporal works of mercy": feeding the hungry, giving drink to the thirsty, clothing the naked, sheltering the homeless, visiting the sick, ransoming the captive, and burying the dead. To this was added a parallel list of "spiritual works of mercy": instructing the ignorant, counseling the doubtful, admonishing sinners, bearing wrongs patiently, forgiving offenses, comforting the afflicted, and praying for the living and the dead. These lists were presented in countless sermons and devotional books and became an integral part of medieval Christian spirituality.

Centuries later, Catholic Workers can readily connect their daily practices to these two lists. The "Hippie Kitchen" at the Los Angeles Catholic Worker, for example, feeds the hungry at a daily meal for more than a thousand people. Haley House in Boston has sheltered the homeless in a variety of transitional housing programs over the years and has recently partnered with a family shelter to create a housing development in which families and seniors, poor and middle-income people will build community together. In Alderson, West Virginia, the Catholic Worker community visits women prisoners at the nearby Federal Prison Camp and provides hospitality to their friends and families. Following in the footsteps of Dorothy Day's original *Catholic Worker* newspaper, most local communities publish newspapers or newsletters to "instruct the ignorant." For thirty years, Catholic Workers from Des Moines have traveled to the Strategic Command center in Nebraska to "admonish the sinners" responsible for the threat of nuclear weapons; when they are arrested for these protests they are able to "bear wrongs patiently." In the Polk Street neighborhood of San Francisco, Temenos Catholic Worker comforts the afflicted by providing sacramental and pastoral ministries to "those who find themselves abandoned and isolated in their suffering, in particular male and female sex workers and homeless gay/lesbian/transgender youth."[5]

Such practices are far from incidental to the identity of Catholic Worker communities. Practicing "the works of mercy . . . is our program, our rule of life," declared Dorothy Day on one occasion.[6] In one of her first attempts to encapsulate the vision of the movement, she identified "the two age-old techniques—*voluntary poverty* and *the Works of Mercy*" as key to the Catholic Worker's "philosophy of labor."[7] A later statement of "Catholic Worker Positions" identified "the Sermon on the Mount (Matthew 5:38-48) and the call to solidarity with the poor (Matthew 25:31-46) as the heart of the Gospel message."[8] Perhaps most provocatively, the website of Casa Juan Diego, the Catholic Worker community in Houston, invites viewers to click on a link to its "Mission Statement" that takes them to the New American Bible's text of Matthew 25:31-46.[9]

Because of the Catholic Worker movement's deep commitment to the works of mercy, it is often perceived as a "charitable" organization, concerned more with social service than with social change. Yet Catholic Workers have always resisted such an understanding. As a young socialist, prior to her conversion to Catholicism, Dorothy Day had been deeply critical of charity as a means of concealing and thus perpetuating social injustices.

Even after her conversion, she "felt that charity was a word to choke over. Who wanted charity? And it was not just human pride but a strong sense of man's dignity and worth, and what was due to him in justice, that made me resent, rather than feel proud of so mighty a sum total of Catholic [charitable] institutions."[10] Gradually, though, she gained a new insight into the transformative potential of directly caring for others. "We consider," she wrote in 1940, "the spiritual and corporal Works of Mercy and the following of Christ to be the best revolutionary technique and a means for changing the social order rather than perpetuating it. Did not the thousands of monasteries, with their hospitality change the entire social pattern of their day? They did not wait for a paternal state to step in nor did they stand by to see destitution precipitate bloody revolt."[11]

This position reflected the Catholic philosophical tradition of personalism, one of the greatest influences on both Peter Maurin and Dorothy Day. According to Emmanuel Mounier, the French thinker who coined the term, personalism began with the affirmation that the human person, created in the image of God, is "an absolute in comparison with any other material or social reality . . . and can never be considered merely as a part of a whole, whether of family, class, state, nation or even humanity."[12] Mounier's emphasis on the person made him deeply skeptical of the modern tendency to invest more and more power in the centralized state, and both Peter Maurin and Dorothy Day pressed this skepticism to the point of rejecting all state-sponsored programs of social service. It was the impersonal charity of "Holy Mother the State," they believed, that perpetuated an unjust status quo, while the practice of caring for the poor "at a personal sacrifice" had the potential to create an entirely new community. Maurin drew the contrast pointedly in one of his most frequently quoted "easy essays":

> In the first centuries of Christianity
> the poor were fed, clothed, and sheltered
> at a personal sacrifice

and the Pagans
said about the Christians:
"See how they love each other."
Today the poor are fed, clothed, and sheltered
by the politicians
at the expense
of the taxpayers.
And because the poor
are no longer
fed, clothed, and sheltered
at a personal sacrifice
but at the expense
of taxpayers
Pagans say about the Christians:
"See how they pass the buck."[13]

Not everyone who serves soup or sweeps floors at a Catholic Worker house of hospitality would agree that there is no place for taxpayer-funded charity. But virtually all would agree that they have been changed by their practice of the works of mercy. Much more than writing a check to the United Way or the Internal Revenue Service, taking personal responsibility for the needs of the stranger changes the way one sees the world.

When Catholic Workers must spend hours standing in line to help their guests receive a few dollars worth of food stamps, they gain new insight into the destructive consequences of weapons systems that cost billions of dollars. Many have traveled from the soup kitchen to the picket line as the result of such experiences. At the same time, the practice of "bearing wrongs" and seeing Christ in guests who are often unpleasant or abusive helps Catholic Workers to recognize the human dignity of the soldiers, police officers, generals, and politicians who are often the target of their protests. At many antiwar protests, Catholic Workers take the lead in engaging their opponents at a personal level, striking up conversations rather than taunting them with harsh invective. As a result of such experiences, the works of mercy have come to function not only as the unifying practice of the Catholic

Worker movement but also its hermeneutical principle—its way of interpreting both the past and the present.

As a hermeneutical principle, the works of mercy help account for the extraordinary depth of the Catholic Worker movement. Catholic Workers readily make connections among seemingly diverse issues, linking the crisis of homelessness to Cold War military budgets and to the experiences of gay and lesbian Catholics who feel bereft of their church home. They are also quick to place their practices within the centuries-old tradition of the Church, appealing to the Benedictine integration of work and prayer, to Saint Francis's vision of life-giving poverty, or to John Chrysostom's suggestion that every family provide a "Christ room" for one stranger in need of shelter.

At the same time, the works of mercy have made possible the movement's equally extraordinary breadth. For if everyone sees the world anew after practicing the works of mercy, not everyone's vision is changed in the same way. In the practice of breaking bread with the poor, many Catholic Workers have discovered the true meaning of the Eucharist and have been drawn to make daily communion part of their spiritual discipline. Others have decided, on the basis of the same experience, that the Eucharist is superfluous—that the true communion is every shared meal. For some Catholic Workers, likewise, the experience of life in a house of hospitality proves the personalist dictum that state welfare programs are a threat to human dignity, while others have been led to work for the dramatic expansion of such programs. Even the War on Poverty can be traced to the years its principal architect, Michael Harrington, spent at the New York Catholic Worker.

It might seem that such diverse conclusions should have ripped the movement apart years ago. But the peculiarly unifying genius of the Catholic Worker lies in the fact that everyone can practice the works of mercy. One does not need to be a Catholic or a Christian to welcome the stranger, even though the Catholic Worker movement as a whole might see this action as a welcoming of Christ. One does not need to be a pacifist to calm the tensions that sometimes break out in the soup line, even though other Catholic Workers may see such actions as preparation for civil disobedience at military bases. One does not even need to live in a Catholic Worker community, as Dorothy repeatedly pointed out, to practice the works of mercy within one's individual life.

Day's insistence that anyone can practice the works of mercy suggests part of the reason that I do not regard "voluntary poverty" to be as definitive of the Catholic Worker as the works of mercy. This is a risky claim, because Day herself almost invariably linked the two concepts. The works of mercy, she believed, were transformative only if they were practiced "at a personal sacrifice," and this entailed a life of simplicity, in which one did without superfluities and luxuries in order to ensure there was enough to share. Both Day and Maurin emphasized the distinction between poverty of this sort and the "destitution" experienced by persons without enough to eat or places to sleep. By embracing the poverty of simplicity, Day and Maurin believed, people could create a world in which no one would be destitute.

Yet a great many Catholic Workers have not practiced voluntary poverty in this sense. On the one hand, many part-time volunteers—the people who come once a week to serve a meal or join the full-time Workers on the picket line—do not aspire to practice poverty at all but may be wealthy, middle-, or working-class people aspiring to prosperity. On the other hand, many full-time Workers have chosen lifestyles that would better be described as "destitute" than "poor." "Instead of poverty," recalled Stanley Vishnewski, who spent more years at the New York Catholic Worker than any other person, "I was given a taste of destitution. For weeks I have gone without a penny in my pocket. I have known what it is to eat horrible, ill-tasting meals. I have worn cast off clothing and ill-fitting shoes."[14] Despite her clear understanding of the difference between poverty and destitution, Day regularly told stories that glorified such experiences, reinforcing a traditional Catholic piety that treated ascetic poverty as an end in itself rather than a means to justice. Drawing on such stories, one historian has even argued that Day "proposed self-dissolution as the goal and essence of Catholicism."[15] Though this judgment is surely one-sided, it is not entirely wrong.

Fortunately, Day's pursuit of simple holiness is more widely imitated in the movement today than her quest for self-dissolution. Most Catholic Workers work hard to balance their own needs with the needs of the people they serve, though some feel that in so doing they are not living up to Day's heroic standard. The point I would stress, though, is that in most cases the practice of the works of mercy must come *before* an authentic commitment to poverty. Prosperous volunteers, for example, must experience the satisfaction of serving others before they can begin thinking about simplifying their own lifestyles. Those who are initially attracted to ascetic self-denial, moreover, gradually realize the value of showing mercy to themselves and—as it often works out—to their children. The trick, as Catholic Worker Larry Purcell has wisely suggested, "is to love your kids so much that you want what you have for them with the homeless. Not like you want to treat your kids like you treat the homeless, but that you want the homeless to have what your kids have."[16]

Catholic, Leftist, and American

The capacity of the works of mercy to transform different sorts of lives helps explain the historical significance of the Catholic Worker: it is the place where the American Catholic Church, taken as a whole, has encountered the American Left, also taken as a whole. In forging a vision for their movement, Day, Maurin, and their early companions drew on an extraordinary range of other Catholic movements, many of them anticipating the renewal of the Second Vatican Council. They were among the most devoted readers of papal encyclicals on social issues, as well as of the distributist writers who taught that the Catholic vision could best be fulfilled in a decentralized rural economy. From the nascent liturgical movement, they imbibed a vivid sense of the liturgy's capacity to transform the social order and a keen awareness of the Church (and all of humanity) as the Mystical Body of Christ. Jacques Maritain reminded them of Thomas Aquinas's doctrine of the common good. The retreat movement of Father Onesimus Lacouture inspired them to aspire to the personal holiness of the saints. Drawing on these rich traditions, Dorothy Day was a Benedictine oblate, a practitioner of Franciscan poverty, and a lover of the Eastern rite liturgy. She corresponded with Thomas Merton, professed her loyalty to the Cold War cardinal Francis Spellman, attended the Second Vatican Council with an ecumenical group of pacifist women, and bemoaned what she saw as a lack of reverence in the post-Vatican II church. Day first joined the Catholic Church because of its inclusiveness—"it held the allegiance of the masses of people in all the cities where I had lived"—and both she and her movement embraced all of it.[17]

Yet the Catholic Worker has never been exclusively Catholic in its inspiration or its membership. Dorothy Day spent her young adulthood as a socialist journalist, and to the end of her life she professed admiration for the ideals and the discipline of the Communists and anarchists she met during those years. At least a few of Day's radical friends continued to associate with the Worker into the 1960s. The anarchist martyrs Sacco and Vanzetti were regularly commemorated in the pages of the *Catholic Worker,* and the movement's approach to labor organizing was as indebted to the "one big union" of the International Workers of the World as it was to the social encyclicals. (One of the Worker's most memorable slogans, "to build a new society within the shell of the old," was borrowed from the Wobblies.)

In its pacifism, moreover, the Catholic Worker stood within one of the most venerable traditions of the American Left. Its American roots go back to William Lloyd Garrison and Adin Ballou, radical abolitionists who took the Sermon on the Mount as a binding rule while discarding most of the doctrinal heritage of Christianity. The Catholic Worker embraced Gandhian methods of civil disobedience years before they were embraced by the civil rights movement, and at least some Catholic Workers were quite conscious of the chain of influences connecting Gandhi to Leo Tolstoy to Garrison and Ballou. In the last years of her life, Dorothy Day was a fierce advocate of E. F. Schumacher's "small is beautiful" philosophy. And despite her personal commitment to Christian anarchism, her socialist sympathies were catholic enough that she paid a friendly visit to Fidel Castro's Cuba.

The recent history of the Worker reveals an equally broad engagement with both the Church and the Left. In the years after Vatican II, Catholic Worker communities were among the first to sponsor informal house liturgies, and in more than a few cases allowed lay women and men to preside at house Eucharists. Catholic Workers have been deeply involved in such "liberal" movements as Call to Action and Voice of the Faithful and have been among the most vocal proponents of gay and lesbian liberation in the Church. But in the 1970s the Catholic charismatic revival and the *cursillo* movement also led many idealistic young Catholics to the Worker, and in more recent years the Worker communities in Houston and South Bend have been among the most enthusiastic admirers of Popes John Paul II and Benedict XVI. Though many Catholic Workers refuse to vote, the Worker influenced both the anti-Vietnam War presidential candidate Eugene McCarthy and more recent candidates for the Green Party and Canada's New Democratic Party. The Worker has also helped to connect non-Christian traditions to the American Left. Boston's Haley House Catholic Worker is an important center for Buddhist peace activism. One of the first Jewish thinkers to declare himself a theologian of liberation, Marc Ellis, was decisively shaped by the year he spent at the New York Catholic Worker as a young adult, just as one of the first thinkers to publish a gay theology of liberation, Richard Cleaver, is a longtime Catholic Worker and (more recently) a priest in a gay-friendly branch of Orthodox Christianity.[18] In the spirit of *Nostra aetate* (the Vatican II declaration on non-Christian religions), the Catholic Worker has always identified the "Mystical Body of Christ" not only with the Church but also with the worldwide community of people who have welcomed Christ by feeding the hungry and welcoming the stranger.

What the Catholic Worker Is Not

I have suggested that the works of mercy provide the vital heart of the Catholic Worker movement, and that the movement's historical significance is as a vital meeting ground for both the entirety of the American Catholic Church and the entirety of the American Left. In making these claims, I also intend to challenge a few misconceptions about the Worker movement that are common both among Workers themselves and among the larger public. The first is that the Catholic Worker is essentially a thing of the past: that the movement achieved its glory days during the Great Depression, nearly collapsed as a result of the Second World War, and has remained a shadow of its former self ever since. In fact, I will show that for the past forty years the movement has included more people, in far more places, than it ever did in its first decade. This is largely the work of an outstanding generation of friends who came to the Worker during the Vietnam War, encountered the warm and empowering support of Dorothy Day, and learned together how to make the Worker a lifelong commitment.

A second misconception is that the movement experienced a dramatic break at the time of Dorothy Day's death, to the extent that much of what goes on in the Worker today represents a stark alternative to the original vision of Day and Maurin. Closely related to this is the view that that original vision was essentially a blend of conservative Catholicism and radical politics. If this were true, then certainly the previous point would also be true, for few Catholic Workers today are conservative Catholics. But from the beginning, the Catholic Worker represented a synthesis of Catholicism *as a whole* with the American radical tradition, and particularly with its anarchist strand. It is true that Dorothy Day's Catholic sensibilities were conservative in certain respects: she held great respect for the hierarchy and even greater respect for the saints, and she cherished aspects of the pre–Vatican II liturgy. But in these respects she was a typical mid-twentieth-century Catholic, and her movement at mid-century attracted a cross section of Catholics of that era. Since Vatican II, the movement has continued to attract a cross section of American Catholics, and that cross section now includes neo-traditionalists, Call to Action reformers, and "cultural Catholics" who no longer attend Mass. As was the case from the beginning, the Worker's blend of Catholicism and radicalism also leaves plenty of space for Catholics who aren't especially radical and radicals who aren't Catholic in the slightest.

A third misconception is that there are just two basic models of Catholic Worker community: the urban house of hospitality, in which single volunteers share life with large numbers of homeless persons, and the rural commune or "agronomic university," in which formerly homeless people create a self-sufficient life on the land. These two models do, in fact, correspond to the reality of the two New York City hospitality houses and to the ideal sought (but never achieved) by the farms directly associated with those houses. But Dorothy Day never claimed that one had to live in a community like these in order to be a Catholic Worker. On the contrary, she held that the Catholic Worker is open to anyone who practices the works of mercy in her or his particular circumstances, with due regard for her or his particular vocation. Indeed, as I will argue later in this book, Day was especially supportive of the many families that were drawn to the Catholic Worker ideal.

A final misconception is that the Catholic Worker can best be understood as the antithesis of some other thing. A variety of attempts have been made to define the movement by antithesis. The Catholic Worker, some would say, promoted "justice" rather than traditional Catholic "charity." Others suggest that its agrarian and medievalist interpretation of Catholic social teaching was starkly opposed to the work of John Ryan and others who sought to make industrial society more just. Some say that the Catholic Worker's "old" style of Catholic pacifism was challenged in the 1960s by the "new" pacifism of Daniel and Philip Berrigan, or that its "radicalism" was superseded by the "revolutionary" vision of liberation theology. Such antitheses are not surprising, for both Peter Maurin and Dorothy Day occasionally presented their ideas in antithetical form. Ultimately, however, Day's habits of friendship trumped any inclination to set the Worker in fundamental opposition to other groups or ideologies. Labor leader John Cort, War on Poverty architect Michael Harrington, and "ultra resistance" priest Daniel Berrigan all represent ideologies that have sometimes been set in opposition to the Catholic Worker, but they were also dear friends of Dorothy Day whose views are shared by many Catholic Workers today. What's more, the works of mercy have always created a platform for people of diverse ideologies—or no ideologies—to participate in the daily work of the Worker.

There is one antithesis, however, that is not so easily dismissed. Many observers have drawn a sharp line between the "radicalism" of the Catholic Worker and the more tepid "liberalism" of mainstream American society. This antithesis traces back to Peter Maurin, whose "easy essays" were filled with jabs at liberals:

> Liberals
> are too liberal
> to be radicals.
> To be a radical
> is to go to the roots.
> Liberals
> don't go to the roots;
> they only
> scratch the surface.[19]

Maurin's hostility to liberalism is echoed in the analyses of both longtime Workers and more dispassionate historians.

Geoffrey Gneuhs of the New York Catholic Worker, for example, describes attempts to associate the Catholic Worker with liberalism and the Left as a "gross misreading [that] not only reveals a lack of understanding of the Catholic Worker but also diminishes the radical critique of modernity and the liberal bourgeois world that is at the heart of the Catholic Worker and the orthodox Catholic faith of Dorothy Day."[20] Michael Baxter, a Holy Cross priest who has been associated with Catholic Workers in both Phoenix and South Bend, explained it more poetically in his interview with Rosalie Riegle: "You know, the Catholic Worker is not a liberal movement. It's a radical movement, and there's a sharp difference. Liberals say, 'Hey! The homeless aren't being fed. Let's march on City Hall.' Radicals say, 'The homeless aren't being fed. Let's feed them.'"[21] And historian James T. Fisher, author of one of the few studies of the Catholic Worker that does not explicitly champion the movement, challenged earlier studies that linked the Catholic Worker to the Americanization of immigrant Catholics. The "view of the Catholic Worker movement as a sign of the Church's security in America," wrote Fisher, "obscures Dorothy Day's original intent, which was radically separatist."[22]

Given the amount of emphasis both Maurin and Day put on the word "radical," this antithesis deserves some unpacking. Its validity depends, to a large extent, on the precise meaning one ascribes to the word "liberal." At the most basic level, liberalism is linked to individual liberty and, by extension, to individualism. The Catholic Worker emphasis on the Mystical Body of Christ is often presented as an antidote to the rampant individualism of American society. Some Catholic Workers would even extend their critique of individualistic liberalism to ideologies, particularly feminism and gay liberation, that they (rightly) see as indebted to the liberal tradition. The problem, of course, is that feminism and gay liberation are very much alive and well in the Catholic Worker movement. Many, probably most, Catholic Workers see no contradiction between efforts to liberate women, gays, and lesbians from unjust traditions and the simultaneous project of building a new, "beloved community" in which all are free. One of the deepest insights of Catholic Worker personalism is that authentic individual freedom and genuine community are not opposites, but interdependent. And this idea is not a monopoly of Catholic personalism: many of the best exponents of the American Left, from the communitarian wing of the Transcendentalists through the Social Gospelers and on to the civil rights movement, have insisted that there is no ultimate opposition between individual freedom and communal solidarity.

Other Catholic Worker critics of liberalism identify it not with individualism but with "reformism"—that is, with efforts to make existing social institutions more just rather than to build a new society within the shell of the old. From this perspective, liberalism is not the polar opposite of radicalism, but simply a watered-down variant of it. This sort of antithesis informs, for example, the refusal of many Catholic Worker communities to apply for federal nonprofit status or to receive support from governmental programs, and the movement has developed a profound body of writing criticizing reformist approaches to social evils. It would certainly be a mistake to regard the Worker as primarily a movement of social reform! And yet the Catholic Worker practice of the works of mercy has inspired such well-known social reformers as Eugene McCarthy and Michael Harrington, and even many Catholic Worker communities have sought government funds to feed the hungry and house the homeless.

Michael Baxter's comment about liberals marching on city hall might be interpreted as a critique of reformism, but it also contains a deeper level of analysis. The problem with liberalism, from Baxter's (and Gneuhs's) perspective, is not only that it is willing to work within the "system"—and particularly with the militarist state—but that in so doing it subtly reinforces the power of systems and states. When liberals march on city hall, or on the White House, they contribute to the mistaken belief that city hall and the White House are truly the centers of power. This argument is indebted to the critique of liberalism developed by Alasdair MacIntyre and Stanley Hauerwas, according to which the modern state, with its monopoly of violence and tremendous destructive potential, and the modern corporation, with its unconstrained devotion to profit, emerged only because liberal movements for individual freedom had broken down the traditional, more human-scaled structures of family, village, craft guild, and church, as well as the transcendent reference point of orthodox Christianity. From this perspective, the unrestrained corporate capitalism espoused by the Republican Party and the welfare stateism championed by the Democrats (and, more fully, by most Western European societies) are the twin children of classical liberalism, and both are opposed to the common good.[23]

This book is certainly not the place for a full response to this argument. But even if one concedes the liberal roots of both capitalism and the omnipotent state, it is worth asking whether they are the only heirs of classical liberalism. Much of the American Left, and particularly the anarchist tradition that has been so important for the Catholic Worker, has at least as strong a claim to the liberal mantle. Pure anarchists (if there is such a thing) are adamantly opposed to hierarchy wherever it may be found—in state, corporation, church, or family. The position espoused by Baxter—and by Peter Maurin and Dorothy Day—might best be understood as a variant on pure anarchism, for it rejects not hierarchy per se, but the idolatrous and self-serving hierarchies of institutions that refuse any transcendent point of reference. At least since the late 1950s, this sort of anarchism has coexisted with the more classical variety in the Catholic Worker movement. If, as I suspect, there is some measure of truth to be found in both strands of anarchism, as well as in the reformism espoused by such renegade Workers as John Cort and Michael Harrington, then it is a great and good thing that the Worker practice of the works of mercy has created a community in which advocates of all three positions can meet and learn from one another.[24]

Leadership through Friendship

It is also something of a wonder that the Catholic Worker has endured so long, when its defining practice brings together such strange bedfellows. Yet the Worker has endured for

three-quarters of a century, all the while maintaining its identity as a decentralized lay movement in which families, individuals, and small communities practice the works of mercy
in a wide variety of urban and rural settings. Some observers
have marveled at the movement's avoidance of the process of
bureaucratization that Max Weber saw as the inevitable fate of
new religious movements after the death of a charismatic
founder.[25] But the more remarkable fact is that it has not simply
disintegrated into hundreds of local houses and farms, without
any sense of connection to a larger movement. After all, as
Dorothy Day often pointed out, one does not need to be part
of a movement to practice the works of mercy. Any family, any
parish, perhaps any individual can take personal responsibility
for the "least" of Christ's brothers and sisters without signing
up as a Catholic Worker.

Yet herein lies the key to the Catholic Worker's endurance:
it has never really tried to endure. While many short-lived radical
movements have sought to usher in the kingdom of God within
a generation, the Catholic Worker declared from the beginning
that "success" was not its highest priority. "What we do is so
little we may seem to be constantly failing," Day explained in
1940. "But so did He fail. He met with apparent failure on the
Cross. But unless the seed fall into the earth and die, there is no
harvest."[26] A fervent admirer of Saint Thérèse of Lisieux, Dorothy
Day consistently advocated the "little way" and urged Worker
houses to remain as small as possible. The consequence of this
stress on smallness and lack of concern for success is that the
Catholic Worker movement has rarely been so turned in on itself
as to become cut off from the larger world. Following Dorothy
Day's example, Catholic Workers have always been interested
in the works of mercy wherever they have been practiced, and
as a result countless practitioners of the works of mercy have
become interested in the Catholic Worker.

Dorothy Day, I believe, deserves much of the credit for the
endurance of the Catholic Worker movement not because she
was a powerful, charismatic leader—though she was that—but

because she modeled a practice of friendship that reached beyond the boundaries of her movement. As a journalist with a roving spirit, she traveled widely, and everywhere she traveled she befriended people who were practicing the works of mercy. Though some of these friends eventually made their way to the New York Catholic Worker, she counseled most to craft their own communities in response to local needs, and she then passed on the New York houses' excess donations to these fledgling communities. When individuals left the movement, even if the reason was a sharp ideological disagreement, she stayed in touch and publicized their future accomplishments. "The gold moves on," she declared repeatedly, "and the dross remains." She took a lively interest in other efforts to practice the communitarian ideals of the Gospel, from Koinonia and Taena in the 1950s to Sojourners in the 1970s. Though she never tried to turn these communities into Catholic Workers, many became integral parts of the Catholic Worker network, initiating young people who would go on to join or found Catholic Worker communities. Some movements that have been perceived as rivals to the Catholic Worker—most notably the "ultra resistance" movement of the Berrigan brothers in the 1960s—have eventually become sources of renewal for the Worker, simply because Dorothy Day and other Workers have treated them as friends rather than as rivals.

This is not to say that Dorothy Day did nothing to promote the institutional survival of the Catholic Worker. In fact, it was Peter Maurin who most fully embodied the values of smallness and openness to failure that Day espoused. His practice, during all the years he was associated with the movement, was simply to outline his "program" and provide a personal example of a life of scholarship and manual labor, then leave it to others to follow suit or not. If an academic host mistook him for a plumber, he would quietly sit in the basement rather than give a planned talk about the Worker. When conflict broke out in the movement, Maurin repeatedly counseled Day simply to walk away, leaving projects and property to her antagonists. He himself walked out on her when he first realized that the *Catholic Worker* newspaper would include a variety of perspectives on social justice, rather than devoting itself entirely to the publication of his "easy essays." Had Day always followed Maurin's example, the Catholic Worker movement may never have gotten off the ground.

Dorothy Day was, by contrast, both strong-willed and charismatic. She drew people to the Worker by the force of her personality and sometimes by her physical attractiveness. Once they were in, she did not hesitate to tell them what to do—with the soup or with their lives. Tom Cornell has often commented that Dorothy Day wanted to be an anarchist but only if she got to be the "anarch," while Michael Harrington recalled that the early Worker "was run on a führer concept, and Dorothy was the führer."[27] On occasion, she expelled volunteers unilaterally and without explanation or berated them and then made up awkwardly with flowers.[28] More than a few Workers, especially in the New York houses, were scarred by Day's authoritarian streak. But her authoritarianism had little influence on the movement beyond New York. The one time she seriously tried to assert her authority on a national level, the attempt backfired. This occurred a few months before the Japanese attack on Pearl Harbor, when the United States was gearing up for what would be by far the most popular war in its history.

Dorothy Day had first articulated her pacifist commitments in the pages of the *Catholic Worker* during the Spanish Civil War; since that struggle pitted socialists against conservative Catholics, her stance partly reflected her refusal to choose between Catholicism and socialism. Many of her supporters in roughly thirty Worker communities founded during the Depression thus expected her stance to soften in the face of a war in which both Catholics and socialists were fighting against the threat of Nazism. Throughout the 1930s the Catholic Worker had spoken out more vigorously against anti-Semitism than virtually any other Catholic organization. Yet even as Nazi tanks rolled across Europe, the *Catholic Worker* published headline after headline denouncing military conscription and declaring the Sermon on the Mount its manifesto of nonviolence. When some local houses began refusing to distribute the paper, Day dug in her heels, writing a strongly worded circular letter insisting that houses that would not circulate the New York paper should disassociate themselves from the movement. A great many did so willingly, while others shut down because their leading volunteers had enlisted in the military. Within a span of three years, the movement had shrunk from a peak of nearly forty communities to just ten. Many observers assumed that it was only a matter of time before it would collapse completely.

Dorothy Day never publicly admitted that she had been wrong to insist on the pacifist character of her movement. Indeed, it may be that this early instance of authoritarianism ultimately served the movement well. In the context of the Korean, Vietnam, and Iraq wars, the fact that the Catholic Worker had maintained its pacifist commitment even in the most challenging circumstances gave it immense prestige among peace activists. Yet she never again chose to impose a boundary on the movement as a whole. Instead, she slowly and steadily built it back up again through supportive visits and correspondence with the handful of houses and farms that were still in operation at the end of the war. When later houses expressed support for the revolutionary violence of the 1960s or challenged aspects of the Catholic tradition that she treasured deeply, she persistently reaffirmed her pacifist and Catholic commitments but also maintained a supportive dialogue with any community that committed itself to the works of mercy.

One consequence of this hands-off approach is that Catholic Worker communities have always been diverse in their organizational structures, and this diversity has been one key to the endurance of both individual communities and the movement as a whole. Day's personal preference was for the "Benedictine" model, in which a fatherly abbot (either male or female) exercises an authority that is deeply attentive to the individual needs of each member of the community. Especially in the Depression years, Dorothy sometimes took it upon herself to appoint (or replace) "house managers" to play this role in local houses of hospitality. Both then and later, this structure has worked well in many places, in part because it allows a house to sustain itself for many years even if most of its volunteers are willing to commit to only a year or two of full-time service. Many, perhaps most, of the Catholic Worker communities that have lasted more than a decade have been anchored either by a charismatic founder or by a couple for whom the Catholic Worker house is also a family home. On the other hand, local communities of this sort have almost never outlived the "abbot" figure or figures.

In many places, moreover, Catholic Worker communities have not been able to identify even one individual who is willing to make the Catholic Worker a full-time, lifelong vocation. Another common model, therefore, is for a cluster of part-time volunteers—usually referred to as the "extended community"—to provide the continuity for a house whose full-time staff people typically serve for only a year or two. Several of the communities utilizing this model are formally registered as 501(c)(3) nonprofit corporations, and the extended community members are organized as formal boards of directors. This is a controversial approach within the movement, for Dorothy Day considered even this degree of cooperation with "Holy Mother the State" to be a violation of personalist principle. Yet the three most enduring houses of hospitality outside of New York City—Saint Joseph's House in Rochester, New York, Blanchet House in Portland, Oregon, and Benedict Labre House in Montreal—all established nonprofit boards early in their history. Dorothy Day did less to support these communities than those adhering to the first model, but she never attempted to force them out of the movement. (Blanchet House did choose to disassociate itself from the movement early in its history.) More recently, a number of small houses of hospitality have found that extended community can provide a sustaining structure even without formal nonprofit status.

Most Catholic Workers, I suspect, would find both these models—longevity based on a single leader or couple and longevity based on extended community or a formal board—less than ideal. Explicitly or implicitly, most houses aspire to forge a self-sustaining community of full-time Workers who have made a long-term commitment. In this model, no one individual is indispensable: people may come and go quite frequently, but enough others remain to keep the newcomers connected to the house's identity and tradition. However sought after, this model of shared leadership has rarely been achieved in the movement. To my knowledge, none of the first generation of Catholic Worker communities was able to sustain itself on this basis. Even the New York houses relied on Day's charismatic leadership for most of their history and underwent extended periods when there were no live-in Workers with more than a year or two of experience. (The New York houses today come closer to the ideal.) It was only in the 1960s that a number of houses began to achieve a sustainability rooted in a common communal life. As a result of their achievement, a number of communities today come close to the ideal: the Des Moines Catholic Worker, the Loaves and Fishes community in Duluth, Haley House in Boston, to name a few with which I am familiar. Yet their achievement should not obscure the equally significant work being done by the many communities that still rely on the abbot or extended community model.

Just as a local house can achieve sustainability in a number of ways, so can a movement. During both the ferment of the movement's first decade and the fallow period from 1945 to 1965, Dorothy Day's charismatic leadership was the glue of the movement. Most communities, in other words, had more intense relationships with Day herself than they did with other communities in the movement. By the time of her death in 1980, however, the movement had successfully evolved into a genuine "community of communities," relying on one another for support and encouragement in difficult times. In this model, no one community—not even New York—is indispensable for the survival of the movement, for there are always many others to which a struggling community may turn in time of crisis.

To make the point somewhat differently, beginning in the late 1960s the Catholic Worker movement as a whole began playing the friendship role that Dorothy Day had honed in the previous decades. Individual Catholic Workers traveled frequently from house to house, sharing much more than recipes for soup. The "Catholic Worker tour" of existing houses became a common exercise for those who wished to start Catholic Worker communities of their own. A series of regional and national gatherings, many providing opportunities for intense bonding through shared civil disobedience, helped Catholic Workers form and sustain life-giving friendships. Remarkably, no individual and no community presumed to step into the leadership vacuum that had been left by Dorothy Day. Yet perhaps it would be better to say that almost everyone did so: because so many individuals and communities took personal responsibility for some of the tasks needed to sustain a vital movement, there was no need for a central leader or bureaucratic structure to take charge of all of those tasks. In the last years of its founder's life, the Catholic Worker movement became what Dorothy Day had always said it was: an organism rather than an organization. And as such it has endured.

[1] Dorothy Day, *The Long Loneliness* (New York: Harper, 1952), 285–86.

[2] Rosabeth Moss Kanter, *Commitment and Community: Communes and Utopias in Sociological Perspective* (Cambridge, MA: Harvard University Press, 1972). This study has justly been criticized for equating longevity with success.

[3] William Miller, *A Harsh and Dreadful Love: Dorothy Day and the Catholic Worker Movement* (New York: Liveright, 1973); Mel Piehl, *Breaking Bread: The Catholic Worker and the Origin of Catholic Radicalism in America* (Philadelphia: Temple University Press, 1982); Patrick G. Coy, ed., *Revolution of the Heart: Essays on the Catholic Worker* (Philadelphia: New Society Publishers, 1988); and William Thorn, Philip Runkel, and Susan Mountin, eds.,

Dorothy Day and the Catholic Worker Movement: Centenary Essays (Milwaukee: Marquette University Press, 2001). A more comprehensive picture of the movement can be found in Rosalie Riegle Troester's oral history, *Voices from the Catholic Worker* (Philadelphia: Temple University Press, 1993), which is the best starting point for any reader interested in the Catholic Worker movement as a whole. My previous study, *Touching the World: Christian Communities Transforming Society* (Collegeville, MN: Liturgical Press, 2007), focuses on both the contemporary Catholic Worker and the Camphill Movement.

[4] Timothy Fry, O.S.B., ed., *The Rule of Saint Benedict in English* (Collegeville, MN: Liturgical Press, 1982), 74.

[5] "Los Angeles Catholic Worker: Who We Are," http://lacatholicworker.org/who-we-are/; "Housing," at http://www.haleyhouse.org/housing.htm; "Alderson Hospitality House," http://www.catholicworker.org/communities/commdetail.cfm; "The History of Stratcom," at http://www.desmoines catholicworker.org/stratcom.htm; and "The Mission of Temenos," http://www.temenos.org/mission/index.html.

[6] Day, "On Pilgrimage," *Catholic Worker* 13, no. 5 (June 1946): 1–2, 8. Searchable access to Day's columns and other writings in the *Worker* is available online at http://www.catholicworker.org/dorothyday/.

[7] "Aims and Purposes," *Catholic Worker* 6, no. 7 (January 1939): 7.

[8] "'Making a path from things as they are to things as they should be'— Peter Maurin," *Catholic Worker* 45, no. 4 (May 1979): 4–5.

[9] "About Casa Juan Diego," at http://www.cjd.org/cjd.html.

[10] Day, *Long Loneliness,* 150.

[11] Day, "Catholic Worker Ideas on Hospitality," *Catholic Worker* 7, no. 8 (May 1940): 10.

[12] Emmanuel Mounier, *A Personalist Manifesto,* trans. Monks of Saint John's Abbey (New York: Longmans, 1938), 69.

[13] Peter Maurin, "Passing the Buck," available at http://www.catholic worker.org/roundtable/easyessays.cfm. The collection of "easy essays" was also published as *Easy Essays* (Chicago: Franciscan Herald Press, 1977).

[14] Stanley Vishnewski, *Wings of Dawn* (New York: Catholic Worker, 1984), 230.

[15] James T. Fisher, *The Catholic Counterculture in America, 1933–1962* (Chapel Hill: University of North Carolina Press, 1989), 47.

[16] Lawrence Purcell, interviewed by Chris Gamm, 14 July 2000.

[17] Day, *Long Loneliness,* 139. The best overview of the specifically Catholic sources for the Catholic Worker movement is Mark and Louise Zwick, *The Catholic Worker Movement: Intellectual and Spiritual Origins* (Mahwah, NJ: Paulist Press, 2005).

[18] Marc H. Ellis, *Toward a Jewish Theology of Liberation* (Maryknoll, NY: Orbis, 1987); and Richard Cleaver, *Know My Name: A Gay Liberation Theology* (Louisville, KY: Westminster John Knox, 1995).

[19] Peter Maurin, "Not Liberals but Radicals," *Easy Essays,* 156–57.

[20] Geoffrey Gneuhs, "Radical Orthodoxy: Dorothy Day's Challenge to Liberal America," in Thorn et al., *Dorothy Day,* 205.

[21] Michael Baxter in Troester, *Voices,* vi.

[22] Fisher, *Catholic Counterculture,* 72.

[23] For a fuller presentation of this argument, see Michael J. Baxter, C.S.C., "'Blowing the Dynamite of the Church': Catholic Radicalism from a Catholic Radicalist Perspective," in Thorn et al., *Dorothy Day,* 79–94.

[24] One recent study that attempts to reconcile the radical and reformist strands in Catholic social ethics, with specific reference to Mike Baxter and the Catholic Worker, is Kristen E. Heyer, *Prophetic and Public: The Social Witness of U.S. Catholicism* (Washington, DC: Georgetown University Press, 2006).

[25] Michele Teresa Aronica, R.S.M., *Beyond Charismatic Leadership: The New York Catholic Worker Movement* (New Brunswick, NJ: Transaction Books, 1987).

[26] "Aims and Purposes," *Catholic Worker* 7, no. 6 (February 1940): 7.

[27] Michael Harrington, cited in Troester, *Voices,* 131.

[28] Terry Rogers, cited in Troester, *Voices,* 88.

Part I

Four Generations of Catholic Workers

Chapter 1

The Founders

The story of the Catholic Worker begins with the interest Dorothy Day took in Peter Maurin—an eccentric, brilliant, self-absorbed, and boundlessly generous French peasant whom she found waiting in the kitchen of her New York City apartment on December 9, 1932. Catholic Workers still delight in telling the story: Day had just returned from Washington, D.C., where she had been covering a Communist hunger march for the Catholic journal *Commonweal*. Impressed by the earnestness of the marchers and saddened by the fact that her new Catholic faith prevented her from participating, she had also stopped at the National Shrine of the Immaculate Conception to offer "a special prayer . . . that some way would open for me to use what talents I possessed for my fellow workers, for the poor."[1] Perhaps in answer to that prayer, Peter Maurin had sought out Day on the recommendation of both the editor of *Commonweal* and one of her Communist friends, who had told Maurin that they thought alike. As he would do to countless Workers after, Maurin immediately began "indoctrinating" Day, telling her of the social encyclicals, of personalist philosophy, and of his own "three-point-program" for a "green revolution" that would bring about a society in which "it is easier for people to be good."

Despite his eccentric manner, Maurin immediately impressed Day. "Peter," she would explain in her autobiography, "made you feel a sense of his mission as soon as you met him. . . . He aroused in you a sense of your own capacities for work, for accomplishment. He made you feel that you and all men had great and generous hearts with which to love God."[2] These words say as much about Day as they do about Maurin. She had an intuitive sense of saintliness, even when it came in strange disguises, and an intense desire to see the heroic potential of every person whom she met. Maurin was woefully incapable of bringing his ideas to fruition, but Day immediately grasped the connection between his vision and her background as a socialist journalist. Their vocations, she realized, could flow together in the project of a newspaper that would bring his ideas to the unemployed workers who filled the streets of New York. Though Maurin quickly proved himself to be an erratic coworker, his vision was inspiring enough to guide her through a six-month process that culminated in the publication of the first issue of the *Catholic Worker* on May Day 1933.

In the throes of the Great Depression, American Catholics were eager for a new vision, and the fledgling paper achieved a circulation of 100,000 by its first anniversary. It then fell upon Day and Maurin—but especially upon Day—to begin implementing the three points of Maurin's program. He had called for "roundtable discussions for the clarification of thought," and so they rented a series of meeting rooms for presentations on such topics as "The History of Nationalism," "Cultural Interests vs. Business Interests," scholastic theology, Jewish spirituality, and racial justice. He had called for "houses of hospitality" to practice the corporal works of mercy, and so when unemployed Workers began arriving at their apartment, they made room, eventually sponsoring houses of hospitality for both women and men. Finally, Maurin had called for farming communes or "agronomic universities" where unemployed urban workers would find a more fulfilling life on the land, and the division between "workers" and "scholars" would be abolished. Accordingly, the first Catholic Worker farm—really more of a garden—was established on Staten Island, and in 1936 the Workers purchased a more substantial property in Easton, Pennsylvania. Though the precise locations have changed repeatedly, for seventy years the New York Catholic Worker has always included at least one farm and one or two urban houses of hospitality.

As editor of the *Catholic Worker,* Dorothy Day publicized all of these ventures, as well as printing and reprinting the "easy essays" in which Peter Maurin laid out his own vision or synopsized the ideas of philosophers who had inspired him. Maurin, in fact, had originally imagined that the paper would consist of nothing but his own writings, but Day had wisely resisted him on this point. Instead, the paper became a vehicle for her wide-ranging interests and sympathies. Despite Peter's insistence that "strikes don't strike me," she covered dozens of strikes, establishing her paper as one of organized labor's best friends in the Catholic Church. Like her former Communist associates, she covered the trial of the "Scottsboro boys," a group of Southern blacks who were being tried on dubious charges of rape. She covered the Spanish Civil War, espousing a pacifist stance that irritated both socialist supporters of the Loyalists and Catholic supporters of Franco. And she wrote adamantly against anti-Semitism, both as it was expressed in the rising Nazi government of Germany and in the popular radio sermons of Father Charles Coughlin.

None of these topics was calculated to build up the Worker's local projects in New York City. But Day's capacity to see the heroism in other people's projects, even if those people did not share her religious convictions or economic theories, made it easier for those others to take an interest in her work. Soon she began combining her journalistic travels with talks at Catholic universities, and everywhere she spoke she encountered earnest young people who wanted to participate in the budding movement. She quickly honed the advice she would give to new Catholic Workers for the next forty years. Start where you are: identify the gifts and needs present in your neighborhood, and practice the works of mercy there. Stay small: remember that massive houses of hospitality would not be necessary if everyone took personal responsibility for those around them. Honor your vocation: choose the work where you feel the most joy, and don't be afraid to move on in response to the spirit's call. Accept failure: remember that God's work is like a seed that must fall to the ground before it can bear fruit. These simple ideas, repeated time and again, empowered individuals and communities to craft countless variations on the Catholic Worker ideal, while remaining in fruitful dialogue with both Day herself and one another.

As a national movement, the Catholic Worker grew at a remarkable rate during its first decade. Between the launch of the newspaper in 1933 and the attack on Pearl Harbor in 1941, at least forty-three houses of hospitality or farms sprang up in locations as diverse as Boston, Los Angeles, Aitkin, Minnesota, and Houma, Louisiana.[3] Day's commitment to local self-determination is reflected in the fact that this first generation of Catholic Worker houses anticipated almost the full range of variants that are present in the movement today. There were houses of hospitality in major urban centers and in smaller cities, some managed primarily by live-in Workers and others by volunteers with more conventional lifestyles. There were actual communal farms and more traditional family farms inspired by the Catholic Worker ideal. In some Catholic Worker communities, a charismatic founder operated as an abbot, while in others authority was shared widely among a founding group. Some Catholic Workers were equally enthusiastic about care for the homeless, Catholic pacifism, and decentralist economics, while others quietly practiced the works of mercy but ignored Day and Maurin's larger social vision.

Despite these differences, most Worker communities of this era began in the same way: with a visit from Dorothy Day. Just two years after the founding of the paper, for example, Day spoke to a crowd of eight hundred people at Saint Louis University. One of those in attendance, Cyril Echele, then wrote to New York for a list of local subscribers to the *Catholic Worker,* and soon a nascent group dubbed the Campion Propaganda Committee was formed. By the following spring, Echele was at the Worker farm in Easton, Pennsylvania, but he returned to Saint Louis to launch "Catholic Worker Farming Commune NO. 2" on two hundred fifty acres of donated land. Unfortunately, 1936 was a dry summer. In what he would later call "a glorious failure," Echele "almost starved to death and even my chickens died." Meanwhile, though, the Saint Louis Workers had launched a bookstore that competed in a friendly way with a nearby Communist shop. When a customer suggested that they should dispense more than ideas, they launched a soup line, distributing day-old bread and donated coffee to the city's unemployed workers. The Worker regularly hosted roundtable discussions, and these conversations led them to agitate for the admission of African Americans to Saint Louis University, to support a sit-down strike at Emerson Electric, and to champion the ideals of the liturgical movement. Finally, in April 1938, they opened a full-fledged house of hospitality; for the next four years, this house would provide shelter for about twenty men, and food for close to three hundred, on a daily basis.[4]

If one assumes that a Catholic Worker "community" is a cluster of committed Workers voluntarily living with the poor for an extended period of time, then Saint Louis never achieved "community" status. Typically, there was just one full-time Worker at a time: Cy Echele managed the short-lived farm; Don Gallagher lived in a back room of the bookstore; Herb Welsh and Bill Camp alternated as managers of the house of hospitality. This lack of communal commitment troubled the Saint Louisans: "Our chief problem," they wrote to Day in 1939, "is that there is none of us except Bill Camp who sleeps, eats, and breathes Catholic Worker day and night." The challenge of conforming to Worker ideals became even more difficult after Nazi Germany launched World War II by invading Poland. Though the Saint Louis Worker did not repudiate Day's pacifism as publicly as the communities in Chicago and Los Angeles, both Herb Welsh and Don Gallagher quietly dissented, while Cy Echele supported his young family by taking a job in a tank factory. The booming war economy also meant that fewer people needed the services of the hospitality house. Key volunteers married or moved away from Saint Louis, and in 1942 the house closed its doors.[5]

Despite its brief and haphazard lifespan, the Saint Louis Catholic Worker had a transformative impact on many lives. "If I hadn't found the Catholic Worker, it's hard telling what I would have done," Cy Echele told a researcher in the early 1980s, while another founder said that "I don't think there's been a stronger influence in our lives." Just after the house closed, several participants formed the Saint Louis Logos Study Group, which continued to meet monthly for reflection on Catholic social teaching for more than four decades. Some of these people were still available to offer advice when a new Catholic Worker community, Karen House, was launched in 1977. This enduring impact had a lot to do with the personal interest Day took in the struggling community, for nearly everyone who met her was touched by her luminous example of Christian commitment. "She really put into practice the beatitudes more than anybody that I ever met," recalled one Worker, while another mused, "Once you waken to an appreciation of Dorothy, she gets under your skin . . . it's a rare and beautiful thing."[6]

If the Saint Louis Workers struggled to conform to the model of the New York Catholic Worker, Chicago was home to two communities that actively dissented from important aspects of Dorothy Day's vision. Yet, significantly, she retained an intense interest in both of these communities, publicizing their efforts tirelessly in the pages of the *Catholic Worker*. The first of these dissident Catholic Workers was the work of Dr. Arthur Falls, one of the few African American Catholics to take a strong leadership role in the movement. Falls began corresponding with Dorothy Day after the first issue of the *Worker* was published, and by 1935 he had his own column in the paper, the "Chicago Letter." He also persuaded Day to alter the paper's masthead, so that it would feature a white and a black workingman in a gesture of solidarity. He opened his house in 1936, shortly after a visit from Peter Maurin. From the beginning, Falls rejected the notion that one could build a new society simply by performing the works of mercy. Instead of a soup line or a hospitality house, he sponsored a credit union and a lending library of books on cooperatives and self-help for the poor. Under his leadership, the Worker became a major voice for racial equality within the Chicago Church, even as his emphasis on leading African Americans into the bourgeoisie troubled Dorothy Day and her more idealistic followers. Still, Falls's house on Taylor Street endured until 1950, in part because a dapper and eccentric house manager, John Bowers, devoted the last decade and a half of his life to the work.[7]

One of the young idealists who was turned off by Arthur Falls's version of the Catholic Worker was John Cogley. He met Dorothy Day when she visited Chicago in 1937, and by the end of the visit she had entrusted a newly rented house of hospitality to his leadership. Though that project lasted only for a summer, a year later (after a brief trial stint with the Dominicans and some time at the New York Catholic Worker) Cogley and a cluster of friends launched a large house of hospitality in an abandoned factory. They also launched what quickly became the second most significant *Catholic Worker* paper in the country. "If you have one quarter," they urged readers, spend it on a subscription to the New York paper, but "if you have two quarters take a chance on Blue Island Avenue [the address of their house], we shall do our best." The paper featured sharp attacks on Father Coughlin's anti-Semitic brand of Catholic social teaching and fervent support for the new industrial unions of the Council of Industrial Organizations. Dorothy Day was so impressed that she wrote to say that the *Chicago Catholic Worker* "far outshines our own poor effort."[8]

Despite this strong show of support, the Chicago paper helped spark the most significant crisis in the long history of the Catholic Worker, for it consistently dissented from the pacifist views that appeared with increasing prominence in the New York paper. Dorothy Day's pacifist sentiments had crystallized during the Spanish Civil War, which pitted her old socialist comrades against her Catholic coreligionists. When World War II broke out in Europe, she began publishing fierce criticisms of the new conscription law and explaining her pacifism in stridently biblical terms. "We consider that we have inherited the Beatitudes," declared one editorial, "and that our duty is clear. The Sermon on the Mount is our Christian manifesto."[9] The Chicagoans, whose personal views on the war varied, responded with an appeal to church authority and personal conscience. "Until the Pope speaks," they editorialized, "it is the right and obligation of every Catholic to form his own conscience on the issue of the war." A like-minded community in Seattle began distributing the Chicago paper in place of the *New York Catholic Worker,* and Workers in Los Angeles went so far as to burn copies of Day's paper.[10]

Such defiant actions prompted Day to issue what Chicagoan Tom Sullivan would dub "Dorothy's encyclical." In a circular letter distributed to most existing houses, she called for all heads of houses to be pacifists and urged those who "take it upon themselves to suppress the paper" to "disassociate themselves from the Catholic Worker movement." In a more conciliatory note, she added that "there is no reason why we should not be associated together as friends and fellow workers, but there is every reason for not continuing to use The Catholic Worker name."[11]

At least in Chicago, this profession of friendship was accepted as sincere and was earnestly reciprocated. A year later, John Cogley attended the movement's annual retreat, even though he knew it would be led by the adamantly pacifist Father John Hugo. Though Day's invitation to the retreat had urged participants to "drop everything, listening to the Lord who will only speak if we keep silent," Cogley engaged both Day and Hugo in vigorous debate at the retreat. Once it was over, he and his companions decided to shut down their paper out of respect for Day's leadership of the movement. A few months later, the Pearl Harbor attack propelled the United States into the war. Cogley enlisted, while his companions Jim O'Gara and Tom Sullivan were drafted. Yet both Cogley and Sullivan took time to visit Dorothy in New York before shipping out, and they corresponded with her regularly throughout the war. When she took a year's sabbatical from the Worker in 1943, she wrote about Sullivan and O'Gara's service in the Pacific, promising to "gather and hold in my prayers all those members of our family so dear to us."[12]

With its base of volunteers gone, Cogley's house of hospitality folded, as did similar communities in Boston, Baltimore, Milwaukee, and a few dozen other places. Most left in their wake a cluster of committed activists who would promote aspects of the Worker vision in other venues. Chicago's Ed Marciniak, for example, had a long career as a labor and human rights activist, culminating in his service as executive director of the Chicago Commission on Human Relations. Tom Sullivan returned from the war with a new appreciation of pacifism; he spent many years managing the house of hospitality in New York City and serving as an editor of the *Catholic Worker* before joining the Trappists in 1955. John Cogley himself had a long career as a radical journalist. Similarly, Nina Polcyn Moore of the Milwaukee house remained Day's devoted friend for decades afterward and steadfastly promoted the Catholic Worker vision at her Catholic bookstore in Chicago.[13]

A handful of early Worker communities managed to survive the war, usually because they were anchored by a single leader (or a committed couple) who had made a lifelong commitment to the Worker vision. This was the case for John Bowers at the Taylor Street house in Chicago, for Llewellyn Scott in Washington, D.C., for Mary Frecon at Saint Martin's House in Pittsburgh, for the Gauchat family in Cleveland, and for the Murphy family in Detroit. In most cases, these individuals were local versions of Dorothy Day, inspiring short-term or part-time volunteers with the depth of their Christian commitment. Unlike Day, however, none of these leaders was able to forge a self-sustaining community that could survive the founder's death. Apart from the New York houses of hospitality, the only first-generation

Catholic Worker community to survive the death of its founder was Saint Joseph's house of hospitality in Rochester, New York. Like virtually every enduring Catholic Worker community, the Rochester community survived in part because of Day's willingness to tolerate a significant departure from the New York City model.

The Catholic Worker in Rochester started early, when Dorothy Day spoke to the Catholic Women's Club in 1933. A cluster of seminarians who heard her formed a study group, and soon other clusters of *Catholic Worker* readers also crystallized. By 1937 they were distributing food and clothing and running a Sunday school program. In 1939 they obtained a house and launched a meal program that fed two hundred fifty people each day, but still had no live-in community. In 1941 the Worker moved to a new location, and took the significant step of incorporating as a nonprofit corporation. This violated Dorothy Day's anarchist principle of not cooperating with the militarist state, but it did not compromise the Rochester Workers' commitment to performing the works of mercy. Two of the original five board members moved into the house, albeit for only a short time. Throughout the war years, the house was managed by a single live-in director, with the assistance of board members and other volunteers. After the war, he left to get married but returned with his family in 1948 and stayed for another four years. By this time, the homeless guests had developed a strong sense of community, and for the next fifteen years they managed themselves, with some supervision from a board member. Though the board itself met only irregularly, its members never lost their sense of connection to the house, and in 1968 the son of the board director moved in as resident director. By this time, the Catholic Worker movement nationally was beginning to expand again, and the new director was especially committed to Worker peace activism. When his draft resistance took him away from the house, the son and daughter of another board member took over. The house almost closed in 1976, but by that time the movement was booming nationally, and a series of individuals who had experienced the Worker elsewhere began arriving to revitalize the community.[14]

Just as the communities in Rochester and elsewhere pioneered new strategies in order to survive the war years, so Dorothy Day's approach to leading the movement also evolved over the course of these years. The notorious "encyclical" on pacifism was in fact one of a series of "circular letters" that Day wrote to the local houses between 1938 and 1940. In these letters, she laid out her vision for the "lay apostolate," offering tips to people starting new houses of hospitality but also insisting that one could be part of the movement simply by taking personal responsibility for performing the works of mercy in one's own circumstances. Not all Workers needed to be at houses of hospitality; indeed, even if a hostile government were to shut down all Catholic Worker houses "our cells could never be suppressed or stopped from the works of mercy program laid down by Christ." Families could, for example, set aside one bedroom as a "Christ room" for a stranger who needed it. "The thing for us all to remember," Day wrote at Christmas 1938, "is the necessity of remaining *small* and progressing along the *little way* laid down by St. Therese." A few months later she announced the opening of several new houses but then added: "We must never cease emphasizing the fact that the work must be kept small. It is better to have many small places than a few big ones."[15]

In keeping with this advice, Dorothy Day maintained an active interest even in people who were not able to "join" the Catholic Worker movement. Indeed, one of the most decisive contributors to the Catholic Worker idea spent relatively little time at the houses of hospitality but stayed connected to the movement for nearly half a century. This was the artist Ade Bethune. Educated at a New York Catholic school, she was referred to the *Catholic Worker* by the editor of *Liturgical Arts* magazine in 1934, and her work has graced both the masthead and the pages of the newspaper ever since. A master of the woodcut, Bethune followed Maurin's advice to portray the saints as workers, and as a result she created an iconography that translated traditional Catholic devotion into a new key. But she did much more than that to sustain the movement. After establishing an art studio in Newport, Rhode Island, she welcomed a series of young Catholic Worker women as "apprentices," often conspiring with their mothers to delay early marriages. (This was the case for Day's daughter Tamar.) She also took a long-term interest in promoting the works of mercy in her own community, and Day in turn took an interest in this work. As late as 1974, Day wrote proudly of Bethune's involvement in the Church Community Corporation, whose mission was to provide "decent housing and home ownership for families of low and moderate income in Newport." This program had allowed thirty families to become homeowners, but Day also took pleasure in the fact that most of its staff were volunteers, and that a group of high school students "had the satisfaction of building one entire house." The transformative potential of the works of mercy was clearly apparent.[16]

By 1940 Day seems to have realized that offering standardized advice to all the communities was unlikely to generate this sort of commitment; in any event, the circular letters stopped. But Day began promoting what she considered a better strategy for holding the movement together: an experience that became known among Catholic Workers simply as "The Retreat." This was a weeklong silent retreat, developed by the Canadian Jesuit Father Onesimus Lacouture, that combined the Ignatian *Spiritual Exercises* with a strong emphasis on the study of Scripture. (Participants were asked to bring only a Bible and a writing pad.) The retreat offered a lofty vision of personal holiness, urging every Christian to aspire to the "counsels of perfection" that mainstream Catholicism enjoined only on members of religious orders. Participants were urged to take the Sermon on the Mount literally—to turn the other cheek and go the second mile—and to give up even minor indulgences if these stood in the way of loving Christ and the poor. In the retreat, Day explained, "We had to aim at perfection; we had to be guided by the folly of the Cross."[17]

Day first learned of Lacouture's retreat from Catholic publisher Maisie Ward, though she was more captivated when she heard of it again from Father Pacifique Roy, who began visiting the New York Catholic Worker in 1939. A Canadian Josephite stationed in Baltimore, Roy was instrumental in popularizing the Lacouture retreat in the United States, and his testimony may have inspired Day to replace the movement's biennial "colloquium" with an annual retreat. Reflecting that "we are all agreed that three days of praying together will solve more problems than three days of talk," she urged Workers to borrow whatever money they needed to get to the Easton farm in August of 1939. "It will be showing a lack of faith," she wrote in one circular letter, "to doubt it and to urge as an excuse that the money is needed for bread."[18] The result, as reported in the pages of the *Catholic Worker,* confirmed the expectation: the colloquiums had been marked by "hours of discussion" in which "problems did not seem to get settled," yet when the retreat participants broke their silence they "found such unity amongst us all, that there seemed no reason for discussion."[19] Accordingly, Stanley Vishnewski echoed Day's admonition in 1940: "With the chaotic condition of the world we cannot speak too strongly of the imperative need for making a Retreat at this time. We seek all heads of Houses of Hospitality to drop whatever work they may be doing and come to the Retreat."[20]

The first retreat was led by Father Joachim Benson and the second by Father Paul Hanly Furfey, and neither followed the Lacouture format. By 1941, though, Day and "members of our Catholic Worker family" from Milwaukee, Toledo, South Bend, Cleveland, Detroit, Pittsburgh, Baltimore, and New York had experienced the full retreat under the tutelage of Father John Hugo, whom Father Roy had recommended as the preeminent English speaking retreat master. Father Hugo was a priest of the diocese of Pittsburgh, and during the summer months he regularly conducted retreats in the empty classrooms of a Catholic orphanage. Day persuaded him to travel to the Easton farm in August 1941 to conduct a special retreat for the Catholic Worker movement as a whole. Day's insistence reached new heights as she wrote: "No material work is being accomplished by the Catholic Worker, in any part of the country, that is as important as this retreat. . . . If you are part of The Catholic Worker movement, it is your obligation." (At the same time, she asked that "only those connected with the CW movement come to the retreat" because of limited space.)[21] This retreat was repeated annually at Easton for most of the remainder of the decade, until the farm closed amidst controversy. Day personally continued to make an annual retreat for the rest of her life. Though Father Hugo was for a time restricted in his pastoral activities because of accusations of Jansenism, he retained a close tie to the Catholic Worker, and as late as 1985 a cluster of young Workers from New York City traveled to Pittsburgh for a retreat where "Father Hugo warmly welcomed the renewed presence of young Catholic Workers."[22]

Different participants reached very different judgments about the significance of the retreat. For Dorothy Gauchat of the Cleveland community, it provided an opportunity to "reach the goal of really living the way Christ wanted us to live. Living the Sermon on the Mount."[23] Yet Julian Pleasants of South Bend, who also attended the 1941 retreat, worried that Father Hugo's Jansenist emphasis on self-sacrifice did not fit with Day's deepest insights: "Father Hugo said that the best thing to do with good things was to give them up. And I just didn't think that was Dorothy's attitude at all. She didn't want to give them up, she wanted to give them *away*."[24] Even Stanley Vishnewski, for decades the most loyal member of the New York community, sensed a troubling dualism in the retreat. "As far as I could understand from making the retreat," he wrote in his memoir, "it advocated a complete renunciation of everything that was in the natural order. . . . For the love of this world is at enmity with God and he who loves the world is an enemy of God."[25]

These diverse reactions suggest that the retreat's influence on the movement may have been more mixed than historian William Miller suggested when he wrote (in 1973) that the 1941 retreat was "the high tide of the Worker movement. It was then that

Worker houses were most numerous and Worker belief in a Church-centered social reformation strongest. One hundred and twenty-five persons were there, a figure that probably still stands as the largest get-together of Workers in the history of the movement."[26] It certainly seems possible that the retreat saved the Catholic Worker movement from complete collapse by coalescing a core group of people through an intense shared experience. But undoubtedly it also accelerated the departure of those individuals who objected either to Hugo's asceticism or to his pacifism.

Diverse judgments about the retreat are still alive and well in the Catholic Worker movement. Lawrence Holben, a longtime associate of the Los Angeles Catholic Worker who published a book-length study of Catholic Worker theology in 1997, contended that the retreat had created "Gnostic divisions . . . between those who had made the retreat and those who had not" and had even left some of its most enthusiastic proponents "psychologically and spiritually wounded." Ultimately, Holben concluded, the retreat was not central to the movement as a whole because it "represented a deviation from Maurin's message, which celebrated the good things of the natural creation and our intended place in it." In a still more recent study, though, Mark and Louise Zwick of the Houston Catholic Worker insist that those who neglect the retreat miss the "spiritual base" for all of Dorothy Day's work.[27]

Whatever the retreat's effect on the movement as a whole, it had a profound impact on Dorothy Day's self-understanding, both as a Catholic and as a movement leader. "I saw things as a whole for the first time with a delight, a joy, an excitement which is hard to describe," she wrote during one retreat. "This is what I expected when I became a Catholic."[28] The retreat gave her the time to read the Bible and the lives of the saints, and to move toward a more integrated vocation as a writer and contemplative as well as a movement leader. As Mel Piehl has perceptively suggested, the retreat taught Day to emulate not only Teresa of Avila, the energetic and intellectual reformer of her order, but also Thérèse of Lisieux, the quietly contemplative advocate of the "Little Way" of prayer and small actions.[29] She learned, finally, that any outward work she might perform depended on her willingness to water her own garden. "It is not only for others that I must have these retreats," Day wrote in her autobiography. "It is because I too am hungry and thirsty for the bread of the strong. I too must nourish myself to do the work I have undertaken; I too must drink at these good springs so that I may not be an empty cistern and unable to help others."[30]

All of this happened because Day felt free to take an interest in Fathers Pacifique Roy and John Hugo, just as she had taken an interest in Peter Maurin almost a decade earlier. Neither man was a prospective recruit for the Worker movement: as priests, their primary work would always lie elsewhere. When she first met them, they were already somewhat controversial and would soon become more so; for a time, both Hugo and Father Lacouture himself were forbidden by their superiors from giving retreats. Day's account of her first meeting with Father Roy gives a lively sense both of the man's eccentricity and of her own capacity for reverence:

> We were sitting in the dining room having our morning coffee when Father Roy started to talk to us about the love of God and what it should mean in our lives. He began with the Sermon on the Mount, holding us spellbound, so glowing was his talk, so heartfelt. People came and went, we were called to the telephone again and again, but still Father Roy went on talking to all who would listen. The men came in from the soup kettles in the kitchen which were being prepared for the soup line and stayed to listen, tables were set around us and the people came in and were fed and went out again, and still Father talked, and so the day went. It was like the story in the Gospels, when the two apostles were talking on the way to Emmaus, grieving and fearful and lamenting over the death of their Leader; suddenly a fellow traveler came along and began to explain the Scriptures, going as far as the town with them and even going to an inn to break bread with them. They knew Him then in the breaking of bread. They had said to each other, 'Was not our heart burning within us, whilst he spoke in that way?'"[31]

Day's reaction to John Hugo was similar, and soon his ideas appeared in the pages of the *Catholic Worker* with as much regularity as those of Peter Maurin. In a series of front page articles that occupied as much as a third of some issues, Hugo provided a comprehensive justification for the Worker's understanding of the lay apostolate. Lamenting what he described as a "failure of Christian effort," Hugo drew a distinction (borrowed from Father Paul Hanly Furfey) between "two rules," a "minimum" and a "maximum" standard of Christianity. The minimum rule was simply to avoid mortal sin and thus achieve salvation. Though this was the advice that many Catholic preachers of the time offered to laypeople, Hugo decried it as a "misleading" and "inadequate statement of the truth" that "reduces Christian practice to the level of paganism." The alternative, which he provocatively called "totalitarian Christianity," took its starting point from the Beatitudes and Jesus's instruction to "Be ye perfect as your heavenly Father is perfect." "This is totalitarian Christianity," Hugo thundered, "the pursuit of holiness, divine holiness. All men are called to it, and the whole plan of God for men can be summarized by saying that God wills all men to have it."[32] Dorothy Day responded to this vision by repeatedly insisting that the traditional "counsels of perfection" applied to laypeople as well as to those in religious orders, and by reprinting a series of magisterial statements to this effect.[33] Hugo also penned a series of articles that articulated the most comprehensive case for Catholic pacifism that the *Worker*—or perhaps any American Catholic publication—had yet published.[34] These articles provided the theological basis for what had been a somewhat intuitive sense of pacifism on the part of Dorothy Day and ensured that nonviolent action would remain central to the work of the Worker for the rest of its history.

Just as Dorothy Day took an interest in John Hugo, so Hugo took an interest in her. For years he served as her spiritual director and confessor but also—as he said in his homily at a memorial Mass for Day—as a disciple who "went to her for counsel."[35] Perhaps the most important piece of counsel that Hugo offered to Day was that she take an entire year of retreat in order to renew her spirituality. Thus, in September 1943—as World War II raged in Europe and the Pacific, and Worker houses continued to close at an alarming rate—Day risked the complete collapse of her movement in order to devote a year to prayer and reflection. With her daughter Tamar, then a precocious teenager, she traveled first to the Grail (a Catholic women's movement located in Ohio) and then to an abandoned orphanage on Long Island, near an agricultural school that Tamar wished to attend.

Though the sabbatical wound up lasting only six months, a number of important things happened during that period. First, Day was able to confirm through direct experience something that she had long claimed—that no one individual was indispensable to the Catholic Worker movement, nor to the larger practice of the works of mercy. Second, she had time to heal some of the wounds in the movement by corresponding with the many Catholic Worker men who were serving in the military, as well as with the pacifists who had been sent to camps for conscientious objectors.[36] Third, because she had to rely on the income she received as a writer, she was able to renew her sense of her core vocation. And finally, she was able to devote more attention to another neglected vocation, that of mother. Tamar had fallen deeply in love with David Hennessy, one of the young volunteers at Maryfarm in Easton, and it was all Dorothy could do to delay the marriage until April 1944, just after Tamar's seventeenth birthday. The wedding provided the occasion for Day's return to the Catholic Worker, though in the quiet years that followed she devoted an increasing amount of attention to her grandchildren, to journal writing, and to caring for Peter Maurin, whose physical and mental health began to decline markedly at the time of the wedding.

---

[1] Day, *The Long Loneliness* (New York: Harper, 1952), 166.
[2] Ibid., 171.

[3] The numbers cited in this and subsequent chapters are drawn from a master list I compiled by consulting several sources: the files on specific communities held at the Dorothy Day/Catholic Worker Collection at Marquette University (DD/CWC); the lists of communities published in the New York *Catholic Worker* from time to time; incidental references to communities in the pages of the New York *Catholic Worker;* my personal knowledge of a few communities; and the list of currently active communities maintained at www.catholicworker.org (accessed in both 2004 and 2006). These numbers should be considered approximate for a variety of reasons. First, although many ephemeral communities appear on at least one list, there were undoubtedly others that went unnoticed by the archive, the New York paper, and the website. (I have personally identified only one community that has not appeared in any of those places.) Second, these sources don't provide clear information about exactly when (or if) a community has shut down, and the website in particular includes listings for a few communities that are definitely defunct. I do not, therefore, describe a community as surviving unless I have information beyond the mere website listing. Third, the lists include a number of entries that probably should not be classified as "communities," such as the individuals listed as Catholic Worker "cells" in the 1952 list and a handful of contemporary listings that simply advertise "rest and recreation" sites for tired Workers. Fourth, many "communities" sponsor multiple "houses," and it is not always possible to distinguish these from truly independent houses within a single city. In such circumstances, I have guessed to the best of my ability, generally erring on the side of counting distinct houses separately. Altogether, I have identified 393 local units of the Catholic Worker movement, 189 of which appear on the most current website. Though I am not at all confident that all of those 189 are still operating, I have identified at least 100 current communities that have survived more than a decade.

[4] Janice Brandon-Falcone, "Experiments in Truth: An Oral History of the St. Louis Catholic Worker, 1935–1942," in Patrick G. Coy, ed., *Revolution of the Heart: Essays on the Catholic Worker* (Philadelphia: New Society Publishers, 1988), 313–36.

[5] Ibid.

[6] Ibid.

[7] Francis Sicius, "The Chicago Catholic Worker," in ibid., 337–46.

[8] Ibid., 344–49.

[9] "Our Stand—An Editorial," *Catholic Worker* 7, no. 9 (June 1940): 1.

[10] Day mentioned the burning of the papers in an interview with James Finn, *Protest: Pacifism and Politics: Some Passionate Views on War and Nonviolence* (New York: Random House, 1967), 375, and two Los Angeles

Workers, John Hollow, Sr., and E. Virginia Newell, both apologized for the incident in letters to Dorothy Day, 6 September 1940 and 22 October 1940, DD/CWC, series W-4, box 1.

[11] Dorothy Day to "Fellow Worker," 10 August 1940, DD/CWC, series W-1, box 1; and Catholic Worker Editors to "Fellow Workers in Christ," 12 December 1941, DD/CWC, series W-1, box 1.

[12] Sicius, "The Chicago Catholic Worker," 349–51.

[13] Brigid O'Shea Merriman, O.S.F., *Searching for Christ: The Spirituality of Dorothy Day* (Notre Dame, IN: University of Notre Dame Press, 1994), 206–11.

[14] Harry Murray, *Do Not Neglect Hospitality: The Catholic Worker and the Homeless* (Philadelphia: Temple University Press, 1990), 127–33.

[15] Dorothy Day to "Fellow Workers in Christ," Christmas Season 1938, DD/CWC, series W-1, box 1; and Dorothy Day to "Fellow Workers in Christ," 21 February 1939, DD/CWC, series W-1, box 1.

[16] William Miller, *A Harsh and Dreadful Love: Dorothy Day and the Catholic Worker Movement* (New York: Liveright, 1973), 77; and Dorothy Day, "On Pilgrimage," *Catholic Worker* 40, no. 2 (February 1974): 8. For more on Bethune, see Judith Stoughton, *Proud Donkey of Schaerbeek: Ade Bethune, Catholic Worker Artist* (Saint Cloud, MN: North Star Press, 1988).

[17] Day, *Long Loneliness,* 246–47.

[18] Dorothy Day to "Fellow Workers," 9 July 1939, DD/CWC, series W-1, box 1.

[19] "C. W. Retreat," *Catholic Worker* 7, no. 1 (September 1939): 4.

[20] S. V., "Retreat," *Catholic Worker* 7, no. 10 (July-August 1940): 2.

[21] Dorothy Day to "Fellow Workers in Christ," 22 July 1941, DD/CWC, series W-1, box 1.

[22] Meg Hyre, "St. Joseph House," *Catholic Worker* 52, no. 5A (August 1985): 2.

[23] Dorothy Gauchat, in Rosalie Riegle Troester, *Voices from the Catholic Worker* (Philadelphia: Temple University Press, 1993), 19.

[24] Cited in ibid., 20.

[25] Stanley Vishnewski, *Wings of the Dawn* (New York: Catholic Worker, 1984), 213–14.

[26] Miller, *Harsh and Dreadful Love,* 188.

[27] Lawrence Holben, *All the Way to Heaven: A Theological Reflection on Dorothy Day, Peter Maurin and the Catholic Worker* (Marion, SD: Rose Hill Books, 1997), 143; and Mark and Louise Zwick, *The Catholic Worker Movement: Intellectual and Spiritual Origins* (Mahwah, NJ: Paulist Press, 2005), 247. For other reflections on the significance of the retreat, see Merriman, *Searching for Christ,* 131–69; James T. Fisher, *The Catholic Counterculture in*

America, 1933-1962 (Chapel Hill: University of North Carolina Press, 1989), 54–60; William D. Miller, *All Is Grace: The Spirituality of Dorothy Day* (Garden City, NY: Doubleday and Company, 1987), 39–150; and William D. Miller, *Dorothy Day: A Biography* (New York: Harper & Row, 1982), 335–41.

[28] Cited in Jim Forest, *Love Is the Measure: A Biography of Dorothy Day* (Mahwah, NJ: Paulist Press, 1986), 114.

[29] Mel Piehl, *Breaking Bread: The Catholic Worker and the Origin of Catholic Radicalism in America* (Philadelphia: Temple University Press, 1982), 89.

[30] Day, *Long Loneliness,* 263.

[31] Ibid., 246.

[32] Hugo, "In the Vineyard," *Catholic Worker* 8, no. 10 (September 1941): 1, 5, 8; "In the Vineyard VIII: The Two Rules," *Catholic Worker* 9, no. 7 (May 1942): 1–2; and Paul Hanly Furfey, "Maximum—Minimum," *Catholic Worker* 3 (May 1935): 5.

[33] Day, "Counsel and Precepts," *Catholic Worker* 8, no. 9 (July–August 1941): 2; Day, "Day after Day," *Catholic Worker* 10, no. 1 (December 1942): 6; Archbishop of Moncton, "Holiness for All," *Catholic Worker* 13, no. 1 (February 1946): 4; and Stephen Thomas Krupa, "Dorothy Day and the Spirituality of Nonviolence," Ph.D. thesis, Graduate Theological Union, 1997, 354.

[34] John Hugo, "Catholics Can Be Conscientious Objectors," *Catholic Worker* 10, no. 6 (May 1943): 6–8, and 10, no. 7 (June 1943): 6–9; "The Gospel of Peace: The Need for Supernatural Ethics," *Catholic Worker* 10, no. 9 (September 1943); and "The Immorality of Conscription," *Catholic Worker* 11, no. 9 (November 1944): 3–10.

[35] Cited in Zwick and Zwick, *Catholic Worker Movement,* 248.

[36] Dorothy Day, "And for Our Absent Brethren," *Catholic Worker* 10, no. 11 (December 1943): 2–3.

Chapter 2

On Pilgrimage

Just as Dorothy Day's life was settling down, the end of World War II ushered in an era that was both quieter and more challenging for the Catholic Worker. The postwar economic boom reduced the need for urban hospitality, though especially in places like New York City the problem of homelessness never disappeared altogether. More significantly perhaps, the institutionalization of social welfare programs after the New Deal diminished the appeal of the Worker's more radical alternative. Most of the Catholics who might have been drawn to the Worker were moving instead into the middle class, while socialist radicals were reeling under the onslaught of McCarthyite propaganda. Over the course of two decades, only thirty-four new "communities" were added to the movement, and this number includes local "cells" that did not necessarily do hospitality, family farms that were sympathetic to Worker ideals, and farms closely associated with urban houses founded earlier. (Day's inclusive vision of the Worker was reflected in the fact that all of these entities could appear in published lists of Worker communities.)

Between World War II and the Vietnam War, in short, Dorothy Day was the revered leader of a national movement that rarely included more than twenty local communities. With a deep sense of her spiritual identity, Day led in this period through her travels, her writings, and her friendships with kindred communities and with a series of individuals who would each leave a distinctive mark on the Worker.

The tenor of Day's leadership in this period is aptly conveyed by the new title she chose for her monthly column at the beginning of 1946: "On Pilgrimage." She had previously used both "Day after Day" and "Notes by the Way" but, she noted, other papers also used those titles. "We should always be thinking of ourselves as pilgrims anyway," Day explained, and she stuck with the new title until the end of her life, ultimately applying it as well to two published books. Day deftly played on both the inner and outer senses of the word "pilgrimage," using the column as both a spiritual journal in which she plumbed the depths of her devotion and a travelogue charting her nearly constant travels.[1] The first installment, for example, began with two quotes that are still repeated often in the movement—Teresa of Avila's "life is a night spent in an uncomfortable inn" and Catherine of Siena's "All the Way to Heaven is Heaven"—and then continued with a daily log of conversations, anecdotes, and reflections on her reading. In the months that followed, she wrote of the births of her grandchildren, of her vision for the farm at Easton, and of daily life at the New York houses of hospitality and around the nation.

Even a cursory reading of the columns from 1946 and 1947 reveals a few notable aspects of Day's life during the period. First, she read constantly. In May 1946 she wrote of *The Snake Pit,* a book describing a young woman's yearlong ordeal in a mental hospital that reminded her of the gospel obligation to visit the prisoner.[2] June's column linked her vision for the Easton Farm to a *Blackfriars* article about lay retreat houses, and in January 1947 she was praising Frank Sheed's *Theology and Sanity* because "it is theology simply written by a layman" and thus a reminder that the pope had "urged all, without exception, to work for the salvation of souls."[3]

Second, she was traveling almost as often as she was either at the farm or the New York houses. "Every year I like to make a real pilgrimage and visit some of our groups around the country," she declared in the November 1946 column and then recounted a trip that had taken her as far west as Minnesota. Two months later, she described her Christmas visit to Peter Maurin, who was spending the winter in Rochester with the Worker's longtime friend Teresa Weider, and her plans to visit Pacifique Roy in Montreal and attend the Detroit wedding of Louis Murphy and Justine L'Esperance.[4] The next month's column told the story of this trip, noting that in addition to visiting Catholic Worker friends, Day had found time for the Young Christian Workers and Catholic Women's League in Montreal and for the widow of Paul St. Marie, first president of the union for workers in the Ford automobile plant.[5]

Third, Day demonstrated that she was still deeply interested in people outside the Catholic Worker movement, including both Catholics and radicals whose social vision differed sharply from her own. In July and August 1946 she wrote at length about Joe Curran, a labor leader and former Catholic who had recently been profiled in the *New Yorker*. Recalling the aid that the Catholic Worker had provided Curran's National Maritime Union during the 1936 strike, she faulted him for saying that "there was no one else to help us" but the Communists, then admitted that "our help was but a drop in the bucket and the Communists must have poured money in." Even as Day explained that Curran's Catholicism had lapsed after his divorce and remarriage, she praised him for his integrity: though his first marriage had not been before a priest, he refused to exploit what he considered a mere loophole. Finally, she explained to her readers that her goal was not to provide them "with interesting and spicy bits of information" but because "he is well worth praying for." "There will be results," she promised; "of that I am sure."[6]

Day's interest also extended to other Christian community movements, including those whose inspiration might seem to contrast with that of the Catholic Worker. In October 1947 she wrote of the Canadian Doukhobors, a radical Russian sect whose members had begun reading the *Catholic Worker*. "These religious people," Day explained with a mixture of admiration and chagrin, "first burned icons in the Russian Church to protest against the State Church, then they burned firearms to protest against war. Last month they were burning their own homes to protest against greed, and also the homes of those they considered faithless Doukhobors who had gotten rich during the war while professing pacifism." After suggesting gently that such judgments are also a form of violence, she wrote about the eighteenth-century Shakers—noting that her nephew was currently working on the restoration of a Shaker village—and the celibate Pietists who had formed the Ephrata Cloister in Pennsylvania. Visits to these communities, she concluded, were "most interesting" to her as she continued to reflect on how to realize Peter Maurin's vision of the agronomic university.[7]

As she always had, Day used these occasional writings as the raw material for published books. In 1948 she published the first book titled *On Pilgrimage,* a month-by-month collection of journal entries from the previous year. In the spirit of Thérèse of Lisieux, she struck a humble, self-effacing tone, opening the book with a description of herself singing to her grandchildren in a rocking chair. Though she wrote of "all those in *The Catholic Worker* movement, scattered throughout the country, all the readers of the paper, all the people on the breadlines," she put the accent on "things of concern to us all, the family, the home, how to live, with what to live and what we live by."[8] A similar tone of concern for the everyday, mixed with a great deal of hagiographical reverence for both Catholic and socialist saints, would infuse *The Long Loneliness* (her final autobiography, published in 1952), *Therese* (a book-length hagiography of the Little Flower), and *Loaves and Fishes* (an overview of the Catholic Worker movement that updated the 1939 *House of Hospitality*).

Whether they encountered her columns or her books, many readers were inspired by Dorothy Day between 1945 and 1965. But relatively few were moved to launch new houses of hospitality.

Much more than the years before or after, this period was dominated by the agrarian dimension of the Worker philosophy. Long after the closure of the Boston house of hospitality, several families who had been involved in that project maintained Saint Benedict's Farm Commune at Upton, Massachusetts. The land was divided into separate family homesteads in the 1950s, but as late as 1985 several of the children who had grown up there still lived on the land, farming and maintaining a stained glass studio.[9] Another farm was launched in 1947 by Larry and Ruth Heaney and Marty and Gertrude Paul, two couples who had been involved in the first Milwaukee house of hospitality and at the Easton farm. Though their dreams for Holy Family Farm were shattered by Larry's death in 1949—just weeks before the death of Peter Maurin—Ruth Heaney raised her children on the farm before joining a nearby Benedictine monastery in her old age. Meanwhile, Julian Pleasants of the South Bend house maintained his employment at Notre Dame while building up an informal community of part-time family farmers.

The closure of the Easton farm in 1947 led not only to the purchase of a new farm and retreat center at Newburgh, New York, but also to the establishment of at least two new family farms by couples displaced from Easton. Tamar and David Hennessy, with help from Tamar's father, Forster Batterham, as well as from Dorothy, settled in a farmhouse in Berkeley Springs, West Virginia, while Jack and Mary Thornton raised their large family on a series of farms in Pennsylvania, writing regularly to the *Worker* about the challenges of the changing rural economy.[10] Both the Murphys in Detroit and the Gauchats in Cleveland also launched farms in this period, and short-lived farms appeared in California, Minnesota, and (in 1960) Nova Scotia. In most cases, these farms aspired at first to be communities of families but endured for most of their history with just one family on site.

During the 1950s and 1960s, Day also took a keen interest in other movements that had created communities of families. The German Bruderhof community, which espoused total community ownership of goods and staunch opposition to war, settled near the New York Worker farm in the 1950s. Both Day and several other Workers visited Koinonia, a communal farm in Georgia that took a strong stand for integration during the civil rights movement and suffered considerable violence as a consequence. During visits to England she came to know Taena, a community that began without religious affiliation but evolved into a community of Benedictine oblates. And in the early 1960s, Ed Willock, a Catholic magazine editor who had been involved in the original Worker house in Boston, helped found Marycrest, a rural community that at one point included eighty children and their parents. Each of these movements was featured repeatedly in the pages of the *Worker*.[11]

Day was also generously attentive to the handful of urban hospitality houses founded in the 1950s and 1960s. One of these was Blessed Martin House, a Memphis day nursery that lasted from 1951 to 1956. This was the project of Helen Caldwell Day Riley, an African American nurse who had volunteered at the New York house of hospitality while she attended nursing school and whose community was an important center for racial reconciliation as well as direct service. Dorothy Day managed to visit at least twice, in 1953 and again in 1956.[12] The 1950s also saw the formation of hospitality houses in Chicago and Oakland, both of them named for the recently deceased Peter Maurin.[13] Ultimately, though, the two most enduring houses of this period relied less on Dorothy Day and more on conventional nonprofit structures to ensure their longevity. Blanchet House was started in 1952 in Portland, Oregon, by members of a University of Portland fraternity, with assistance from Father Kennard, then the assistant pastor at the cathedral. Within a few years, it formally disassociated itself from the Worker. Fifty years later, it continues to sponsor an emergency shelter, transitional housing program, and working farm staffed by forty homeless men. Despite its autonomy from the Worker, it has retained several important dimensions of the Worker vision. It receives no funding from church or government, though it is incorporated as a nonprofit. Its staff is unpaid, and most are drawn from the people who have received services at the house. Performing "all of the daily tasks involved in [the house's] operation," they are able to develop self-esteem and "a community spirit."[14]

Montreal's Benedict Labre House was also founded in 1952 by a diverse group who had been influenced not only by the Catholic Worker but also by the Grail, Friendship House, and other movements popularizing the idea of the "lay apostolate." As one of the group explained in an early letter to the *Catholic Worker,* they were convinced that "the Lay Apostolate was for everyone" but unsure about the distinction between the "lay vocation of a Catholic Worker or a Friendship House staffer and the general vocation of all Catholics to Christian Life." After a series of discussions they agreed that each would continue to practice the works of mercy according to his or her circumstances. Physician Marcus Seng opened a free medical clinic; college professor Betty McCabe maintained a Christ room for girls and sponsored activities for neighborhood children; and Tony Walsh served as full-time staff for a house of hospitality. Initially, they decided that it was "inadvisable" to use the Catholic Worker name because of "several differences of theory and practice," particularly with regard to Catholic Worker pacifism. But by 1959 the house, now called Benedict Labre House, had declared itself a Catholic Worker, and it has appeared on every published list of houses since. Still, as its work has expanded it has downplayed the Catholic Worker connection. Today, Benedict Labre House maintains an array of services similar to that at Blanchet House, and its website mentions the Catholic Worker movement only on the page devoted to "history."[15]

If Dorothy Day had relatively little influence on the ongoing development of Blanchet House and Benedict Labre House, her influence on a series of significant individuals she encountered during this period proved much more momentous for the movement as a whole. The first of these was Robert Ludlow, an intellectual convert to Catholicism who began writing for the *Catholic Worker* when he was working at the Rosewood Training School, a home for adults with mental retardation and mental illness staffed by Catholic conscientious objectors. Even earlier, he had demonstrated an interest in integrating Catholicism with the American Left by writing articles linking Thomas Aquinas to the prominent American reformer Henry George.[16] When World War II ended, Ludlow was free to move to the New York Catholic Worker, where he stayed from 1946 to 1954. During those years, he served on the editorial board and published articles or book reviews in virtually every issue of the newspaper. Though Dorothy Day worried that many of these contributions were too intellectual for their readership, Ludlow proved to be the great synthesizer of the Worker movement, demonstrating how decentralism, pacifism, and anarchism (a word he did not hesitate to use) fit with Thomas Aquinas's doctrine of the common good and with more recent papal encyclicals. Ludlow was the primary author of the statement of "Catholic Worker Positions" that would provide a blueprint for many of the new houses founded in the 1960s and 1970s. He also wrote widely on psychology (drawing on his Rosewood experience), on Eastern rite Catholicism, and on the thought of Gandhi.[17]

Another newcomer shared Ludlow's interest in Eastern religion. Fritz Eichenberg was a German Jewish artist who had immigrated to the Americas just before Hitler's rise to power. Inspired by the muralists Rivera and Orozco in Mexico, he then settled in New York City where he worked as a book illustrator and studio art professor. After his wife's death, a spiritual crisis led him first to Zen Buddhism and then to Quakerism, and it was at the Quaker conference center, Pendle Hill, that he met Dorothy Day in 1949. Day was familiar with the illustrations Eichenberg had done for Dostoyevsky's novels and she invited him to begin publishing his woodcuts in the *Worker*. "She wanted something that would express without words the spirit of the Catholic Worker movement, especially to people who couldn't read," Eichenberg later recalled. "I was so pleased to be asked! . . . I was drawn to the Christ-centeredness of the Catholic Worker, the way that they saw Christ in everyone." Along with Ade Bethune, Eichenberg came to define the Catholic Worker aesthetic. His

distinctive woodcuts portraying Christ in the breadline of homeless people or showing a black man on the cross, like Bethune's
more simple images of the saints, appear on the walls of virtually every Catholic Worker community.[18]

Yet the influence of Ludlow and Eichenberg, and even of John
Hugo, pales in comparison to that of Ammon Hennacy. Hennacy
arrived at the New York Catholic Worker in 1952; a decade later
he was the only person apart from Peter Maurin who merited
his own chapter in Day's updated story of the movement, *Loaves
and Fishes*. Like Maurin, moreover, Hennacy was a single-minded
eccentric who needed someone of Day's generous spirit to draw
forth his true gifts. The child of Appalachian farmers, Hennacy
became a socialist in his youth and spent World War I in solitary
confinement for draft resistance. His only prison reading was
the Bible, and his reading of the Sermon on the Mount—and
later of Leo Tolstoy—transformed him from an atheist into what
he called a "Tolstoian Christian," committed to absolute nonviolence and individual initiative. He first met Dorothy Day after
she spoke at a rally in Milwaukee during the Depression; like
Peter Maurin and Pacifique Roy his technique was to get her attention and then just keep talking: "He wanted me to know that,
though he was not a Catholic and thought the Catholic Church
one of the most evil institutions in the world, he *was* a Tolstoian
Christian, having become one in prison. 'And what jails have *you*
been in and how long did *you* serve?'"[19]

Though Day's prison record paled by comparison, they were
mutually impressed, and over the next several years Day published both the story of his prison experience during World War
I and a series of reports on "Life at Hard Labor," in which he
described his work as a day laborer in the Southwest (a calling
that allowed him to avoid income tax but still pay his daughters'
college tuition) and his efforts to distribute the *Catholic Worker*
in as many different places as possible. By 1952 he had made
his way to the New York Catholic Worker and converted to Catholicism, at least in part because of his infatuation with Dorothy
Day. After several years as an editor of the *Catholic Worker,* he

went back west to found the Joe Hill House of Hospitality in Salt Lake City, which for its seven-year history was featured more prominently in the *Catholic Worker* than any other community outside New York.[20]

Hennacy transformed the Catholic Worker movement in two ways. First, he took the Worker's strong and theologically grounded pacifism and turned it into a concrete program of action that could, for some Workers, occupy as much time and attention as the running of hospitality houses. Declaring himself a "one-man revolution," Hennacy pursued peace by picketing, fasting, and resisting the payment of income taxes. Soon after his arrival in New York, he persuaded a group of Workers and other local pacifists to defy the compulsory air raid drills mandated by the Civil Defense Act. In 1955 around thirty demonstrators were arrested for this defiance; by 1961 their numbers had swelled to two thousand, prompting the city to discontinue compulsory drills. This action put the Catholic Worker on the map as a leading opponent of Cold War hysteria and set a precedent for the larger scale nonviolence of the Vietnam era.

Hennacy also transformed the Worker by renewing its connection to the American Left. Just as Peter Maurin, John Hugo, and Robert Ludlow had all deepened Day's understanding of her adopted faith, so Hennacy renewed her appreciation of her socialist roots. Hennacy knew radical history inside out, and he was catholic enough in his sensibilities to draw inspiration from the Hopi Indians, the Russian Doukhobor sect, Mormon polygamists, and Christian Scientists. His radical pedigree stretched back to the time he had driven Mother Jones to a union meeting in West Virginia, but his greatest love was for the long anarchist tradition that stretched from the "nonresistant" pacifists of the 1840s to the International Workers of the World. As he presented it, Catholic Worker anarchism was the true heir to the Wobbly spirit—and he presented it to almost everyone, in meetings and conversations with Communists, Unitarians, Mormons, and just about anyone who would give him a chance to speak.

Hennacy's presentation of Christian anarchism was also emphatic enough to provoke a reaction among some Catholic Workers. In 1955, shortly after leaving the New York Catholic Worker, Robert Ludlow published "A Re-evaluation," in which he confessed that "I now think it was unwise that we employed the term anarchism or 'Christian' anarchism." He, at least, had been motivated in part by "a somewhat immature desire to appear more radical than the next fellow." More mature reflection had persuaded him that the term "Christian anarchism" was best reserved to the Tolstoyans, whose "religious notions on authority" were clearly contrary to Catholic doctrine. To say that people could reform themselves to the point that they would not need any state at all, moreover, was "like insisting that all become celibates or that all become Trappists"—it was a Jansenist position that "consigned most of mankind to hell." Though Ludlow denied that this change of heart had prompted his departure from the Worker, it was clear that Ammon Hennacy was leading the movement in a direction that Ludlow did not want to go.[21]

A subsequent exchange of articles between the two men further clarified the alternatives. Rather than explaining how his Tolstoyan ideals were compatible with Catholicism, Hennacy acknowledged that "it is not necessary for a pacifist anarchist to accept any certain religion" and asserted that he had simply brought "all that was good from Gandhi and Tolstoy" into the church when he was "baptized by an anarchist priest who uses that term without qualms." "Today in this atomic chaos," he concluded pointedly, "anything less than the Sermon on the Mount is not worth bothering with." Ludlow replied by appealing directly to the teachings of Pope Leo XIII, and even took a step away from Catholic Worker pacifism. Though he personally opposed wars "which of necessity must also use weapons whose very composition makes for their indiscriminate use," the fact was that the church had not made a definitive judgment against war and so "Catholic pacifists should not carry on as though their fellow religionists who go into the army are . . . in mortal sin."[22]

Clearly, Hennacy and Ludlow envisioned two very different religious identities for the Catholic Worker, one that took the Sermon on the Mount as its sole standard and the other privileging communion with the whole of the Catholic Church. Dorothy Day, for her part, did not want to choose: though her personal religious sensibilities were closer to Ludlow's, she continued to offer Hennacy a journalistic platform even after he publicly renounced his Catholicism and announced that "after fifteen years in the Catholic Church I find that any increase in spiritual emphasis that I have gained has been in spite of and not because of attendance at Mass and taking Communion."[23] The reason was simple: he was still practicing the works of mercy, both by feeding the hungry at his house of hospitality and by admonishing sinners through his war resistance. "We cannot judge him, knowing so well his own strong and courageous will to fight the corruption of the world around him."[24] Though this nonjudgmental stance left room in the movement for supporters of both Hennacy's and Ludlow's alternatives, Ludlow's voluntary departure allowed Hennacy to exercise a much stronger influence for the next few decades.

The next major leader of the movement outside New York followed a spiritual trajectory remarkably similar to Hennacy's. Son of a Vermont Congressman, Karl Meyer "started my first Catholic Worker house in Washington, D.C., when I was nineteen years old and not even a Catholic." That first house was not notably successful: Meyer waited several months for guests, then picked up a homeless alcoholic in an alley and lasted three days with him. But Meyer would go on to found perhaps more Catholic Worker houses than any other person. After his Washington experience, he proceeded to New York, where he participated in the civil defense protests of the mid-1950s, and then to Chicago, where he founded Saint Stephen's House of Hospitality in 1958. After a decade in existence, that community was succeeded by the "Chicago Storefront," then by the Saint Francis House of Hospitality, which is today one of several thriving communities in Chicago.[25] Along the way, Meyer found time to trespass at military installations, to join a peace march to Moscow, to publish advice on how to avoid paying the federal income taxes that were used to fund the Cold War, and—picking up on an earlier suggestion by John Hugo—to propose the burning of draft cards.[26] He would later spend time driving around the country in a "Peace Bus," before settling in Nashville to launch an ecologically oriented community called Greenlands.

Like Ammon Hennacy, Karl Meyer eventually lost his Catholic faith. When Meyer wrote Dorothy Day to this effect, she published his letter in the *Catholic Worker,* retained him as a member of the editorial board, and wrote back to say, "Your letter caused me grief but I know all works out for good eventually and of course you are always part of the Catholic Worker family." In keeping with Meyer's religious stance, Greenlands is one of many communities today that finesses its affiliation with the Catholic Worker. "We are a non-sectarian community, not based in prayer or in religious doctrine," explains their mission statement, "affiliated with the Catholic Worker movement through many years of personal association, and a deeply shared ethical and social vision."[27]

In part because of the gifts brought by John Hugo, Robert Ludlow, Fritz Eichenberg, Ammon Hennacy, and Karl Meyer, and in part because of the continuing dedication of others who had joined earlier, the Catholic Worker was a richer movement in 1965 than in 1945. It had a solid theological foundation, a deep spirituality, and a broad political platform that attracted both Catholic and non-Catholic radicals. People such as Stanley Vishnewski, Justine and Lou Murphy, Bill and Dorothy Gauchat knew—as no one had known in 1945—what it meant to practice the works of mercy over the long term, rather than merely as an expression of youthful idealism. The movement included thriving houses of hospitality, struggling farms, and families who opened their homes to strangers without ever saying a word about it in print. Yet the overall scope of the movement had scarcely changed since the end of World War II. In 1965 as in 1945, there were houses of hospitality in New York City, Rochester, Detroit, and Washington, D.C. There were no longer houses in Cleveland, Pittsburgh, or Philadelphia, but Worker communities had been added in Portland, Montreal, Chicago, Salt Lake City, and Oakland. There were perhaps more farms seeking to embody the Catholic Worker ideal, but only the New York community's new farm at Tivoli was truly communal. Few people in any of these places, not even Dorothy Day herself, anticipated the dramatic growth that was just ahead.

[1] Day, "On Pilgrimage," *Catholic Worker* 13, no. 1 (February 1946): 1; Day, *On Pilgrimage* (New York: Catholic Worker Books, 1948); and Day, *On Pilgrimage: The Sixties* (New York: Curtiss Books, 1972).

[2] Day, "On Pilgrimage," *Catholic Worker* 13, no. 4 (May 1946): 2.

[3] Day, "On Pilgrimage," *Catholic Worker* 13, no. 5 (June 1946): 1–2, 8; Day, "Review of *Theology and Sanity*," *Catholic Worker* 13, no. 11 (January 1947): 1–2, 4.

[4] Day, "On Pilgrimage," *Catholic Worker* 13, no. 11 (January 1947): 1–2, 4.

[5] Day, "On Pilgrimage," *Catholic Worker* 13, no. 12 (February 1947): 2.

[6] Day, "On Pilgrimage, *Catholic Worker* 13, no. 6 (July–August 1946): 1–2, 7–8.

[7] Day, "On Pilgrimage," *Catholic Worker* 14, no. 7 (October 1947): 1–2, 8.

[8] Dorothy Day, *On Pilgrimage,* 2.

[9] Dorothy Day, "On Pilgrimage," *Catholic Worker* 41, no. 7 (September 1975): 2; and Carl Paulson, "Massachusetts," *Catholic Worker* 52, no. 8 (December 1985): 8.

[10] Jack and Mary Thornton, "Five Years on the Farm," *Catholic Worker* 18, no. 18 (February 1953): 1, 5; Jon Thornton, "Mo. and Penn. Farms Write," *Catholic Worker* 24, no. 3 (October 1957): 8; and Jack and Mary Thornton, "The Thorntons," *Catholic Worker* 30, no. 1 (July–August 1963): 5.

[11] Day, "Community of Brothers," *Catholic Worker* 22, no. 5 (December 1955): 1, and "Pacifist Community Suffers Fire," *Catholic Worker* 23, no. 8 (March 1957): 1 on the Bruderhof; "Bombing at Koinonia Farm, Americus, Ga.," *Catholic Worker* 23, no. 2 (September 1956): 1; "Developments at Koinonia," *Catholic Worker* 23, no. 3 (October 1956): 5; "The Story of

Koinonia," *Catholic Worker* 23, no. 6 (January 1957): 8; Kerran Dugan, "Interracial Community Attacked," *Catholic Worker* 23, no. 8 (March 1957): 1; Robert Steed, "Two Weeks at Koinonia," *Catholic Worker* 24, no. 1 (July–August 1957): 8, on Koinonia; Frank Goodridge, review of *Community Journey,* by George Ineson, *Catholic Worker* 23, no. 2 (September 1956): 5; and "Taena Community," *Catholic Worker* 23, no. 4 (November 1956): 3, on Taena; Arthur Sheehan, "News from Marycrest," *Catholic Worker* 29, no. 2 (September 1962): 7, on Marycrest. For more on these communities, see Benjamin Zablocki, *The Joyful Community: An Account of the Bruder-hof, a Communal Movement Now in Its Third Generation* (Baltimore: Penguin Books, 1971); Markus Baum, *Against the Wind: Eberhard Arnold and the Bruderhof* (Farmington, PA: Plough Publishing, 1998); Tracy Elaine K'Meyer, *Interracialism and Christian Community in the Postwar South: The Story of Koinonia Farm* (Charlottesville, VA: University Press of Virginia, 1997); James T. Fisher, *The Catholic Counterculture in America, 1933–1962* (Chapel Hill: University of North Carolina Press, 1989), 101–29; and Jack Holland, "A Vision on a Hill: Recalling Marycrest, an inspiring experiment in Christian community," at www.irishecho.com/newspaper/story.cfm?id=11704.

[12] Helen Caldwell Day, *Not Without Tears* (New York: Sheed and Ward, 1954).

[13] Dorothy Day, "On Pilgrimage," *Catholic Worker* 18, no. 4 (November 1951): 1, 2, 6; Jack Woltjen, "Chicago's Peter Maurin House," *Catholic Worker* 21, no. 8 (March 1955): 3, 6.

[14] Keith D. Barger, "Hearing the Cry of the Poor: The Catholic Worker Communities in Oregon and Washington 1940 to the Present," senior thesis, University of Portland, 1992, 14–18, at DD/CWC, series W-7.1, box 4, folder 5; and http://www.blanchethouse.org/.

[15] Jim Shaw, "Canadian House," *Catholic Worker* 18, no. 17 (January 1953): 5; Charles Butterworth, "Benedict Labre House, Montreal," *Catholic Worker* 26, no. 1 (August 1959): 1; and http://www.benedictlabre.org/english/home page.htm.

[16] Robert Ludlow, "Georgeism, Thomism, and the Catholic Question," *Land and Freedom* (November–December 1940), available at "The School of Cooperative Individualism," http://www.cooperativeindividualism.org/ludlow-robert_georgeism-thomism-and-catholicism.html.

[17] William Miller, *A Harsh and Dreadful Love: Dorothy Day and the Catholic Worker Movement* (New York: Liveright, 1973), 219–20. Some of Ludlow's most significant contributions to the *Worker* include "Truth and Freedom," *Catholic Worker* 10, no. 10 (October 1943): 3; "Catholicism and Socialism," *Catholic Worker* 14, no. 6 (September 1947): 6; "Revolution

and Compassion," *Catholic Worker* 15, no. 3 (May 1948): 1, 8; "The State and the Christian," *Catholic Worker* 15, no. 7 (October 1948): 1, 6, 8; "Satyagraha: A Christian Way," *Catholic Worker* 16, no. 1 (May 1949): 3, 8; "Christian Anarchism," *Catholic Worker* 16, no. 4 (September 1949): 1–4; "Eastern Rite Catholics and Reunion," *Catholic Worker* 18, no. 7 (February 1952); "Personalist Revolution," *Catholic Worker* 18, no. 15 (November 1952): 1, 4, 5.

[18] Fritz Eichenberg, *Works of Mercy,* ed. Robert Ellsberg (Maryknoll, NY: Orbis, 2004), 18.

[19] Day, *Loaves and Fishes* (New York: Harper and Row, 1963), 109.

[20] See, for example, Ammon Hennacy, "God's Coward," *Catholic Worker* 9, no. 1 (November 1941): 5; "God's Coward," *Catholic Worker* 9, no. 7 (May 1942): 3; "God's Coward," *Catholic Worker* 9, no. 9 (July–August 1942): 3; "Life at Hard Labor," *Catholic Worker* 15, no. 6 (September 1948): 5; "One Man Revolution," *Catholic Worker* 18, no. 12 (July–August 1952): 1, 6; "Hiroshima Fast," *Catholic Worker* 20, no. 3 (October 1953): 2, 7; "Five Days in Jail," *Catholic Worker* 21, no. 5 (December 1954): 2, 6, 7; "Salt Lake City," *Catholic Worker* 27, no. 11 (June 1961): 2; "Joe Hill House," *Catholic Worker* 29, no. 8 (March 1963): 3, 6; "Joe Hill House," *Catholic Worker* 30, no. 8 (March 1964): 4; and Ammon Hennacy, *The Book of Ammon,* 2nd ed. (Baltimore: Fortkamp Publishing, 1994).

[21] Robert Ludlow, "A Re-evaluation," *Catholic Worker* 21, no. 11 (June 1955): 2.

[22] Ammon Hennacy, "Christian Anarchism Defined," *Catholic Worker* 22, no. 1 (July–August 1955): 3, 7; Robert Ludlow, "Anarchism and Leo XIII," *Catholic Worker* 22, no. 2 (September 1955), 3, 8; and Robert Ludlow, "Is Pacifism a Precept?" *Catholic Worker* 22, no. 7 (February 1956): 1, 7.

[23] Hennacy, *Book of Ammon,* 474.

[24] Dorothy Day, "Ammon Hennacy—'Non-Church' Christian," *Catholic Worker* 36, no. 2 (February 1970): 2.

[25] Karl Meyer, "Chicago CW," *Catholic Worker* 25, no. 4 (November 1958): 1, 7; "Chicago House," *Catholic Worker* 34, no. 1 (January 1968): 3; "Chicago Storefront," *Catholic Worker* 34, no. 7 (September 1968): 7; "Chicago Co-op," *Catholic Worker* 38, no. 6 (July–August 1972).

[26] Karl Meyer, "The Walkers," *Catholic Worker* 27, no. 10 (May 1961): 5; "Walk for Peace," *Catholic Worker* 27, no. 11 (June 1961): 3; and Francis Sicius, "The Chicago Catholic Worker," in Patrick G. Coy, ed., *Revolution of the Heart: Essays on the Catholic Worker* (Philadelphia: New Society Publishers, 1988), 355. The peace march was sponsored by the Committee for Nonviolent Action, on whose board Day, Hennacy, and Catholic Worker Ed Turner had all served.

[27] Karl Meyer, roundtable on "Forging Community in Spiritual Diversity," National Catholic Worker Gathering, 2006; Karl Meyer, "From Prison," *Catholic Worker* 37, no. 5 (June 1971): 6; and "Peacemaker Writes," *Catholic Worker* 37, no. 8 (October–November 1971): 4; and "Nashville Greenlands," http://www.catholicworker.org/communities/Commdetail.cfm?Community=33.

Chapter 3

The Flowering of the Sixties

In 1965, Dorothy Day was sixty-eight. She was definitely aging but still vigorous enough to travel around the country and as far away as Cuba and Rome. Much was going on in the world and in the movement she had founded, and Day had ample reason to feel both vindication and mortification. The Second Vatican Council, which finished meeting in that year, was a triumphal moment for the liturgical movement, which Day had long championed. By authorizing the use of local languages in the liturgy, it made possible the "full, conscious, and active" participation in the sacraments that Day earnestly believed would empower people to perform the works of mercy. By defining the church as the "whole people of God," moreover, the council affirmed the centrality of the "lay apostolate" to the life of the church. Perhaps even more important, both Pope John XXIII and the council itself had affirmed pacifism as a legitimate option for Catholics and spoken out in no uncertain terms about the dangers of nuclear war. Day had traveled to Rome twice to advocate for such a statement, the second time with an ecumenical women's group that staged a ten-day fast, and she greeted the council's "Pastoral Constitution on the Church in the Modern World" with joy.[1] Yet many of the first fruits of the council revealed, from Day's perspective, a lack of reverence for the Mystical Body of Christ. She did not like the idea of a priests' union, did not care for the priests who wore plaid shorts when they said Mass at Tivoli, and fretted about the young people who preferred informal house Masses to full participation in their local parishes.[2]

On the world political stage, likewise, the Cuban revolution had stirred Day's old Leftist ardor, and in 1962 she traveled to Cuba expecting to find "concordances . . . that which is of God in every man." As she had during the Spanish Civil War, Day tried to chart a peaceful course between atheist socialism and reactionary Catholicism, though her enthusiasm for Castro's revolutionary program led her to characterize him as Catholic at heart and to compare him more than once with Peter Maurin. (As late as 1970 she was still referring to the Cuban revolution as "one of the most incredible stories in modern times.") Such positions subjected her to intense criticism. Letters poured in accusing her of naïveté and of whitewashing Castro's persecutions, and even Robert Ludlow worried that she had betrayed her pacifism. Meanwhile, the escalating war in Vietnam outraged and distressed her, even as it stirred a new generation of Workers to heroic acts of resistance.[3]

Here too there was reason for both vindication and mortification. Tom Cornell, David Miller, and other Catholic Workers were in the forefront of the movement to burn draft cards. Many, among them Day's close friend and traveling companion Eileen Egan, were also involved in PAX (later Pax Christi), a Catholic pacifist group that held an annual retreat at Tivoli. Jim Forest, who came to the Worker early in the decade, was instrumental in the founding of both PAX and the Catholic Peace Fellowship, an affiliate of the Fellowship of Reconciliation that placed special emphasis on Catholic conscientious objectors and draft resisters. The priest brothers Dan and Phil Berrigan, longtime contributors to the *Catholic Worker,* gradually pushed for more extreme acts of resistance, and their burning of draft files at Catonsville, Maryland, galvanized a new Catholic Left.

Much as Day celebrated this new heroism, she also saw in it a troubling lack of reverence and perhaps an echo of her own unsettled, pre-Catholic youth. The young people flocking to the New York houses were, in many cases, skeptical of traditional sexual morality and attracted to Ammon Hennacy's harsh invective against the church. In a 1962 episode known as the "Great Stomp," Day became furious with a large group of young people who were not only promiscuous but involved in what she considered a pornographic publication called *Fuck You*. She effectively excluded them from the movement by refusing to pay the rent for the apartment where they were staying. Few outside the affected group criticized her for this decision, but longtime friends were less sympathetic when she wrote a letter to Jim Forest (who had defended the Workers who had been stomped out) asking that he be removed from the Catholic Peace Fellowship stationery because his postdivorce romance meant he was no longer truly Catholic. Thomas Merton and Daniel Berrigan both thought she was excessively harsh, and eventually she wrote to Forest promising "to amend my life—or attempt to by 'mortifying my critical faculties.'"[4]

Day's private papers, as analyzed by historian William Miller, reveal the deep anguish she felt and sometimes expressed during the tumult of the 1960s and 1970s. In a chapter titled "The Travail of the Sixties," Miller concluded that for Dorothy the decade was "full of signs of something vital having gone out of the world—a glue that had held things together no longer worked." Ammon Hennacy, Jim Forest, and Phil Berrigan all felt the sting of her judgment regarding their sexual and religious choices. In letters to her friend Sister Peter Claver, she bemoaned the "depressing" disconnection between sex and reproduction, the lack of interest in parish life among young Workers, the open expression of gay and lesbian sexuality in the movement. "I am just not 'with it' any more," she wrote, "and you can imagine the kind of desolation I feel."[5]

Still, Day managed to "mortify my critical faculties" to the point that she did not often express this desolation in public.

Instead, she wrote exultingly of the earnestness of the young people who were drawn to the Catholic Worker and provided new houses with both emotional and financial support. She also continued to reach out to kindred movements. She inspired thousands with her last major public act, getting arrested at a United Farm Workers demonstration in 1973. The sight of a seventy-five-year-old woman putting her body on the line for the sake of her brothers and sisters in Christ inspired many much younger folks to devote their lives to the works of mercy.

In many ways, Day's position came back to the philosophy of personalism. She believed in taking personal responsibility for one's actions, and she was most tolerant of disagreement when the person disagreeing was willing to pay his or her own way. The common thread connecting the many occasions when she excluded people from the Catholic Worker—from a group of labor activists who had wanted to stop doing hospitality in the 1930s, to the families that claimed sole authority over the Easton farm in the 1940s, to the Great Stomp—was that in each case Dorothy prevented people from using donations intended for the poor to pursue their own agendas. When dissenting individuals found their own means of support—as did labor activist John Cort in the early years and Ammon Hennacy in the 1960s—Day was more than willing to accept them as friends and allies. One consequence of this personalist attitude was that the boundaries of the movement were tighter in New York, which relied heavily on donations directed to Day herself, than in the self-supporting communities that were cropping up around the nation. For the new Workers in these communities, Day was what she had always been—a devoted friend who inspired them to transform their lives by devoting them to the works of mercy.

The generation of Workers who responded to this inspiration was, in many respects, the most remarkable in the movement's history. Between 1965 and 1980, seventy-six communities were founded, nearly twice the number launched during the Great Depression. The geographical distribution was similar—Syracuse, Boston, Milwaukee, Baltimore, Washington, D.C., Los Angeles, San Francisco—though the new local founders rarely had direct ties to their predecessors of the previous generation. These communities proved much more enduring than their precursors, with forty-nine lasting more than a decade and thirty-five still going strong today. In most cases, moreover, they have survived as communities, with resident Workers sharing daily life with their homeless guests.

This endurance is all the more remarkable in that these communities were created at a time of intense turmoil in the Catholic Church and in American society more generally. The civil rights movement and the War on Poverty had raised high hopes among idealistic young people, but by 1965 these hopes were gravely threatened by the costly and destructive war in Vietnam. Likewise, the Second Vatican Council, held between 1962 and 1965, had opened the windows of the church to a broader engagement with culture, explicitly affirming several ideas that had been central to the Worker movement, such as the lay apostolate and the Mystical Body of Christ. But the council also left a legacy of uncertainty for precisely those young people who in the past had traditionally entered ordained ministry or the religious orders. If the church was the whole people of God, was there still any reason to get ordained or join an order? If religious life was now out-of-date, was conventional lay life any better? Might there be a more radical, gospel-centered alternative to both? Such questions became more intense and wrenching after 1968, when the church's renewed prohibition of artificial birth control in *Humanae Vitae* took the American laity by surprise and signaled that the hierarchy was willing to place limits on the post-Vatican II transformation of the church.

The Catholic Worker proved to be a place of refuge—and of ongoing transformation—for many of the young people who were most deeply affected by these changes. Some had been student activists against the Vietnam War or draft resisters; others had left seminary or novitiate programs for what they saw as a more authentic model of religious community. Many had participated in the sexual and psychedelic experimentation of the era. Initially, they brought a certain chaos to the movement: stories abound of broken marriages, of Workers and guests feeding off one another's addictions, of hospitality so open that it ceased to be hospitable, and of newly fledged resisters marching off to prison with little sense of the long-term consequences.

For many of these people, the Worker ultimately proved to be a stable anchor amidst the chaos. It offered principles that could be recalled, seasoned Workers who could be consulted, and the opportunity to balance one's activist intensity with the simple labors of cooking a meal or cleaning a bathroom. Some communities that had spun quickly out of the Catholic Worker orbit moved back in, simply because someone suggested a roundtable discussion of Peter Maurin's principles. The stories of most of these communities are still relatively unknown, except to those most directly touched by them. My selective and partial accounting of a few of the communities founded in this period will not do justice to them, but may at least provide a sense of the flowering of the movement during a time in which too many observers thought it was dying.

Haley House

The complexity of the Catholic Worker experience in this era is well illustrated by the story of one of the first Worker houses of this generation, Haley House in Boston. This community began in 1967, when John and Kathe McKenna, young Catholics inspired by the vision of Dorothy Day, rented a cheap apartment and began combing the streets for homeless persons who would be willing to live with them. Early on, the community embraced nonprofit status, primarily to accommodate a cluster of conscientious objectors who were required to work at a registered nonprofit. At the time of the founding, both McKennas were serious young Catholics with close ties to the church—indeed, eight priests were listed as Haley House "members" when the community applied for nonprofit status a few years later. Yet Catholicism was far from the only influence on the fledgling community. Faced with the escalation of the Vietnam War and the radicalization of the civil rights movement, the McKennas were impressed by such non-Catholic and non-pacifist organizations as the Black Panthers. Other community members were impressed by the burgeoning "commune" movement, and Haley House was one of relatively few Catholic Worker houses to try to build a community consisting of multiple families under a single roof. By the time the McKennas left to pursue other forms of activism in 1969, the community had dropped most references to Catholicism or the Catholic Worker from its flyers and newsletters.[6]

Yet Dorothy Day did not drop Haley House. Throughout the 1970s, the Boston community benefited from her willingness to redistribute funds contributed to the well-known New York houses. "We got such an abundance of Christmas gifts, we are passing it around," she wrote to Haley House (and other communities) in 1972, while in 1976 she scribbled a note to an assistant on a Haley House fund-raising letter: "Send something! Sow and reap!"[7] Kathe McKenna also recalled a more direct way in which Day expressed support for the diversity present at Haley House. At the height of the Vietnam War, Day visited Boston and joined the McKennas in a presentation about the war. Though Kathe was "trembling in my boots," she nevertheless took the occasion to dissent publicly from Day's pacifism. Still, "after it was all over," she recalled, "Dorothy came up to us and said in her wonderfully stiff, warm way, 'You must feel very strongly about what you believe.' And she just smiled and left it at that."[8]

This attitude of affirmation made it easy for Haley House to renew a sense of connection to the Catholic Worker in the 1970s, even as its individual members explored a variety of ideological and religious identities. Donations continued to come from Catholic churches; student volunteers continued to come from Catholic universities such as Boston College. Quite significantly, the community kept up the practices of holding "roundtable discussions" for clarification of thought, and the records of these discussions reveal a pattern of radical openness. Between 1977 and 1985, the community repeatedly hosted veteran New York

Catholic Worker Stanley Vishnewski, along with Robert Coles, one of the movement's strongest academic supporters, and such Catholic peace activists as Gordon Zahn, Michael True, Charlie McCarthy, Liz McAlister, and Phil Berrigan. They also sponsored talks on such topics as "Amnesty International and Gay Human Rights," "The Feminine Dynamic: Women in the Church," "Meditation and Political Change," "Fearless Generosity: A Buddhist Approach to Working with Others," and "Exploring Human Growth from an Eastern Perspective."[9]

The last three topics are especially significant, for by the time of Day's death, Haley House was drawing as fervently on Buddhist as Catholic sources for its identity. By the early 1980s, Buddhist monks were regular visitors to the community, and Kathe McKenna, who along with John had returned to Haley House by that time, had embraced Buddhist practice. Beth Ingham, who arrived at Haley House in 1980, would eventually become a nun in the Nipponzan Myohoji Order of Buddhists, a group devoted to walking through places suffering violence. All of these new ideas made for a rich community life, but also a certain level of incoherence. In 1981, for example, a newsletter announced the arrival of several new community members and explained that "their long-range hope is that a Christian community will be created, rooted in hospitality, peace work and prayer." But an undated brochure that appears next to this newsletter in the archival file scrupulously avoids any reference to the Catholic Worker or Christianity, and begins, "Haley House is a nonprofit corporation chartered by the State of Massachusetts for the purpose of helping the skid row alcoholic."[10]

By November 1984, the community was ready to address this incoherence head-on. In a series of community meetings that stretched through March, they discussed their relationship to the Catholic Church and the Catholic Worker movement, the relationship between peacemaking and hospitality, and their desire to adopt more formal processes of consensus decision making. They even discussed the hot-button issue of abortion, discovering that community members held a wide range of views on that topic. Through this process, they realized that they had a strong sense of "communal bondedness" and that "there are deep Christian beliefs that underpin the communal bondedness and the work that flows from that."[11] At the same time, they recognized that not all members of their community were Catholic or Christian, and so they developed a new identity statement that defined a nuanced relationship to the Worker movement:

> We have affirmed that Haley House is a spiritually based community nurtured by the Catholic Worker tradition. Its activity is focused on the works of mercy and challenging the system. It has committed itself to a communal consensus process for all its decision making. While not insisting that any of the sub-committees engage in hospitality, we have affirmed that hospitality is an essential dimension of our communal life. In addition, our commitment to peacemaking through various forms of non-violent resistance has been reincorporated in a very explicit way into our work.[12]

I cite this text at length because it exemplifies what has become a widespread pattern of communities that identify themselves as "in the Catholic Worker tradition" rather than simply "Catholic Workers." Coming as it does in the mid-1980s, this statement might readily be interpreted as evidence of the movement's drift away from orthodox Catholicism in the years immediately following Day's death. Seen in the context of Haley House's earlier history, however, it reflects more revival than deterioration: far from abandoning their Catholic Worker roots, the Haley House members were returning to them even as they affirmed their diversity. To a degree that probably would not have been possible a decade earlier, Haley House could in 1985 affirm a rich liturgical life, featuring twice-monthly Eucharists, "Baptisms, House Blessings, First Communions . . . and Days of Reflection." They could also affirm that "[w]e happily count Quakers, Jews, Protestants, Deists and Agnostics as well as devout and not so devout Roman Catholics as partners in our endeavors. And, we have experienced 'Church,' those called to be people of God, as wider than any specific faith community." This commitment to a centered diversity made it possible for one community member, Louise Cochran, to convert to Catholicism even as her Jewish husband was reflecting on the relationship between Chanukah and resistance, and her community-mate Beth Ingham was becoming a Buddhist nun![13]

Even as it was clarifying its spiritual identity, Haley House was also articulating a more diversified model of community membership. When John and Kathe moved back to Boston, Kathe resumed her work with Haley House while John pursued a new career as a policeman, lawyer, and judge. In keeping with these new directions, they decided not to live directly in Haley House but purchased a building across the street. That building quickly evolved into an extended community house that was especially attractive to individuals exhausted by the intensity of Haley House itself. Since Haley House also sponsored a farm seventy miles away, the community could thus offer its members three very distinct sorts of commitment. At Noonday Farm, McKenna wrote in a 1991 newsletter, "three families hold most things in common including the collective purse and a long-term commitment to this experiment has been made (present members have been together 3 to 6 years)." The "live-in community" at Haley House held "most things in common except the purse strings" but typically involved less than a year's commitment; while the neighbors who "live more independently from one another but share common values and goals and work" included several whose length of commitment was much greater. Through this diversity, Haley House honored the very diverse life stages and vocational commitments of individuals drawn to the Catholic Worker.[14]

Perhaps the most fascinating aspect of the Haley House story is the fact that it never drifted out of the Catholic Worker orbit altogether. As more members were drawn to Buddhism, they continued to host roundtable discussions on Catholic as well as Buddhist spirituality. They maintained a strong relationship with Boston College, which provided them with a steady stream of young Catholic volunteers. The simple fact that they continued to call themselves a Catholic Worker has also ensured that individuals with a more classical understanding of the movement would continue to appear at their doors. My primary informant during my visit was just such an individual. Matt Daloisio clearly shared Dorothy Day's reluctance to accept nonprofit status and longed for a more intensely Catholic community situation, and as a result he was planning a move to the New York Catholic Worker. But he also expressed a strong admiration for Haley House's distinctive path. "How boring would it be if we all looked like the New York Catholic Worker," he said. "The genius of the anarchist movement is that . . . it doesn't allow all of us to look the same."[15] The same admiration was echoed in my interviews with members of the more traditional Worker communities in New England, many of which work closely with Haley House in their resistance activities.

Viva House

As this history suggests, the practice of the corporal works of mercy quickly led the founders of Haley House to emphasize the spiritual work of resisting war. By the late 1960s, the trajectory had reversed itself for some founders of Worker communities: a commitment to resisting the war in Vietnam led them to embrace hospitality as a way of anchoring a nonviolent life. This was the case for Brendan Walsh and Willa Bickham, founders of Viva House in Baltimore. During the early years of the war, Walsh was a seminarian and Bickham was a member of the Sisters of Saint Joseph. Influenced by such Catholic peace activists as Dan and Phil Berrigan, they found their way to the Catholic Worker movement just as Workers were getting involved in draft card burning. After their marriage, the Walsh-Bickhams spent time at Saint James the Apostle Catholic Worker during the months before cofounder David Miller went to jail for burning his draft card in New York City. They then headed to Baltimore to support their friends Phil Berrigan and Tom Lewis, both of whom faced substantial prison terms for their involvement in destroying draft records in Catonsville, Maryland.

Walsh and Bickham launched Viva House Catholic Worker in 1968, and from the beginning one of their central tasks was providing support to war resisters. As the "Catonsville Nine" and "Baltimore Four" prepared for their trials, they needed a place to stay, to plan legal strategy, and to ready themselves spiritually for the prison experience. Viva House played all these functions, but from the beginning it was more than simply a center for antiwar work. Baltimore, like most major cities, had experienced race riots in the aftermath of Martin Luther King's assassination, and so they took particular care to choose a house along a racial boundary, with a black neighborhood to the north and a white area to the south. As the Catonsville Nine defendants moved on, they began doing long-term hospitality on a small scale, hosting "a woman and her child, an elderly guy in bad health," along with individuals who stayed for a few days or weeks. As a conscientious objector, Walsh was obliged to do alternative service at a psychiatric hospital, but they also found time to open a soup kitchen a few blocks from the house. Within their first year in Baltimore, moreover, they welcomed their daughter Kate into the Catholic Worker family.

"There wasn't any blueprint for a Catholic Worker house," Walsh would later recall. "About the best blueprint there was was a blueprint for how to make soup." Still, the support and encouragement of Dorothy Day played a vital role in getting the community started. Like other community founders, they published a letter in the New York paper announcing their plans, and then the Workers in New York sent them a list of Maryland subscribers from whom they might solicit support. As was the case at Haley House, Day continued to be generous with excess donations received in New York, passing on about a thousand dollars during the early years. She was more skeptical, though, of their plan to combine family with the Catholic Worker. For their part, Walsh and Bickham simply took to heart her advice to "make real space for raising the family within the family." They altered the style of their hospitality repeatedly to accommodate Kate's developmental stages, but they never stopped performing the works of mercy. At times their community was augmented by other individuals or even families; at other times they relied on an "extended community" of nonresident Workers and volunteers. This "flowing approach" to hospitality and resistance has kept Viva House going for nearly four decades.[16]

Viva House's blend of resistance, hospitality, and family was soon echoed in dozens of other places. At Milwaukee's Casa Maria, founder Mike Cullen was deported for his involvement in the Milwaukee Fourteen, but the community quickly attracted others willing to carry on the work. Dan and Chris Delany started the Los Angeles Catholic Worker in 1970, when their son was just fifteen months old; after their departure the community would continue to be anchored by Jeff Dietrich and Catherine Morris and would eventually sponsor a vital cluster of daughter communities. The Catholic Worker farm in West Hamlin, West Virginia, was launched by gay couple Chuck Smith and Sandy Adams in 1969. They were among the most vociferous advocates of the agrarian ideal in this era, and by the 1980s they were also "storming heaven for more recognition of gay, lesbian, and women's rights in the C.W. movement and the church."[17]

Family Clusters

As more couples and families were drawn to the movement, they consciously began developing new strategies to facilitate long-term commitment. The founders of Saint Martin de Porres House in San Francisco, for example, had been troubled by the revolving door membership of the New York Catholic Worker, and so they made a number of deliberate choices to help members pursue individual vocations while remaining involved in the Catholic Worker. They made sure that everyone had a day off and some private space so that they would not be obliged to do hospitality seven days a week. Since the founders were mostly single, this initially meant maintaining both a soup kitchen restaurant and a separate residence; as couples formed, the community agreed to pay rent on separate family apartments in which each family would practice hospitality on a small scale. In order to pay the bills, some community members took part-time jobs while others worked full-time in their shared ministries. These responsibilities rotated to allow individuals to pursue particular vocations, whether these involved paid employment or a specific activist cause. Early members of the community chose projects ranging from prison visitation to working at a baby clinic to publicizing the work of the United Farm Workers, thus covering a wide range of the works of mercy.[18]

Despite these efforts, however, the community saw more than twenty members come and go during the first three years. Still, several of the founding members, including Chris and Joan Montesano, were able to make a lifelong commitment to the Catholic Worker movement, both at Saint Martin's and at the associated Sheep Ranch Catholic Worker farm. The core community at Saint Martin's has continued to shift, but the presence of a strong extended community, and the fact that San Francisco attracts a wide range of social activists, has allowed this Worker house to thrive for nearly forty years.

Though the founders of Saint Martin's had been deeply influenced by the Catholic *cursillo* movement, the community quickly moved away from Dorothy Day's attitude of intense loyalty to the Catholic Church. By 1974 an observer reported that they had a weekly house Mass (officiated by the activist priest of a local parish) but were divided about the importance of participating in parish life. At least one member had renounced his Catholic faith because of opposition to the church's hierarchy, yet most others described themselves as theologically conservative, at least in their inclination to take the Sermon on the Mount as a literal guide for life. "Members of the community," wrote this observer, "derive spiritual sustenance from the support of the community itself and from the Scriptures, as much as from the formal sacraments of the Roman Catholic Church."[19] This spiritual evolution continued and today the community's website explains: "We are a community of people with diverse spiritual practices although our roots are in, and we continue to be inspired by, the Catholic Worker movement."[20] Members of Saint Martin's sometimes jokingly describe themselves as the "Jewish Worker" or the "Gay Worker," reflecting the diversity of their membership.

The San Francisco pattern of separate households working together was soon adopted in a number of other places. In Portland, Oregon, Pat and Mufti McNassar began doing small-scale hospitality in their home in 1968, but it was not until 1972 that they took the step of hammering up a sign identifying themselves as Ammon Hennacy House. In 1974 Jim and Genny Barnhardt followed suit with Emmaus House. A year later the two families, along with others, began running a soup kitchen out of a nearby Methodist church, and in 1976 Catholic Worker families began moving to available houses on the site of what had been an urban commune. "The block," as it became known, evolved into something like a traditional village, with spontaneous potlucks in unfenced backyards, several families' worth of children growing up together, and the entire group taking responsibility for raising turkeys, rabbits, and chickens. The group also protested regularly at a nuclear power plant and at a Trident submarine base. But the 1982 sale of the land where they lived presaged the end of the community, as the members found they could not sustain a common spirit without living in close proximity.[21]

The Des Moines Catholic Worker

Well into the 1970s, new houses continued to be founded that would evolve into regional "motherhouses," supporting smaller communities and inspiring a variety of individuals who have gone on to support the movement in other places. The Des Moines Catholic Worker was founded in 1976 by Frank "Sonny" Cordaro and Joe da Via. Cordaro, who stayed on much longer than his cofounder, was the son of a prominent local Catholic family whose spirituality had been shaped by both the Catholic charismatic movement and the Berrigans' resistance activities. His charismatic personality attracted everyone from traditional Des Moines Catholics to hippies just passing through town. The first volunteer was Helen Tichy, a retired schoolteacher who came to the door during the community's first summer and said, "I've been reading the Catholic Worker since the 1940s, [and] I never ever thought I'd see a Catholic Worker in Des Moines." Though she did not move in, she continued as a regular volunteer well into her nineties. Richard Cleaver, an alumnus of both Grinnell College and the New York Catholic Worker, arrived a few years later and began serving "as our community expert on the Catholic Worker and its history."[22] His example would soon lead a steady stream of Grinnell students and graduates to the Des Moines house, and in some cases beyond it to New York City and other Worker houses. Though he no longer lives at the house, Cleaver continues to be closely associated with both the Worker and the emerging movement of gay liberation theology. Another hippy attracted to the house was Mike Sprong, who has embodied the Worker's artisanal ethos by starting both a farm and a publishing house that has issued a variety of Catholic Worker books, including Richard Cleaver's.

Drawing on such a wide range of personalities, the Des Moines Catholic Worker quickly established itself as a local center for both hospitality and resistance. Within a year the live-in volunteer community had expanded to eight members; they added a second hospitality house in 1978 and a third in 1981. At the same time, they branched out to establish a Peace and Justice Center, dubbed Isaiah House, with other local peace activists. Though Isaiah House was short-lived, it hosted a national gathering of the antinuclear organization Mobilization for Survival in 1978. After its closing, the space was transformed into Hansen House, a hospitality center for men leaving prison directed by a Presbyterian minister whom Frank Cordaro had befriended. Richard Cleaver, along with another recent Grinnell graduate named Kristin Layng, launched a small Catholic Worker farm in a struggling rural town in 1981. In 1985 the Workers lent one of their houses to the Kindred Hospitality House, apparently an attempt to do Worker-style hospitality without an explicit connection to Catholicism. Though that house returned to the Catholic Worker fold a few years later, its creation is emblematic of the Des Moines Worker's longstanding commitment to support others "doing the work" of hospitality and resistance, regardless of their religious affiliations. That spirit of partnership has been evident in more recent years in the community's partnership with a local development center in Chiapas.[23]

Over the years, cofounder Frank Cordaro has continued to be a vital presence in the life of the Des Moines Catholic Worker. But he has not always been a member of the live-in community of Catholic Workers. His commitment to Berrigan-style resistance has repeatedly landed him in prison, for both short and long terms, and his letters from prison have always been featured prominently in the pages of the community's newspaper (and, more recently, in its e-mail distribution list). Cordaro also left the community early in the 1980s in order to complete his studies for the priesthood at Saint John's University in Collegeville, Minnesota. After his ordination, he was assigned to a series of parishes in the Des Moines diocese, and did not move back to the Worker until the late 1990s. During his absence, according to Cordaro's report, the live-in volunteer community continued to practice good hospitality but gradually lost a sense of connection to the larger Catholic Worker movement and its spiritual underpinnings. "They didn't come in here looking to take over the place," Cordaro explained in a 2002 interview. Instead, "everyone who had any kind of background just disappeared, and they were left with the place. And they had no affinity for the church or faith." Cordaro realized the situation during the community's fifteenth anniversary, when the full-time Workers refused to join him in an anniversary dialogue "on the tradition and Dorothy Day and some of the religious aspects."[24]

Though Cordaro might have used his position on the board of the community's land trust to press for a change, he recognized that the "sweat equity" of the full-time Workers gave them the right to determine the spirit of the house. So his approach, instead, was to draw on the larger movement—by that time quite vigorous—to shift the balance in Des Moines. He encouraged Joanne Kennedy, who had cut her teeth at the Los Angeles Catholic Worker, to join the Des Moines community, and gradually he increased his involvement until he was ready to move back in personally. "If you're going to regain the community," Cordaro explained, "have some influence on the community, you've got to move back into the community, pay your price, you've got to put your time in, you've got to put the sweat equity of leadership, and once you've done that, then you can say your piece."

Cordaro's return, to be sure, did not result in a monolithic or exclusively Catholic community. The Des Moines Catholic Worker continues to be a rich blend of Catholics, Quakers, Baptists, and others. What happened was simply that the local community reconnected with the diverse influences that are present in the Worker movement as a whole. More so than many other houses, moreover, it succeeded in blurring the distinction between "guests" and "Workers." One of the most prominent Des Moines Workers, Carla Dawson, came originally as a homeless single mother; she has since raised her children in the Worker and continues to function as what Cordaro calls the "franchise player" of the community. The contrasting yet compatible temperaments of Cordaro and Dawson have helped create space for a wide range of personalities at the Des Moines Worker, and the community takes pride in being both interracial and significantly older, on average, than the typical Catholic Worker house.

Jonah House

Though Los Angeles, Des Moines, and other communities have inspired dozens of new Catholic Worker houses, perhaps the community that has come closest to supplanting New York's role as national motherhouse is not a Catholic Worker house at all. Jonah House in Baltimore was founded in 1973 by Phil

Berrigan and Liz McAlister. Building on the work of the Catons-ville Nine, they hoped that a supportive community would allow them and others to continue engaging in acts of resistance over the course of a lifetime. Parents living at Jonah House, for example, often choose to engage in acts of civil disobedience that might result in a year or more of jail time, knowing that the community will support their spouse in caring for the children. (Both Berrigan and McAlister, for example, spent significant chunks of their children's early years in prison, though never both at once.) In 1980 Jonah House became the launching pad for the Plowshares movement, in which peace activists court lengthy prison sentences by physically damaging weapons and military equipment. (The name, of course, is a reference to Isaiah's prophecy that "they shall beat swords into plowshares and their spears into pruning hooks.") Phil Berrigan and seven others went to the General Electric plant in King of Prussia, Pennsylvania, where they hammered components of the Mark 12A nuclear missile, and spilled their own blood on the damaged equipment. That initial action has inspired more than eighty subsequent actions, many of them carried out by members of Jonah House or of Catholic Worker communities.

Jonah House has never identified as a Catholic Worker, in part because they have never been willing to place hospitality on a par with resistance. (They do, however, maintain a food pantry that serves about one hundred people every week.) Still, its members articulate their identity as a "faith-based" community, rooted in Roman Catholicism but open to people of all faiths, in terms quite similar to those used at Haley House and other Catholic Worker houses. They sponsor weekly Scripture studies and lay Eucharists and declare on their website: "We submit ourselves to the over-arching standard of nonviolence: love of enemies (Mt 5:43), love for one another (Jn 13:34), and living by the truth (Jn 3:21)." They also cooperate closely with Worker communities on many levels. They host roundtables to clarify their thought along with neighboring Viva House and cosponsor "faith and resistance retreats" three times a year with

Dorothy Day Catholic Worker in Washington, D.C. (These retreats, held on Good Friday, Hiroshima Day, and the Feast of the
Holy Innocents, reflect an intricate blend of liturgical and activist
sensibilities, often featuring ceremonial blood pouring at the
Pentagon.) Jonah House also plays a leading role in the Atlantic
Life Community, a resistance-oriented network of individuals
and communities that includes many of the Catholic Worker
houses along the East Coast.[25]

The influence of Jonah House and, more broadly, of the
Berrigan family, is now visible almost everywhere in the Catholic
Worker movement. The Des Moines community named one of
its houses after Phil Berrigan shortly after his death in 2002, while
the Los Angeles community had named its resistance center after
him years earlier. Frank Cordaro has declared that "we're not
afraid to call the Berrigan brothers, Dan and Phil, our Rabbis and
Jonah House the Mother House of US faith-based resistance to
war and the ways of war."[26] Jonah House "alumni," including Phil
and Liz's son Jerry Mechtenberg-Berrigan, are well represented
among the recent founders of Worker communities, and countless college students have gravitated to the Worker after participating in spring break service trips to Jonah House. At the most
recent national gathering of Catholic Workers, a prominent dis-
play featured contemporary-style icons of just two movement
"saints": Dorothy Day and Phil Berrigan.

It is important to stress the connection between Jonah House
and the Catholic Worker, because Dorothy Day and the Berrigans
are sometimes portrayed as representing two rival approaches to
Catholic nonviolence. When the Berrigans began promoting "direct action" as the central Christian vocation, Day protested that
"Peter Maurin, co-founder of *The Catholic Worker,* insisted that
the works of mercy are the most direct form of action there is."[27]
She questioned whether the destruction of property could truly
be nonviolent and worried about the personal and familial costs
of long prison terms, especially for young people without a mature
commitment to nonviolence.[28] Catholic Workers continue to hold
a wide range of views on Plowshares actions, but that is just the

point. For the past twenty-five years, the Catholic Worker movement has been the primary carrier of *both* Day's and the Berrigans' version of Christian nonviolence.

The Legacy of the 1960s

In the end, the hippie generation of Catholic Workers achieved something that very few of the founders had: they figured out how to make whole lives out of the Catholic Worker movement. At the time of this writing, a remarkable number of founders (or "second founders") of communities launched in the 1960s and 1970s are still active in the movement. Baltimore's Willa Bickham and Brendan Walsh, Des Moines's Frank Cordaro, Los Angeles's Catherine Morris and Jeff Dietrich, San Francisco's Joan and Chris Montesano, rural Iowa's Betsy Keenan and Brian Terrell, Detroit's Tom Lumpkin, and many others entered the movement during the last years of Dorothy Day's life and still live in houses of hospitality or at Catholic Worker farms.

Perhaps because they came of age during the ferment of Vatican II, this generation of Workers may be somewhat more spiritually cohesive than either their predecessors or their successors. Very few are as harshly anticlerical as Ammon Hennacy or as traditionally pious as Dorothy Day. Many were seminarians or members of religious orders in their early adulthood, then became part of the great exodus of priests and religious that simultaneously enriched the lay apostolate and endangered traditional Catholic patterns of ministry. Many participated in the Catholic charismatic revival, which spawned a variety of intentional communities as well as propelling people toward the Worker. Most eventually gravitated toward the style of liberal Catholicism embodied by such organizations as Call to Action. Typically, they support gay liberation and women's ordination, though they may be more ambivalent about abortion. They value liturgical informality and an approach to the Scriptures that draws direct connections between the Word and the world. They recognize the differences between their own spirituality and that of Dorothy Day but cherish her as a model of what Brian Terrell has called "loving defiance" and "faithful dissent."[29]

The endurance of these Workers, and of the communities they founded, is all the more remarkable because they entered the movement at the time when many observers thought it was dying. When William Miller published *A Harsh and Dreadful Love* in 1973, for example, the movement included hospitality houses in around twenty cities, roughly the same number it had during the early peak year of 1942. Around ten new communities were founded in that year alone, half of them destined to endure for at least thirty years. Yet Miller concluded his history with a tone of elegy: "The crisis of the times fell upon the Catholic Worker movement. There was no longer the sense of community that had marked the early days when Workers had trooped behind Peter Maurin to Union Square." Writing a year later, Paul Hanly Furfey, one of the Worker's most loyal clerical supporters, con-fided that "I rather suspect that we are near the end of the Catholic Worker era. The Catholic Worker people were radicals. The future belongs not to the radicals, but to the revolutionar-ies." A full decade later, when the New York paper was listing about twice as many communities as it had in 1942, Marc Ellis echoed this sentiment, telling Rosalie Riegle Troester that the Worker would "never again be a major [intellectual] force [in the Catholic Church] . . . the movement that informs the North American church . . . is liberation theology." And Mel Piehl chose to conclude his history of the Worker in 1965, on the grounds that in that year "the new Catholic Left emerged amidst a general crisis in American Catholicism."[30]

Such testimonies certainly make me reluctant to make sweep-ing pronouncements about the future of the Catholic Worker! Yet, with hindsight, it is possible to identify two things that these observers did not see. The first is the Catholic Worker's generous capacity to befriend, and eventually incorporate, other move-ments. The "revolutionaries" and "liberationists" that Furfey and Ellis contrasted to the Catholic Worker are now, in many cases, active participants in the movement. The second is the way the

1960s generation of Workers picked up on Dorothy Day's generous example by befriending one another. Many of the long-term
Workers I just mentioned spent time at more than one community, and they visited frequently after moving on. Clusters of
Worker communities in the Midwest, West Coast, and East Coast
began hosting annual gatherings in the mid-1970s, around the
time Tivoli was declining as a gathering center for the movement.
These would set a precedent for the great national gatherings
of the 1980s and beyond, which attracted participants in the
hundreds—far more than the retreats of the 1940s.[31] Both regional and national gatherings often included acts of civil disobedience at nearby military facilities, and the shared experience
of arrest and, in some cases, imprisonment deepened friendships. Moreover, virtually all the houses published newsletters,
and the distribution of these humble publications around the
movement fostered strong relationships.

In short, what Dorothy Day experienced as a generation gap
was, for the younger generation, a remarkable experience of gen-
erational continuity. Many of them came to the movement much
younger than Day had been when she joined the Catholic Church.
She saw them making the political and sexual mistakes of her
youth and was distressed; they saw in her a path from troubled
youth to lifelong commitment. One such young Worker was Jeff
Dietrich of the Los Angeles community. Writing in the *National
Catholic Reporter* just days after her death, he told his story: he
had arrived at the Catholic Worker in 1970 as a "hippie/revolu-
tionary." He was "awaiting the fall of the corrupt ruling class,
which for me also included the church." He was attracted to the
works of mercy but still asked, "What the hell does Catholic have
to do with the revolution anyway?" As he learned Dorothy Day's
life story and immersed himself in the life of the community,
though, things started making sense. Moving from the soup
kitchen to the daily Eucharist, he saw that "Christ meant the eucharist to be a symbol of our lives." And this "profoundly revolutionary insight" allowed him to stay: "Now, because of Dorothy,
my radicalism had taken roots in the last place I would have

suspected: the Catholic Church. While other young radicals fell by the wayside, as their notions of the Woodstock Nation faded, I had the strength to struggle for a greater kingdom."[32] Twenty-seven years after writing those words, Dietrich is still at the Catholic Worker; his commitment is just one token of the remarkable power of Day's vision in a generation not her own.

[1] Day, "On Pilgrimage," *Catholic Worker* 32, no. 4 (December 1965): 1, 2, 7.

[2] William D. Miller, *Dorothy Day: A Biography* (New York: Harper & Row, 1982), 472–73, 480–82.

[3] Ibid., 469–73; Day, "Pilgrimage to Cuba—Part I," *Catholic Worker* 29, no. 2 (September 1962): 1; "Pilgrimage to Cuba—Part II," *Catholic Worker* 29, no. 3 (October 1962): 1–2, 4; "Pilgrimage to Cuba—Part III," *Catholic Worker* 29, no. 4 (November 1962): 1, 3–4, 6–8; "Pilgrimage to Cuba—Part IV," *Catholic Worker* 29, no. 5 (December 1962): 2, 5; and "More about Cuba," *Catholic Worker* 29, no. 7 (February 1963): 1, 4; and "On Pilgrimage," *Catholic Worker* 36, no. 5 (June 1970): 1–2, 7.

[4] Miller, *Dorothy Day,* 484–90.

[5] Ibid., 490, 502.

[6] Interview with Matt Daloisio, 3 January 2002; and Kathe McKenna, "Another Beginning," *Haley House Newsletter,* June 1969, DD/CWC, series W-19, box 1, folder 11.

[7] Dorothy Day to "Fellow Workers" (1972), DD/CWC, series W-19, box 1, folder 4; and Haley House Fund-raising Appeal, DD/CWC, series W-4, box 6, folder 10.

[8] Kathe McKenna, in Rosalie Riegle Troester, *Voices from the Catholic Worker* (Philadelphia: Temple University Press, 1993), 92.

[9] Various brochures and flyers, DD/CWC, series W-19, box 1, folder 11.

[10] Ibid.

[11] Kathe McKenna, interviewed by Rosalie Troester, 9 June 1988, 62, DD/CWC, series W-9, box 6, folder 9; and *Haley House Newsletter,* Easter 1985; and "Developments at Haley House," *Haley House Newsletter,* Hiroshima-Nagasaki-Feast of the Transfiguration 1985, 6–7, both at DD/CWC, series W-19, box 1, folder 12.

[12] "Developments at Haley House," *Haley House Newsletter,* Hiroshima-Nagasaki-Feast of the Transfiguration 1985, 6–7, DD/CWC, series W-19, box 1, folder 12.

[13] "Developments at Haley House," *Haley House Newsletter,* Hiroshima-Nagasaki-Feast of the Transfiguration 1985, 6–7; *Haley House Newsletter,* Hiroshima-Nagasaki, Feast of the Transfiguration 1985, 13; James Levinson, "Chanukah," *Haley House Newsletter,* Feast of the Holy Innocents 1985, 5–6, all at DD/CWC, series W-19, box 1, folder 12.

[14] Kathe McKenna, "A Dangerous Idea," *Haley House Newsletter,* Winter 1991, 8, DD/CWC, series W-19, unboxed folder.

[15] Interview with Matt Daloisio, 3 January 2002.

[16] Interview with Brendan Walsh and Willa Bickham, 25 May 2000.

[17] This statement appears in their community's listing in "Houses of Hospitality," *Catholic Worker* 55, no. 3 (May 1988): 6–7.

[18] Elizabeth B. Flynn, "Catholic Worker Spirituality: A Sect within a Church," M.A. thesis, Graduate Theological Union, 1974, 87–126.

[19] Ibid., 117–19, 132.

[20] "Martin de Porres House of Hospitality," at http://www.martindeporres.org/.

[21] Keith D. Barger, "Hearing the Cry of the Poor: The Catholic Worker Communities in Oregon and Washington 1940 to the Present," senior thesis, University of Portland, 1992, 19–23, at DD/CWC, series W-7.1, box 4, folder 5.

[22] Frank Cordaro, "Book Review: *Know My Name: A Gay Liberation Theology,* by Richard Cleaver," *Via Pacis* 20, no. 2 (Summer 1996): 6.

[23] Early flyers, DD/CWC, series W-21, box 1, folders 1 and 2; Frank Cordaro, "On Hospitality," *Via Pacis* 1, no. 8 (June–July 1977): 2; Frank Cordaro, "The Early Years," *Via Pacis* 11, no. 3 (April–May 1987): 1; "Catholic Worker starts farm project," *Catholic Mirror,* June 11, 1981, 12, in DD/CWC, series W-21, box 3, folder 3; "Kindred Appeal," *Via Pacis* 10, no. 3 (June–July 1986): 2; and interview with Claire Quiner, 2 February 2002.

[24] Interview with Frank Cordaro, 2 February 2002.

[25] "Jonah House: Community—Nonviolence—Resistance," http://www.jonahhouse.org/phil.htm.

[26] Frank Cordaro, "Twenty-Five Years—Reflections from a Co-Founder," *Via Pacis,* 25, no. 2 (June 2001). After Phil Berrigan's death in 2002, one of the Des Moines community's houses was named in his honor, while the Los Angeles Worker named its "Resistance Center" for the Berrigans in 1971. See Dan and Chris Delany et al., "Los Angeles," *Catholic Worker* 37, no. 6 (July–August 1971): 6.

[27] Day, *Loaves and Fishes* (New York: Harper and Row, 1963), xvii.

[28] On Day's response to the ultra-resistance movement, see Anne Klejment, "War Resistance and Property Destruction," in Patrick G. Coy, ed., *Revolution of the Heart: Essays on the Catholic Worker* (Philadelphia: New Society Publishers, 1988), 272–309; Anne Klejment and Nancy L. Roberts, "The Catholic Worker and the Vietnam War," in Klejment and Roberts, eds., *American Catholic Pacifism: The Influence of Dorothy Day and the Catholic Worker Movement* (Westport, CT: Praeger, 1996), 153–69; and Stephen Thomas Krupa, "Dorothy Day and the Spirituality of Nonviolence," Ph.D. thesis, Graduate Theological Union, 1997, 232–36.

[29] Brian Terrell, "Dorothy Day, Rebel Catholic: Living in a State of Permanent Dissatisfaction with the Church," in William Thorn, Philip Runkel, and Susan Mountin, eds., *Dorothy Day and the Catholic Worker Movement: Centenary Essays* (Milwaukee: Marquette University Press, 2001), 145.

[30] William Miller, *A Harsh and Dreadful Love: Dorothy Day and the Catholic Worker Movement* (New York: Liveright, 1973), 348; Anthony William Novitsky, "The Ideological Development of Peter Maurin's Green Revolution," Ph.D. dissertation, State University of New York at Buffalo, 1976, 324; Ellis cited in Troester, *Voices,* 520–21; and Mel Piehl, *Breaking Bread: The Catholic Worker and the Origin of Catholic Radicalism in America* (Philadelphia: Temple University Press, 1982), xii.

[31] Peggy Scherer and Daniel Mauk, "Worker Conference," *Catholic Worker* 42, no. 8 (October–November 1976): 4; Peggy Scherer, "National CW Gathering," *Catholic Worker* 50, no. 5 (August 1983): 2; Tim Lambert, "A Birthday Celebration," *Catholic Worker* 54, no. 8 (December 1987): 1.

[32] Jeff Dietrich, "One Worker's journey: From hippie to Christ," *National Catholic Reporter* 17, no. 8 (12 December 1980): 7.

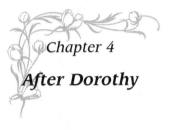

Chapter 4

After Dorothy

For the past twenty-five years, Dorothy Day has not had the opportunity to lead the Catholic Worker movement directly, although many Catholic Workers believe that "Saint Dorothy" is actively interceding for them from beyond the grave. They may well be right, for in many ways her influence is stronger than it was during the last years of her life. In this period she has continued to lead through her writings, which are much more readily available than they were just prior to her death, and even more so through her prestige as the United States' most prominent—if still not canonized—Catholic saint. Few American Christians today who are serious about either peace or urban poverty are unaware of her legacy. Her name graces both Catholic Worker houses and more conventional social service centers, and her books appear on syllabi of hundreds of college courses.

Yet Day's fame is not the only reason for the continued growth of the Catholic Worker movement. The year of her death also saw the election of Ronald Reagan to the presidency, and his policies soon gave new importance to the works of mercy. Over the course of two terms, Reagan cut the budget for the Department of Housing and Urban Development by three-quarters and simultaneously reduced government incentives for the private creation of low-income housing. These changes, coupled with an economic recession and the widespread dein-stitutionalization of persons with mental illness, created an epidemic of homelessness that overwhelmed large urban shel-ters and spread to small cities that had not typically had shelters at all. At the same time, the intensification of the Cold War lent new relevance to Worker protests against nuclear weapons, and Reagan's financing of death squad governments in Central Amer-ica sent a wave of refugees to the United States and Canada. Though Reagan was not personally responsible, the AIDS crisis also erupted during his presidency, creating yet another occasion for Catholic Workers to comfort the afflicted and visit the sick.

Each of these challenges could in itself provide a mission for a Catholic Worker house, and some of the new houses were devoted exclusively to urban hospitality, to antiwar resistance, to sanctuary for Central American refugees, or to AIDS hospice work. At the same time, the previous generation of Workers was more than ready to initiate newcomers into the broader dimen-sions of the movement. National gatherings swelled to five hun-dred people by 1987, when Workers gathered in the Nevada desert to protest at a nuclear test site and to learn, in the words of one participant, about the small things that made up the Catholic Worker: "growing vegetables . . . raising children . . . fixing meals . . . sorting and distributing clothing . . . caring for the sick . . . making candles, and . . . waiting, with the poor, sick, and imprisoned in their various conditions of life. [Catholic Worker life] is not defined by a few bold gestures, but by many little things."[1]

All of these influences helped the movement continue to grow. Ninety new communities were formed during the 1980s; fifty lasted at least a decade, and forty-three are still in existence today. On average, these are somewhat smaller and less influen-tial than the thirty-five survivors from the previous period, in part because so many are located in such smaller cities as Duluth, Minnesota, and Columbia, Missouri. Seventy-nine communities were founded in the 1990s, and seventy-two between 2000 and

2006, suggesting that the rate of community creation has stabi-
lized. It is, of course, impossible to say whether these new communities will achieve the same level of stability as their immediate
predecessors. Certainly a good many are thriving.

One thriving community is Loaves and Fishes in Duluth,
Minnesota, which today includes three houses occupied by a
diverse cluster of live-in Workers and a roughly equal number
of long-term guests. Loaves and Fishes was founded by Angie
Miller and Steve O'Neil a few years after Dorothy Day's death.
During the early years of their marriage, O'Neil worked as a farm
organizer while Miller did legal aid for senior citizens, but even
these service-oriented jobs did not give them sufficient sense of
meaning in life. "We decided," recalled Miller, "we didn't want
to have a boring life." They discussed starting an intentional
community with some friends, but when those friends decided
they weren't ready to take the plunge, they chose to enhance
their own community skills by joining an already existing community. This decision quickly brought them into contact with
the Catholic Worker movement, which by that time had grown
into perhaps the most prominent network of activist communities in the United States. Steve visited a number of Catholic
Worker houses, though the couple eventually settled on Washington, D.C.'s Community of Creative Nonviolence, then a very
large shelter that engaged in Berrigan-style resistance activities
on behalf of the homeless.

Though the Community of Creative Nonviolence did not identify as a Catholic Worker, it cooperated closely with the Worker
houses in Washington. After a year and a half there, O'Neil and
Miller were ready to start a venture closer to home, and by then
it seemed entirely natural that that venture would be part of the
Catholic Worker movement. After waiting briefly for others to
join them, they realized that they had sufficient resources to
start on their own. Taking jobs in Duluth, they purchased a large,
run-down house for $25,000 and began quietly to do hospitality.
A friend who was involved in the sanctuary movement called to
say that she needed space for two teenage Guatemalan boys

who were hoping to reunite with their father in Canada. The younger brother wound up having to wait two years for that re-union, during which time he became like their son: "It was all very informal, he wasn't really legally with us. He wasn't legally in the United States. But he went to high school and he got a driver's permit, and he was great." Around the same time, a friend of theirs who was leaving an abusive marriage moved in with her daughter. These experiences persuaded O'Neil and Miller that they were ready to do hospitality on a larger scale, so they wrote what Catholic Workers call a "begging letter" to friends and family. "A ton of money" poured in, and they were able to put three large bedrooms into the house's attic, room for about ten guests at a time.[2]

They continued to work in social service jobs and to partici-pate in peace activism, and their local prominence gradually drew others to their community. Donna Howard, for example, came to Duluth with two teenage sons in the wake of a difficult divorce. Though she had originally envisioned joining a com-munity only after her children were grown, Loaves and Fishes provided both her and her sons with an important support net-work during the first Gulf War. They decided to join the com-munity by purchasing a new house, opening up space both for themselves and for expanded hospitality. The involvement of Howard's sons made Loaves and Fishes an appealing center for young activists in Duluth, and one of those activists, Joel Kilgour, ultimately devoted more than a decade of his life to the com-munity. The larger Catholic Worker network also proved to be a source of seasoned community members. After several years at Worker communities on the East Coast, Reba and Scott Mathern-Jacobson joined Loaves and Fishes in order to be closer to their extended family; Greg and Michele Obed moved there from Jonah House in order to combine their resistance activities with a deeper experience of hospitality.[3]

Most of the people just mentioned no longer live full-time at Loaves and Fishes, though O'Neil, Miller, and Howard continue to reside in the neighborhood and participate actively as "extended community" members. Since their departures, Loaves and Fishes has continued to attract new members about as quickly as it has lost older ones. Though the "revolving door" creates tension and some abiding concern about the community's long term prospects, the community appears to have achieved a vitality that is not dependent on any single person or family.

Throughout its history, Loaves and Fishes has combined small-scale hospitality with vigorous involvement in a range of activist causes. Yet in other places the continuing crisis of homelessness has led Catholic Worker communities to expand their hospitality activities dramatically, and this expansion has often challenged traditional Catholic Worker notions about personalism. In Syracuse, New York, Dorothy Day House was founded in the early 1980s in response to a rapidly increasing local population of homeless persons. Though the need continued to grow over the course of the decade, by the late 1980s the community had to turn to Catholic Charities to help it resolve a financial crisis. This in turn led to a significant conflict between the community's founders—some of whom were still live-in Workers—and administrators working for Catholic Charities. Citing the Catholic Worker tradition of opposition to state-supported charity, the founders refused to be certified as social workers or to receive formal salaries. Eventually, they were forced out, yet the house continued for several years to identify as a Catholic Worker community. "This [was] a curious claim," noted one observer, "considering that Dorothy Day House is comparable to all other Catholic Charities shelters, with one exception: Dorothy Day House has a picture of Dorothy Day hanging in their living room."[4]

This ironic comment might suggest a sharp division between "true" Catholic Workers that eschew nonprofit status and professionalization, and those that abandon both resistance work and the personalist approach to hospitality in order to serve more people. In fact, there is much gray area between these extremes, as is illustrated in the story of Saint Joseph's House in Minneapolis, known today as the HOPE Community. This community was created in 1977 when three Sisters of Saint Joseph moved into an urban house that they made available as a shelter for battered women. (One of the three, Char Madigan, had previously spent a summer at the New York Catholic Worker, and they had maintained a "Christ room" in a small apartment for a few months.) Following the example of other Catholic Worker houses, they encouraged a few regular volunteers to launch a communal farm in rural Saint Joseph, which provided the house with produce for a few years. They also balanced their hospitality with resistance by protesting at local defense contractors like Honeywell, as well as by speaking out strongly on behalf of gay and lesbian persons. A decade later, their strong sense of connection to the Worker was evident when they hosted a series of roundtable discussions on poverty, pacifism, and personalism, and then declared in a new mission statement that "St. Joseph's House is a shelter and house of hospitality for women and children rooted in the Catholic Worker tradition." A more expanded statement published a few months later explained that the community was "dedicated to 'comforting the afflicted and afflicting the comfortable.' We give comfort by offering shelter in a safe and supportive environment to women in crisis and their children. We afflict the comfortable by publishing writings on issues of love, peace and justice."[5]

Around the same time, however, a variety of factors was reshaping their sense of identity. After ten years of active involvement, founder Char Madigan, by her own account, "began to have kind of the aura of the priest in the rectory." Believing that "the revolution can't work if one person is the chief," she tried to hand over more leadership to former residents and neighbors of the house, and in 1988 the house began hiring these individuals as paid staff. This practice violated the traditional Catholic Worker emphasis on voluntary poverty but also helped them avoid the tendency of many Workers to be dominated by "downwardly mobile" children of the middle class, for whom poverty is a spiritual idea rather than a hard reality, and who are always aware that they can fall back on their family wealth or educational credentials. Around the same time, they spun off two transitional houses for residents who required support for more than the one-month stays allowed by the original shelter. In 1989, moreover, their windows were shattered by gunshots, and they realized that they needed to take "active leadership in changing what wasn't safe and nurturing on our block." Surveying the boarded-up buildings that surrounded them, the St. Joseph's community decided the best response was to buy up houses on their block, then rehab them as affordable housing units. To do so, they created a separate organization, Homes on Portland Enterprises, or HOPE, which was incorporated as a 501(c)(3) nonprofit.[6]

Though this was hardly the first nonprofit established by Catholic Workers, those who made the decision were keenly aware that they were breaking with the ideology of personalism. At first, they sought to resolve the dilemma by maintaining a distinction between St. Joseph's as an unincorporated personalist venture and HOPE as a rapidly growing nonprofit. In practice, the two entities were thoroughly intertwined, and both were committed to the sort of approaches to urban poverty that nonprofit status made possible. So in 1993 St. Joseph's sent a Christmas letter to "our dearest of Kin" asking for advice. "The St. Joseph's House community is changing and our response is being pushed far beyond the limits of the original vision," the card explained. "St. Joe's is the grandmother on our block and many are calling on her to take the lead in the redemption of our neighborhood from the violence, drugs and desperation. . . . We are being asked to make use of funding sources we have avoided in the past. We are being asked to change."[7] Before doing so, they needed to hear about the priorities, hopes, and fears of their core supporters. The response, which was reported in a subsequent newsletter, was cautiously supportive of the change: writers warned against "let[ting] outside sources suppress your voice of protest" but also noted that "change is difficult at best, however, inability to change is almost certain death." Accordingly, St. Joseph's recommitted to its personalist focus on just one city block, but also merged with HOPE in order to receive a million dollar grant for the construction of thirteen affordable housing units.[8]

"St. Joseph's HOPE Community is a catalyst for change, growth and safety in our neighborhood," declared a new mission statement. "We work to build an inclusive, lifegiving community by transforming relationships of fear into creative opportunities of mutual support." The new organization's newsletter continued to highlight the evils of federal military spending, suggesting that they had not let nonprofit status silence their prophetic voice. And though they stopped calling themselves a Catholic Worker and (reluctantly) stopped sending their newsletters to the Catholic Worker archive, they remained clear about their fidelity to the movement that had birthed them. "Our commitments to social justice issues and our Catholic Worker roots remain very strong," wrote director Deanna Carter, while founder Char Madigan declared that "I think Peter and Dorothy would bless our latest efforts, though we have evolved past what they taught us."[9]

As this story suggests, Char Madigan and the other leaders were very conscious of the tensions between classic Catholic Worker ideology and their community's evolving identity. This consciousness was itself the result of a lively, and for the most part friendly, debate that bubbled through the movement during the 1980s. This debate brought to the surface the long-standing tension between the many Catholic Worker communities that refuse to receive government aid or be recognized as 501(c)(3) nonprofits and those that accept nonprofit status and (in some cases) extensive support from the government's social service bureaucracy. The tension can be traced all the way back to the contrast between New York City houses and the community in Rochester, though that contrast should not be overstated. When the federal government tried to collect $300,000 in delinquent income taxes from the New York Catholic Worker in 1972, the community defended itself on the grounds that they were eligible for nonprofit status even though they had never applied, and the government dropped the claim. At least one Rochester

Worker, on the other side, acknowledged to Dorothy Day that "I did . . . and do still regret the necessity of incorporation."[10]

In any case, the stakes were raised in the 1980s, as many Workers came to believe they had a moral obligation to expand into transitional housing and other activities that required a more substantial income stream than donations could provide. The resulting dilemmas were felt especially strongly at Haley House. There was little debate when the community first applied for Federal Emergency Management Agency funds in 1984, but the discussion was much sharper when time came for renewal three years later. As Kathe McKenna explained in a newsletter article, several people who had been very new when the first decision was made wished to adhere more closely to Catholic Worker tradition. They pointed, moreover, to the fact that in the intervening years FEMA had taken on responsibility for establishing evacuation and dissident containment camps in the event of a "national emergency." It was thus easier for it to be portrayed as part of the military establishment that needed to be resisted. Still, McKenna and others wished to honor the hard work of activists who had pushed the federal government to make money available for homelessness programs.[11]

Since the Haley House community was committed to consensus decision making, a final decision did not come quickly. They also shared their discernment process with the larger Catholic Worker movement. McKenna's original article quoted extensively from Ann O'Connor of Unity Kitchen Community, who defended strict anarchism on the grounds that "all human structures and organizations . . . are under demonic control because of their fallen nature, and therefore have an existence that works against human life." McKenna responded that while she was still temperamentally an anarchist, she was troubled by the dualism implicit in O'Connor's position. "The demonic element which is so easy to point out in some governments, corporations, and the real estate industry," she wrote, also "exists in the peace movement, in Haley House, in families, and in myself." McKenna acknowledged that it could be appropriate to refuse government benefits for oneself but wondered if it was acceptable to refuse them on behalf of the homeless persons who might benefit enormously.

In their next newsletter, Haley House published an open letter from Scott Schaeffer-Duffy of Worcester's Saints Francis and Thérèse Catholic Worker, who took up the other side of the debate with vigor. Haley House's commitment to consensus alone, he suggested, should preclude federal funding, since the government by nature is too large and impersonal to practice anything like consensus. In response to McKenna's concerns about dualism, Schaeffer-Duffy noted that there is still a significant distinction between governments and churches insofar as "the Church remains a free association which is not backed up by physical punishment as is the state." Ultimately, Haley House continued to rely on federal funds to build an expansive network of transitional apartments and—unlike many other Catholic Workers with nonprofit status—continued to articulate the reasons for its decisions. "While we support the War Tax Resisters and their courage to refuse to pay taxes for war, we certainly have no problem allowing people to pay fewer taxes to the government without risk of punishment," wrote McKenna in a 2001 article. "The accounting we give to the government becomes a public record of how we spend our money, which is open to anyone's review. It is not much more cumbersome than some of the paperwork demanded to 'register' a newspaper—which Dorothy did in order to publish the *Catholic Worker*. There is a concern that people might give money just to receive tax relief. People's motivation for donating anything is a sticky realm to judge, best left to the individual who is giving and their conscience."[12]

Because the Catholic Worker movement lacks any overarching authority, this debate was never resolved. Though the HOPE Community and many other registered nonprofits have ceased identifying as Catholic Workers, Haley House, like Saint Joseph's in Rochester and Benedict Labre House in Montreal, has continued to affirm its place in the movement. On the other hand, the debate provoked rethinking among some other communities.

Saint Catherine of Genoa House in Chicago, for example, obtained 501(c)(3) status when it was founded early in the 1980s, and the founding documents provide no clues that this was a controversial decision. By the end of the decade, however, community members were aware that many Catholic Workers are unincorporated, and they were also conscious of the practical challenges of nonprofit status. When founder Al Mascia was critically injured in a car accident, for example, the community found itself paralyzed by a lack of leadership and decided to transform the office of "executive director" into a codirectorship shared by all community members. A year later, in 1990, they declined to renew their nonprofit status "in resistance to the war effort." When I began cooking soup at the house a few years later, one of the first things I learned was that the food supply was limited by a conscientious decision to refuse food donations from the government.[13]

The debate over nonprofit status was not the only one to shake the Catholic Worker movement in the 1980s. A significantly more vociferous conversation concerned the degree to which the movement should remain faithful to the Catholic orthodoxy exemplified by Dorothy Day and Peter Maurin. Many commentators have assumed that this debate occurred because the movement began to drift away from its Catholic roots after Dorothy Day's death. As my narrative has already suggested, things were not nearly so simple. As early as the 1960s, Ammon Hennacy and Karl Meyer had opened up space for both dissent and apostasy within the movement, and many of the communities founded during the Vietnam era began challenging aspects of Catholic teaching—particularly with regard to women's roles and sexual orientation—before Day's death. Day may have been troubled by these developments, but she chose not to speak out publicly or push rebellious houses out of the movement. Her silence seems to have precluded a larger debate among Worker houses in the 1970s. What was new after her death, therefore, was that theologically conservative Workers felt a new freedom to call the larger movement to account.

Perhaps the most vocal of these "*Catholic* Catholic Workers" were Ann O'Connor and Peter King of Unity Kitchen Community in Syracuse. Like the communities that bore the brunt of O'Connor's and King's criticism, Unity Kitchen was born during the Vietnam era. The pastor of an inner city parish had encouraged a cluster of laypeople to open a house of hospitality, and for the first decade they offered rather chaotic hospitality to everyone who came to their door. By most accounts, the community was not deeply connected to either Catholicism or the Catholic Worker, though it did host a weekly Mass from the beginning. In 1977 a new volunteer was informed that the Kitchen was "not really a Catholic Worker house" because "there is no effort on our part to spread the economic-social philosophy associated with the Worker."[14] Shortly thereafter, the community underwent a "human service evaluation" from Dr. Wolf Wolfensberger, a researcher at Syracuse University. Wolfensberger's report was harshly critical of the dehumanizing effects of unlimited hospitality and of the "contradictions between what we said we believed and what we were doing" but suggested that the community might improve by connecting more deeply to the core values of the Catholic Worker. In one particularly telling moment, Wolfensberger suggested that the community pray for guidance and was shocked to discover that they never prayed together. And so began a four-year process of discernment about the identity and direction of Unity Kitchen.[15]

The resulting process was as messy as it was prayerful. All the Workers but O'Connor and King left, in at least some cases with quite bitter feelings, though as many as thirty people from outside the community participated in the discernment process. Ultimately, the "base community" changed its name from simply "Unity Kitchen" to "Unity Kitchen Community of the Catholic Worker Movement" and produced three documents—the "Declaration of Faith and Principles" (issued on the movement's fiftieth anniversary in 1983), "A Teaching on Hospitality" (1989), and "Christian Personalism: A Manifesto" (1995)—that spelled out their new sense of identity. From that time on, Unity Kitchen Community was committed to "lavish but limited hospitality," providing sit-down dinners to just twenty-four guests at a time. It was also committed to total fidelity to the Roman Catholic Church.[16]

The "Declaration of Faith and Principles" is one of the most unusual documents produced by the Catholic Worker movement; to my knowledge no other community has produced anything remotely comparable. In structure, it is more like a confession of faith than a mission statement. It begins with a somewhat revised version of the Nicene Creed (God the Father is described as "creator of heaven and earth and both the visible and invisible orders," and a specific reference to "Apostolic Succession" is added to the article on the church), then offers twelve doctrinal articles before moving into sections on "politicization," "hospitality," and "callings, commitments, gifts and talents."

Ann O'Connor has identified four aspects of this document as particularly challenging for others in the Catholic Worker movement.[17] First is the clear statement that "we center our worship around the Catholic Eucharist and sacraments, and we are in communion with our local bishop who stands in obedience to the legitimate Vicar of Christ." (In practice, this means that non-Catholics can serve as volunteers but not as full members of the base community.) Second is the articulation of a "unity of life" position: "Unity Kitchen says 'no' to death in all its forms embodied in our world, and particularly glorified in our nation as oppression, abortion, capital punishment, euthanasia, war and preparations for war."[18]

Though this commitment is shared by a number of Worker communities, a third point is more distinctive: they profess a literal Fall brought about by "demonic spirits led by Satan," teach "that this Fall entailed a profound rupture between the human and God," and thus draw an especially sharp distinction between church and state. On the one hand, "all collective human enterprises, and social and political institutions, function on the fallen level and, therefore, experience demonic bondage," and "the national government is most essentially allied to death." On the other hand, "through the gifts of the Holy Spirit to both individual believers and Christian communalities, and the practice of these gifts, such individuals and communalities will be enabled to 'transcend' the fall." This sharp distinction grounds the fourth challenging point: in addition to hospitality, Unity Kitchen's special "work"—not necessarily shared by "other authentically Christian communities"—is "politicization," which means drawing attention to the "fallenness of the universe" through public witness and the avoidance of "any 'unholy alliances' which may obscure our witness or cause it to be incoherent."[19]

From my perspective, what is even more startling about the Declaration is its lack of connection to the theological heritage of the Catholic Worker movement. There are no quotations from Dorothy Day or Peter Maurin, no mention of the major theologians who influenced them, and no mention of such theological themes as the Mystical Body of Christ. Indeed, it contains a few passages that might be interpreted as veiled criticisms of Day and Maurin. In explaining their opposition to "unholy alliances," the authors criticize Christians who "exalt non-Christian efforts (for instance, strategies of Gandhi) as equal to, or even superior to, the Gospel message" or who "participate with various non-Christian groups in efforts, such as peace marches, for which the non-Christian participants have entirely different motives or even goals." Yet Dorothy Day repeatedly exalted Gandhi and marched alongside Communists as well as members of other secular organizations. In the "Christian Personalism" document, Unity Kitchen Community occasionally places Maurin in a negative light. Maurin was wrong, they say, to hope that the Worker would "create a new society within the shell of the old," for "the proportion of disciples submitted to Christ will always be minuscule." In discussing Maurin's use of the term "gentle personalism," they suggest that contemporary Workers misinterpret it as meaning that "those within the Catholic Worker movement should refrain from taking open or public positions on anti-Christian, anti-Catholic, and anti-church perversions that have come to permeate the Catholic Worker movement," adding that "traditionally, the Catholic Worker movement has strongly confronted the powers of political and economic oppression and warmaking, and not necessarily very gently." Yet it was precisely because of Maurin's call to be "announcers" rather than "denouncers" that Dorothy Day so often refrained from speaking out against practices that troubled her—and so often gently chided herself and others for the lack of gentleness in their resistance to war.[20]

A final passage from the manifesto encapsulates the tension between Unity Kitchen Community's vision and that of the Catholic Worker movement as a whole. In discussing the personalist challenge to state institutions—something certainly shared by most Catholic Workers—the authors write that personalism is most likely to thrive in situations of persecution, in small denominations like the Anabaptists, "and in circles at the margins of their denominations, such as the Catholic Worker."[21] This may well be true at a descriptive level, but it contrasts sharply with the ideals of both Peter Maurin and Dorothy Day. Maurin saw the Catholic Middle Ages, against which the Anabaptists reacted so sharply, as the social ideal, and Dorothy Day was first drawn to the Catholic Church because of its inclusive character as the church of the masses. To the extent that the Worker is at the "margins" of the church, it has failed the vision of its founders.

It is a token of the Worker's commitment to gentle personalism that King and O'Connor continue to be accepted, perhaps even embraced, by the larger Worker movement despite the fact that virtually no one shares their understanding of Catholic Worker identity. At the most recent national gathering of Catholic Workers, for example, they ruffled feathers in a discussion of homosexuality (they were the only ones publicly supportive of the Catholic hierarchy's stance) but were well received in a discussion of technology (they are part of a respected minority of Workers who eschew computers). Their published assessment of the gathering, however, was overwhelmingly negative: "Overall," they wrote in their newsletter, "the Gathering revealed that the CW is worse off than we thought. . . . Non-Catholic, Catholic Workers dominate the CW [movement] assisted by the silence of the more faithful Catholics."[22]

A more widely influential approach to Catholic Worker orthodoxy is exemplified by Houston's Casa Juan Diego and its founders, Mark and Louise Zwick. Their story typifies the transitions of American Catholicism in the second half of the twentieth century. Like many founders of Catholic Worker houses, Mark first learned of the Catholic Worker movement when he was a seminarian; during those years he also made the controversial retreat with Father John Hugo. Like many seminarians of his generation, Mark left the seminary to marry, but both he and Louise remained deeply involved with both radical and liberal currents of Catholicism. As they moved from Youngstown, Ohio, to Chicago and then Northern California, they protested against racism and the Vietnam War, founded an urban neighborhood center, volunteered at Saint Martin de Porres Catholic Worker in San Francisco, organized for the United Farm Workers, and participated in house liturgies. They drew inspiration from both Dorothy Day and Daniel Berrigan, whom they invited to California on several occasions. But the truly transformative moment came when they traveled to El Salvador in 1977, just before Oscar Romero's appointment as archbishop.[23]

In El Salvador, the Zwicks would later recall, they were "brought to our knees," both by the reality of poverty and by their encounter with "the institutional Church redefined." As American Catholics of the Vatican II era, they had been taught to distrust the institutional church, but in El Salvador the institutional church "was all over the place working with the poor, celebrating the liturgy, preparing people for first communion, teaching catechism, sharing with adults in small groups, fighting against slave wages and being killed for standing with the poor—even at leadership roles at the highest level." Back in the United States, they led the social ministry program at a Houston parish just as the city was inundated by refugees from Central American wars during the economic dislocations of globalization. Their response was to start a house of hospitality that has since grown to include ten houses, each offering a distinctive form of hospitality: shelter and legal support for immigrant workers, shelter for women and children, care for sick and wounded immigrants, English classes, food and clothing, Spanish-language liturgies.[24]

Casa Juan Diego not only practices the works of mercy on an unusually large scale, it also publishes one of the most widely distributed and theologically astute of the local Catholic Worker papers. While many Catholic Worker papers focus exclusively on "house news" and antiwar articles, the *Houston Catholic Worker* regularly publishes detailed analyses of papal encyclicals (and critiques of the critics of those encyclicals) and has weighed in on such topics as Benedict XVI's interpretation of Vatican II, the Gnostic Gospels, "The Eschatological Dimension of Money," "Anti-Judaism in Religious Feminist Writing," and "The Drawbacks of Pure Secular Reason."[25] As these titles might suggest, the Zwicks are equally critical of "conservative" approaches to war and the economy and of "liberal" approaches to religion and sexuality, both of which they treat as symptoms of a deeply problematic modern (and American) individualism. They are enormously appreciative of Popes John Paul II and Benedict XVI, whom they portray as charting an alternative path embracing "the fullness of the Church's rich teaching" and bringing together "those who put together adoration and a love of the liturgy with peacemaking and living the Gospel in the marketplace, those who embraced both the Cross and the Resurrection, and the consistent ethic of life, those committed to building up the civilization of love in the Communion of the Trinity together with God's people." (In a tongue-in cheek title, the Zwicks even declared that Pope Benedict had "Unwittingly Complete[d] Zwick Article on 'What Happened to the Tremendous Renewal Possibilities after Vatican II?'")[26]

At times, the Zwicks's presentation of their version of Catholic orthodoxy has taken on sharp tones. They have little patience for pro-choicers, doctrinaire secularists, or members of the Jesus Seminar (whom they accuse of "manipulation of the press" and of having "declared war on Christianity").[27] They are more respectful, but still sharply critical, of some of the most important Catholic theologians of the twentieth century. Karl Rahner, they have written, "emphasized assimilation to the secular culture and de-emphasized transcendence and immortality," while John Courtney Murray undermined the theology of the mystical body of Christ when he "defend[ed] the Liberal model as the only way to have religious freedom." The problematic legacy of Rahner and Murray, they have suggested, is equally present in the work of such Catholic neoconservatives as George Weigel and Michael Novak, who resist papal teaching on war and the economy, and in the liberal columns of John Allen and the *National Catholic Reporter*.[28]

Yet the Zwicks's stance within the Catholic Worker movement has been more subtle. Unlike Peter King and Ann O'Connor, they rarely attack other Catholic Workers directly, preferring to remind them, gently and persistently, of the many ways in which Peter Maurin and Dorothy Day drew deeply from the wells of Catholic orthodoxy. It was the "bombshell" of one of O'Connor's attacks on other Worker houses (published in the *New Oxford Review* in 1994) that inspired them to begin an extended project of reading and rereading the saints, philosophers, theologians, and novelists who influenced Dorothy Day and Peter Maurin. By going "to the roots of the movement," they discovered that Maurin and Day were part of "the great movement in this century in the Church of *ressourcement,* retrieving the tradition, going back to the sources."[29] This research ultimately bore fruit in a series of newspaper articles and a published book titled *The Catholic Worker Movement: Intellectual and Spiritual Origins*. Though this book slights the American and secular sources of the movement (and entirely bypasses Ammon Hennacy), its tone is gentle and invitational, encouraging new generations of Workers to take seriously the thought of Saint Benedict and Saint Thérèse of Lisieux, of Emmanuel Mounier and Virgil Michel and Nicholas Berdyaev, of Dostoyevsky and Day's other favorite novelists.[30]

The Zwicks's approach reflects their conviction that the Catholic Worker practice of the works of mercy is the surest antidote to the ideological divisions besetting their beloved church. In a number of articles, the Zwicks have bemoaned the polarization of the Catholic Church, suggesting that the inclination of both "liberals" and "conservatives" to point fingers at the opposite group has prevented the church from realizing "the tremendous renewal possibilities" of the Second Vatican Council. The personalism of the Catholic Worker, they have argued, starts with "I" not "They." The key, in other words, is not to criticize others for their lack of faithfulness, but to look to the example of saints like Dorothy Day who simply took positive action on behalf of others.[31]

In the past few decades, the Zwicks have acquired some quite influential academic and ecclesial allies. Their conviction that *ressourcement* theologians Henri de Lubac and Hans Urs von Balthasar, rather than Karl Rahner and John Courtney Murray, represent the best legacy of Vatican II has been shared by Popes John Paul II and Benedict XVI, as well as by many of their most influential episcopal appointments. Although the guild of Catholic theologians in the United States is still predominantly Rahnerian, influential scholars such as David Schindler share their emphasis on a theology of communion that is equally opposed to economic and theological liberalism. (Schindler invited them to contribute the introduction when he republished Dorothy Day's *On Pilgrimage* as part of his series of classic texts from the *ressourcement* movement.) The Zwicks's critique of liberalism also owes much to the more ecumenical conversation generated by the work of Alasdair MacIntyre and Stanley Hauerwas. One of the most influential "Catholic Worker theologians" writing today, Mike Baxter, was mentored by both Hauerwas and the Zwicks. Baxter founded Andre House Catholic Worker in Phoenix and is currently active in a new Catholic Worker house near Notre Dame, where he teaches theology. Former students of Hauerwas can be found in at least half a dozen Worker communities around the country.

Hauerwas, along with Protestant theologian Christine Pohl, has also been a big influence on the nascent community movement that calls itself the "New Monasticism." In just a few years, this movement has generated an influential book, a few major conferences, and a vibrant network of communities pledged to simple living, hospitality, peacemaking, and reconciliation, along with "humble submission to Christ's body, the church," and "commitment to a disciplined contemplative life." Although no Catholic Worker communities have identified themselves as New Monastic communities, the Zwicks have praised and publicized the movement in their newspaper, continuing Dorothy Day's tradition of welcoming kindred initiatives without seeking to incorporate them into the Catholic Worker.[32]

In their conviction, shared with Brigid O'Shea Merriman, that "Dorothy Day's life may be understood only in the context of her great faith," the Zwicks stand in the mainstream of the Catholic Worker movement. Their insistence that Day drew on the whole of the Catholic tradition—"the best of the ancient and medieval traditions of the Church with the best of the movements (liturgical, biblical, the social teachings of the Church and the importance of the role of the laity) that paved the way for Vatican II"—is an important antidote to the sectarian orthodoxy of the Unity Kitchen community.[33] But the Zwicks's vision should not be confused with the whole of the Catholic Worker movement. They have drunk deeply from the writings of Day and Maurin, but not so deeply from the transformative experiences of many Catholic Worker communities in the 1960s and 1970s. And it was these experiences, at least implicitly blessed by Dorothy Day, that linked the Worker not only to the whole of the church but also to the whole of the American radical movement.

Other communities founded in the 1980s and beyond drew much more directly from the experience of the communities that came before them. In the mid-1980s, for example, the Los Angeles Catholic Worker began deliberately sponsoring "daughter" communities. This was the indirect result of an experience with "bigness" somewhat comparable to the transitions at Haley House in Boston and Saint Joseph's House in Minneapolis described earlier. Because they were recognized as leading advocates for the homeless poor of Skid Row, the Los Angeles Catholic Workers—and especially Jeff Dietrich—were repeatedly called upon to serve on community development boards and task forces. For a time, Dietrich chaired the Skid Row Task Force of the Community Redevelopment Agency and served on perhaps eight other nonprofit boards. Though the Worker community itself resisted incorporation, several of its sponsored projects, such as a bakery, became incorporated. Eventually, though, Jeff Dietrich and Catherine Morris chose to resist what they saw as a "snowballing" pattern of cooperation with governmental institutions. After an Advent fast, Dietrich abruptly resigned from all the boards on which he served. This challenge to return to Catholic Worker "roots" generated conflict and a series of departures from the community, and soon a small remnant of Workers set about a process of "refoundation." This resulted in a new mission statement that highlighted the goal of sponsoring new communities. Rather than growing too big to practice personalism, the community would deliberately send out experienced Workers to smaller cities, spreading the values of the movement ever more widely.[34]

Today, the Los Angeles Catholic Worker website identifies eleven communities as "sister houses," noting that "usually this means that they were founded by former LACW community members." Though two are in Philadelphia, most are in smaller cities not usually associated with social radicalism: Fresno, Santa Ana, Las Vegas, and Norfolk, Virginia. An accompanying photo of forty-five people, including several families, suggests that this network has remained intimately connected.[35]

In other places, new houses have been founded by individuals who spent time at large urban houses of hospitality, then decided to live out their Catholic Worker vocation closer to home, in small cities more conducive to family. Scott Schaeffer-Duffy, for example, first visited the New York Catholic Worker on the day of Dorothy Day's funeral, which he attended with two other novices in the Capuchin Franciscans. After a year with the Capuchins, he "wanted something a little more concrete and connected to the poor," and so he moved to Saint Benedict's Catholic Worker in Washington, D.C. The founder of this community, Michael Kirwan, is famous in Catholic Worker circles for embodying the extreme idealism of unlimited hospitality. "It was really very, very wild," Scott recalled in an interview. "Open door in an extremely violent neighborhood. Unlimited hospitality for the most part. I got very severe bronchitis there sleeping on the floor in the front hallway. We had no heat 'til December 20th the first year. I mean the poverty was just incredible. We gave away everything at the end of each day. You know, don't take anything for the morrow. Well it was literal, we put a board in front of the house and put all the food we had left in the house and gave it away."[36]

After a year and a half in Washington, Scott married Claire, who had spent time at the Sojourners community as well as two Catholic Worker houses. They moved to Worcester in order to be closer to family while continuing the peace work they had begun at the Catholic Worker. In jail for civil disobedience, Scott befriended a convict who wound up homeless after his release, and so the Schaeffer-Duffys invited him to move into their apartment. "When he stayed with us," said Scott, "it occurred to Claire and me both that our lives weren't complete just doing the peace work without the hospitality." They began holding weekly meals and Bible studies to promote their desire to launch a Catholic Worker house, and by the time they published their first newsletter they had moved into their first house of hospitality. More than twenty years later, they are in a different house but doing the same work, having raised four children in a community that seeks to balance prayer, works of mercy, peace activism, and a lively sense of community.[37]

Just as the Schaeffer-Duffys drew on the model of Worker life they experienced in Washington, D.C., so their friends Chris and Jackie Allen-Doucot adapted the Worcester model (which Chris had experienced as a student at the College of the Holy Cross) to a new community in Hartford, Connecticut. Once they had identified Hartford as a community in need of a Catholic Worker, they chose a neighborhood and began building ties to a local parish. When they initiated a dialogue about possibilities for a Catholic Worker, many people participated, though only the most ambivalent, Brian Kavanagh, actually moved into the house they purchased in June 1993. Since that time, the Allen-Doucots and Kavanagh have anchored a community that has hosted a steady stream of both guests and short-term Workers. Along the way, they have allowed the needs of the neighborhood to set their agenda.

"The original vision for the community was basically to try and open a house of hospitality and practice the works of mercy," explained Chris. "We didn't want to get any more specific than that because we didn't want to dictate to the community, the neighborhood, what its needs were." Though they assumed that they would mostly provide hospitality to persons experiencing homelessness, the neighborhood they chose had far more poor but housed children than actual homeless persons. So their ministries have mostly focused on the needs of children. They host an extremely well-attended afterschool program and also keep a huge basket of fruit by their door, so that children can receive a nutritious snack whenever they wish. Another ministry is a food-buying club that provides fresh organic vegetables during the summer months and other items year-round. And, given Brian and Jackie's strong interest in the arts, they have recently opened a community art center called Saint Brigid House.[38]

Though the Schaeffer-Duffys and Allen-Doucots benefited enormously from their personal connection to the previous generation of Catholic Workers, the movement today also features an increasing number of communities that were founded by individuals who had read Dorothy Day's books but had no previous connection to her movement. Indirectly, this was a consequence of her death, because both the death itself and the subsequent canonization process gave new publicity to the movement and created a wider market for *The Long Loneliness, Loaves and Fishes,* and her other publications. In 1973 Robert Coles reported that all of Day's books were out of print; by the 1980s a steady supply of reprints were both available and widely assigned in college classrooms.[39] (I first read *The Long Loneliness* as a college freshman in 1986, for a class taught by Coles himself.)

A good example of these "book-inspired" communities is Place of Grace Catholic Worker in La Crosse, Wisconsin. This house of hospitality was started around 1997 by a cluster of families who knew one another through their employment at Viterbo University and Franciscan Hospital, both institutions sponsored by the Franciscan Sisters of Perpetual Adoration. A group of friends, including teenager Chuck Berendes as well as several professional adults, began gathering for Monday morning prayer in the hospital's dining room. Few if any had any previous connection to the Worker movement, but all wanted to put their Catholic faith into action, and they shared a sense that Dorothy Day's vision could work in their city. Within a few months, they had identified a house, and in keeping with Day's emphasis on "precarity," they moved in as soon as they could afford a single month's rent. Donations kept coming in when they were most needed, and eventually the community was even bequeathed a few houses. The first house, which hosts a meal for homeless persons and an afterschool program for children, continues to be the hub of community activities. Though the founders all kept their professional jobs and private homes, many spend the bulk of their free time at Place of Grace. The result, according to Berendes, is an appealing model of community life for people who don't want to turn their backs on mainstream society. "It's not this kind of hippie commune where everybody . . . [has] given up all their stuff and they live together and play the guitar or something. . . . They're real people with real jobs, who are . . . making this be a big part of their life. . . . And so this has been a real model for me, that . . . there are ways that you can use the gifts that you have, and try and work for justice. And still have a normal life."[40]

Berendes's aspiration to "still have a normal life" might seem contrary to the high idealism of the Catholic Worker movement. Yet one key to the endurance of the Catholic Worker communities in the past generation is the fact that their members have felt free, in diverse ways, to create "normal lives" within the Worker. For some this has meant staying only a short time;

for others it has meant making room for the family within the house of hospitality; for still others it has meant moving from the city to the countryside to pursue a new vocation. All of this creativity has been possible because of Dorothy Day's refusal to impose a single pattern of life on her movement. Her non-judgmental leadership, clearly, has left room for both the anti-clerical diatribes of Ammon Hennacy and the sectarian zeal of Unity Kitchen, but more important, it has enabled Workers to follow the "little way," to start small and get smaller. For this latest generation of Workers, as for Day herself, the practice of the works of mercy has been a way to engage "things of concern to us all, the family, the home, how to live, with what to live and what we live by."[41]

[1] Tim Lambert, "A Birthday Celebration," *Catholic Worker* 54, no. 8 (December 1987): 1.

[2] Interview with Angie Miller and Steve O'Neal, 25 August 2002.

[3] Interview with Greg and Michele Obed, 24 August 2002.

[4] Fred Boehrer, "Diversity, Plurality and Ambiguity: Anarchism in the Catholic Worker Movement," in William Thorn, Philip Runkel, and Susan Mountin, eds., *Dorothy Day and the Catholic Worker Movement: Centenary Essays* (Milwaukee: Marquette University Press, 2001), 107.

[5] Mary Byers, "Building on Our Catholic Worker Foundations," *St. Joseph's House News* 2, no. 3 (March 1988): 3; Catherine Gillis, "Reflections on Our Mission," *St. Joseph's House News* 3, no. 1 (January 1989): 8; and *St. Joseph's House News* 3, no. 3 (March 1989): 9; all in DD/CWCs, series W-4, box 11, folder 25; and Char Madigan, interviewed by Rosalie Troester, 8 July 1989, in DD/CWCs, series W-9, box 5, folder 21.

[6] *Saint Joseph's House News* 4, no. 9 (September 1990), DD/CWC, series W-4, box 12, folder 23; Deanna Foster, "House News—Planting and Growing in 1992," *Saint Joseph's House News,* 7, no. 2 (March 1993): 4–5, DD/CWC, series W-4, box 14, folder 9; Deanna Foster, "House News—An Anatomy of Change," *St. Joseph's House News,* 7, no. 1 (January–February 1993): 6–7, DD/CWC, series W-4, box 14, folder 9; St. Joseph's House Brochure, ca.

Christmas 1993, DD/CWC, series W-4, box 14, folder 9; and Char Madigan, interviewed by Rosalie Troester, 8 July 1989, in DD/CWCs, series W-9, box 5, folder 21.

[7] St. Joseph's House Christmas card, 1993, DD/CWC, series W-4, box 14, folder 9.

[8] Deanna Foster, "Change," *St. Joseph's House News,* 8, no. 1 (January–February 1994): 2–3, DD/CWC, series W-4, box 14, folder 9.

[9] *St. Joseph's House News* 8, no. 5 (June–July 1994); Deanna Foster, "Change," *St. Joseph's House News,* 8, no. 1 (January–February 1994): 2–3; and Char Madigan, "Inpulse," *St. Joseph's House News,* 8, no. 1 (January–February 1994): 6; all in DD/CWC, series W-4, box 14, folder 9.

[10] Dorothy Day, "On Pilgrimage," *Catholic Worker* 38, no. 6 (July–August 1972): 1; and Harry Murray, *Do Not Neglect Hospitality: The Catholic Worker and the Homeless* (Philadelphia: Temple University Press, 1990), 129.

[11] Kathe McKenna, "To Apply or Not to Apply," *Haley House Newsletter,* Easter 1987, 6–9, DD/CWC, series W-19, box 1, folder 12.

[12] Ibid.; Scott Schaeffer-Duffy, "Open Letter to Kathe McKenna, 8 May 1987," *Haley House Newsletter,* August 1987, 3–4, DD/CWC, series W-19, box 1, folder 12; Kathe McKenna, "Why We Have a Tax Exempt Status," *Haley House Newsletter,* Spring 2001, 7, DD/CWC, series W-19, unboxed folder.

[13] "A Brief History of St. Catherine of Genoa Catholic Worker," DD/CWC, series W-63.

[14] Murray, *Do Not Neglect Hospitality,* 9.

[15] Ann O'Connor, "From Soup Line to Soup Tureen: Twenty Years of Gracious, Dinner Hospitality in Unity Kitchen," *The Unity Grapevine* (Spring–Summer 2002): 1; and Rosalie Riegle Troester, *Voices from the Catholic Worker* (Philadelphia: Temple University Press, 1993), 446.

[16] "Declaration of Faith and Principles of Unity Kitchen Community of the Catholic Worker," 3rd rev., January 1, 1989; "A Teaching on Hospitality," January 1, 1989; and "Christian Personalism: A Manifesto," September 14, 1995, all available from Unity Kitchen Community. Harry Murray, *Do Not Neglect Hospitality,* 9–14, tells the story from his perspective as one of the people who left the community as a result of this discernment. Interestingly, he is more directly critical of the new approach to hospitality than of the new approach to Catholicism, though he describes his puzzlement over appeals to the "Holy Spirit" and "Biblical numbers" to justify the new policy.

[17] Troester, *Voices,* 449.

[18] "Declaration of Faith and Principles," 2.

[19] Ibid., 1, 2, 4.

[20] Ibid., 4; "Christian Personalism," 12, 19.

[21] "Christian Personalism," 14.

[22] Ann O'Connor, "What Is the Current State of the Catholic Worker Movement and What Can Be Expected for Its Future?" *The Unity Grapevine* (Spring 2007): 5.

[23] Mark and Louise Zwick, "Roots of the Catholic Worker Movement: Saints and Philosophers Who Influenced Dorothy Day and Peter Maurin," in Thorn et al., *Dorothy Day,* 60; Mark and Louise Zwick to Dan McKanan, 24 March 2007; and Mark and Louise Zwick to Dan McKanan, 13 May 2007.

[24] Mark and Louise Zwick, "No Federal Funds: What Now?" *Houston Catholic Worker* 16, no. 7 (December 1996), available at http://www.cjd. org/paper/funds.html, and "What Is Casa Juan Diego?" at http://www.cjd. org/whatis.html.

[25] For links to these and related articles, see "Houston Catholic Worker Newspaper: Faith and Culture," at http://www.cjd.org/paper/faith.html.

[26] Editors' introduction to "Pope Benedict XVI Interprets Vatican Council II: Holy Father Unwittingly Completes Zwick Article on 'What Happened To the tremendous Renewal Possibilities After Vatican II?'" *Houston Catholic Worker* 24, no. 2 (March–April 2006), at http://www.cjd.org/paper/vatcoun2. html.

[27] Mark and Louise Zwick, "Fraudulent Scholarship, Whether Archaeological or Neo-Gnostic, Misleads Christians," *Houston Catholic Worker* 25, no. 2 (March–April 2006).

[28] Zwick and Zwick, "What Happened to the Tremendous Renewal Possibilities after the Second Vatican Council?" *Houston Catholic Worker* 24, no. 2 (March–April 2006), at http://www.cjd.org/paper/vatcoun2.html .

[29] Zwick and Zwick, "Roots," 61–63.

[30] Mark and Louise Zwick, *The Catholic Worker Movement: Intellectual and Spiritual Origins* (Mahwah, NJ: Paulist Press, 2005). One Catholic Worker who has faulted the Zwicks for their neglect of Leftist sources is Brian Terrell, "Weeds Sown Among the Wheat: Omissions and Exaggerations Distort CW Spirit," *The New Southern Catholic Radical* (Spring 2006): 4–6.

[31] Zwick and Zwick, "What Happened"; and Zwick and Zwick, "How Can We Reform the Church? Personalist Revolution Starts with 'I,' Not 'They,'" *Houston Catholic Worker* 25, no. 3 (May–June 2005), at http://www.cjd.org/ paper/reform.html.

[32] The Rutba House, *School(s) for Conversion: 12 Marks of a New Monasticism* (Eugene, OR: Cascade Books, 2005).

[33] Zwick and Zwick, "Who Will Inherit the Legacy of Dorothy Day?" *Houston Catholic Worker* 14, no. 3 (May 1994), at http://www.cjd.org/paper/legacy. html. The Zwicks take the first quote from Brigid O'Shea Merriman, *Searching for Christ: The Spirituality of Dorothy Day* (Notre Dame, IN: University of Notre Dame Press, 1994), vii.

[34] Troester, *Voices,* 52–56.

[35] "Sister Houses," at http://lacatholicworker.org/sister-houses/.

[36] Interview with Scott Schaeffer-Dufy, 5 January 2002.

[37] Ibid.

[38] Interview with Chris Allen-Doucot, 4 January 2002; and interview with Brian Kavanagh, 4 January 2002.

[39] Robert Coles and Jon Erikson, *A Spectacle Unto the World: The Catholic Worker Movement* (New York: Viking, 1973), 52.

[40] Interview with Chuck Berendes, 10 April 2002.

[41] Dorothy Day, *On Pilgrimage* (New York: Catholic Worker Books, 1948), 2.

Part II

Rules, Families, and the Church

Chapter 5

Aims and Means

In the previous chapter, I have tried to show that Dorothy Day nurtured the full diversity of the Catholic Worker movement. Given that diversity, what, if anything, holds the Catholic Worker movement together? Is there a distinct identity that sets the Worker apart from other movements in church and society? Some, especially those who are most critical of the religious diversity within the movement, would say that there is no common identity and that since Dorothy Day's death the movement has lapsed into utter incoherence. Others, more sympathetic to contemporary Workers, insist that the movement's unity can be experienced but not put into words. Rosalie Riegle, who has probably explored the contemporary movement more broadly than anyone else, initially thought that "if I just looked long enough and deep enough and at enough Workers, the truth would emerge and I'd be able to define the Catholic Worker." But, after collecting hundreds of oral histories, she concluded that Catholic historian Jay Dolan was right to say that "trying to define the Catholic Worker is like trying to bottle morning fog." The Catholic Worker, Riegle added, can be expressed only through "many descriptions, not one, many truths, not *the* truth."[1]

If by "definition," Dolan and Riegle mean a sharp line separating *all* Catholic Workers from *everything* else, they are certainly correct. At the same time, it is not hard to identify specific ideas and themes that resonate with the vast majority of Workers. Since Vatican II, most Catholic religious orders have stressed the importance of having a particular "charism," or leading value, and though Catholic Workers insist that they are not a religious order, they can readily point to some short phrases that might encapsulate their charism. This facility is, in part, the legacy of Peter Maurin, who certainly had a knack with catchy phrases. By the time he first encountered Dorothy Day, he had already worked out a "three point program" consisting of roundtable discussions for the "clarification of thought," "houses of hospitality" for the urban poor, and "agronomic universities" to give those poor a new start through farming and traditional crafts on the land.[2] Remarkably, many Catholic Worker communities still understand their mission in just those terms, while the more common formulation of "hospitality and resistance" incorporates the nonviolent legacy of Ammon Hennacy, Karl Meyer, and the Berrigan family. Maurin also coined the phrase "cult, culture, and cultivation" to express the Worker's desire to break down the boundaries between prayer, scholarship, and physical labor.

If Peter Maurin excelled in the creation of catchphrases, Dorothy Day's gift was as a storyteller. Almost as soon as she had met Peter, Dorothy began telling stories about the man she called the "Peasant of the Pavements" and a modern Saint Francis. By the time he died, she had composed a complete biography of him, though it was too disjointed to be published during her lifetime. Her sense of his personal holiness, she said, is what prompted, her to write: "Who knows, he may be a saint, he may be a canonized saint some day, and we need a new kind of hagiography."[3]

One of the characteristics of Day's new hagiography—and one of the features that made it so disjointed—was that she could not tell Peter's story without telling countless other stories. Indeed, she began Peter's story by describing New York City and the neighborhood of the Catholic Worker, "this dark narrow street, full always with parked cars, children, boys playing games, men playing cards, and mothers sitting by baby carriages, winter and summer."[4] She could not tell of Peter without telling of the many people whose lives he touched, because for her Peter's saintliness lay precisely in his awareness of the holiness of other people:

> Perhaps that is what makes Peter so important a person, this tremendous faith he has, not only in God, but also in men. He was an apostle to the world. It is this which set him apart from other men, from other saints of the Church who went around preaching penance, reminding men of their relationship with God and eternity. . . . Peter so felt the tremendous importance of this life, that he made one feel the magnificent significance of our work, our daily lives, the material of God's universe and what we did with it, how we used it.[5]

Day practiced the same "new hagiography" in her study of her favorite saint, Thérèse of Lisieux. That book begins not with the saint herself, but with the two Catholics who first introduced Dorothy to the Little Flower: the young woman in the next bed when she gave birth to Tamar, and Father Zachary, the priest who prepared Dorothy for confirmation. Though she dwells on the homely details of these two individuals—the girl fishes a Little Flower medal from the pocketbook "where she kept her powder and lipstick, tissues and rosary beads, money to buy candy and the *Daily News*"—Day's clear intention was to suggest that they too were humble saints, following Thérèse's "little way," and that they helped her understand that "we are all 'called to be saints.'"[6]

Indeed, this is the point of all the little stories that crowd *The Long Loneliness* and *Loaves and Fishes*. Ade Bethune called Day to greater holiness simply in the way she gave lessons in calligraphy: "'If you are going to put a cross bar on an H,' she said, 'you have to aim *higher* than your sense of sight tells you.'" Steve Hergenhan, another early Worker, refused to attend church and dismissed the works of mercy as a coddling of shirkers, but Day could still write that, like Peter Maurin, he was a "lamb in the simplicity of [his] program [who] wanted to see the grass spring up between the cobbles of the city streets." Day glimpsed holiness even in the ravings of a mentally ill guest who walked barefoot through the garden, saying that "I can feel things growing. . . . I look at the little plants, and I draw them up out of the earth with the power of love in my eyes."[7] For forty years she nurtured the movement primarily by telling such stories, as Tom Cornell recalled: "Maybe Dorothy Day had a special gift, but she didn't even have to have one I suppose. She told stories of people in houses who went through the same thing that your house was going through . . . stories with what everyone needed to hear. But when she said it . . . they'd find what they needed in her story. It happened all the time."[8]

By telling these stories, Day lifted a mirror up to the movement, helping Workers both in New York and in distant states see their place in the Gospel narrative. Nevertheless, she constantly received requests from new Workers and sympathetic outsiders for a more systematic statement—perhaps, implicitly, for a "rule" as distinctive as the documents governing the Benedictines and other religious orders. Her response to these requests is quite revealing: rather than preparing a single definitive rule, she published a great many rule-like documents in the *Catholic Worker,* written either by herself or by other individuals involved with the Worker at one point or another. Typically, she published these without identifying the individual author, and many individual statements were edited to reflect the views of the community as a whole. In keeping with the Worker's emphasis on personal responsibility, she rarely ascribed any specific authority to these documents. In a sense, these multiple rules underscore Riegle's point that in the Catholic Worker there are "many truths, not *the* truth," but a careful analysis of the collections can shed intriguing light on the way the Worker drew its identity simultaneously from Catholic and anarchist sources, and on Day's role in safeguarding that compound identity.

The diversity of Catholic Worker "rules" is not always recognized within the movement today. If you ask an individual Worker about the movement's rule, he or she might well point you to a document called "Aims and Means." Look at the Catholic Worker website (which has no "official" authority but represents a broad cross section of the movement) and you will find this phrase atop a list of links. It connects to a document titled "The Aims and Means of the Catholic Worker," published (according to the website) in the New York paper in 2002. This document begins with a ringing summary and a liturgical quote: "The aim of the Catholic Worker movement is to live in accordance with the justice and charity of Jesus Christ. Our sources are the Hebrew and Greek Scriptures as handed down in the teachings of the Roman Catholic Church, with our inspiration coming from the lives of the saints, 'men and women outstanding in holiness, living witnesses to Your unchanging love' (Eucharistic Prayer)." This is followed by a pair of quotes from Day and Maurin that simultaneously underscore the authority of "our founders" and give a sense of the personalist expectation that Catholic Workers will "begin living in a different way." Day is quoted saying that "God meant things to be much easier than we have made them," while Maurin's vision of a society "where it is easier for people to be good" concludes the preamble.[9]

The body of "Aims and Means" is then divided into three major parts. The first, which diagnoses the ills besetting American society, is unabashedly rooted in classical socialist thought: "When we examine our society, which is generally called capitalist (because of its methods of producing and controlling wealth) and is bourgeois . . . we find it far from God's justice." More specifically, this section continues, "those in power live off the sweat of others' brows. . . . Laborers are trapped in work that does not contribute to human welfare. . . . We tend toward government by bureaucracy—that is, government by nobody. . . . Class, race and sex often determine personal worth and position within society. . . . The arms race stands as a clear sign of the direction and spirit of our age." This last point is underscored by a quote from Vatican II—"The arms race is an utterly treacherous trap"—that is the only explicit reference to Catholic or Christian teaching in this section.

The second part describes the Catholic Worker alternative, or the "aims" alluded to in the title. This part begins on a more theological note, appealing to "St Thomas Aquinas' doctrine of the Common Good, a vision of a society where the good of each member is bound to the good of the whole in service of God." The three marks of this vision are "personalism," defined as "a philosophy which regards the freedom and dignity of each person as the basis, focus and goal of all metaphysics and morals," a "decentralized society" composed of family farms, land trusts, and cooperative enterprises, and a "green revolution" in which people will live on the land and "rely on the fruits of their own toil and labor." Apart from the appeal to Aquinas, the only explicitly religious reference in this section appears to be a gentle critique of current Catholic practice: "We pray for a Church renewed by [personalism] and for a time when all those who feel excluded from participation are welcomed with love."

The third major part identifies the appropriate "means" to the ends just described, and it is emphatically biblical in tone: "We believe this needed personal and social transformation should be pursued by the means Jesus revealed in his sacrificial love," striven for "by prayer and communion with His Body and Blood." The document identifies this means as "nonviolence," "the works of mercy," "manual labor," and "voluntary poverty," and all are illustrated with quotes or references from the Gospels, Christian tradition, or Dorothy Day. Nonviolence is found in the Beatitudes ("Blessed are the peacemakers," Matthew 5:9); the works of mercy in the story of the Last Judgment (Matthew 25:31-46); manual labor in the Benedictine motto of "*Ora et Labora,*" and voluntary poverty in both a quote from Day and the recent Catholic teaching of the "preferential option for the poor." The biblical tone continues in the conclusion to the entire document, which alludes indirectly to the gospel teaching that a seed must die before it can bear fruit:

"We must be prepared to accept seeming failure with these aims, for sacrifice and suffering are part of the Christian life. Success, as the world determines it, is not the final criterion for judgments. The most important thing is the love of Jesus Christ and how to live His truth."

A careful reader might discern that Dorothy Day is not the author of this document, since she is quoted in it, but the website provides no further clues about either its provenance or the extent of its authority. As it happens, this particular version of "Aims and Means" is identical to one first published in the New York *Catholic Worker* in May 1987, evidently after an extended process of deliberation by the Worker community in New York City. This process was just one step in a long series of revisions to an original text titled "Catholic Worker Positions" prepared by Robert Ludlow in 1954—ironically, just before he personally left the movement. The story of Worker rule making began much earlier, however, with a series of similarly titled articles published in the New York paper in the 1930s.[10]

The Catholic Worker website features links to three of these articles, just after its link to the 1987 "Aims and Means." These include Day's letter "To Our Readers" from the very first issue of the newspaper, an outline of "Maurin's Program" from the second issue, and an article titled "Aims and Purposes," published in February 1940. The first addresses itself to the poor of New York City and describes the paper's goal as publicizing "the encyclicals of the Popes in regard to social justice" but does not spell out the content of those encyclicals. The second highlights the three points of roundtable discussions, houses of hospitality, and agronomic universities but also notes that Maurin had refused to be listed among the paper's editors. Both of these appeared before Day and Maurin had launched their first house of hospitality, much less envisioned a nationwide movement. The third article, written after dozens of Worker communities had crystallized, is much more systematic in outlining a vision for a movement. But it is neither the only nor the first article published under the title of "Aims and Purposes."

Four years earlier, Day had published "A Restatement of C. W. Aims and Ideals" in honor of the paper's third anniversary. That article was hardly systematic, focusing primarily on differences with Communists and Fascists regarding private property and class war. It did, however, provide one early signal of Day's respect for both Catholic teaching and indigenous American radicalism, for she urged "all Americans" to "recall what Thomas Jefferson stood for in the minds of his countrymen, look around them and contemplate the state we are in today."[11] The first article specifically titled "Aims and Purposes" appeared in January 1939, and here Day first articulated the idea that the Worker would be guided not by a definitive rule but by a series of attempts to encapsulate an evolving ideal. "From now on each issue of *The Catholic Worker* will contain a brief statement of principles, of our aims and purposes. We receive so many letters each month from new readers asking us for these statements that we will try to make each as complete and as simple as possible."

This article went on to explain that the *Catholic Worker* sought to provide "all those employed in manual and mental labor" with a "philosophy of labor," using "the two age-old techniques—*voluntary poverty* and *the Works of Mercy*." Day came close to articulating a binding principle by writing that "all our fellow workers in our twenty-one branches throughout the country have pledged themselves to voluntary poverty and manual labor." After explaining that voluntary poverty meant not ascetic destitution but "taking less so that others may have more," Day wrote at length of Maurin's three-point program, drawing heavily on examples from medieval church tradition. (She credits Saint Jerome, for example, with the idea that "every home should have a Christ's room.") A second large section, on "Brotherhood," noted that "the Holy Father has said that we must *go to the worker, especially to the poorest*," and then used the doctrine of the "Mystical Body of Christ" to condemn anti-Semitism and racism. Day concluded by appealing to a phrase from the Lord's Prayer: "We beg all our readers to work with us and to pray with us for Christ's kingdom on earth. 'Thy will be done *on earth* as it is in Heaven.'"[12]

As promised, Day published several additional articles with the same title in the *Catholic Worker*. Many touched on just one aspect of the Worker program, and in some cases the editing was careless.[13] By far the most comprehensive was the February 1940 version featured on the website. Day's intent, in composing this version, was clearly to balance the specifics of Maurin's program with a fuller elaboration of its religious underpinnings, which she found above all in the Catholic doctrine of the Mystical Body of Christ. "Together with the Works of Mercy, feeding, clothing and sheltering our brothers," she explained, "we must indoctrinate. We must 'give reason for the faith that is in us.' Otherwise we are scattered members of the Body of Christ, we are not 'all members one of another.'" She underscored the corporate vision of the movement by quoting Péguy's comment that God's question at the gates of heaven will be "where are the others?" The Mystical Body, she stressed, was the basis for specific activities like Houses of Hospitality and farming communes.[14]

Though this version was more explicitly Catholic than either what had gone before or the later "Catholic Worker Positions," Day couched many of her ideas in terms that Protestant Americans could relate to. She identified the "Mystical Body" with "the brotherhood of man and the Fatherhood of God," language favored both by the seventeenth-century Puritans and the Protestant Social Gospelers. She also placed a stronger emphasis on Christian action than Christian belief, specifically rejecting an exclusive emphasis on heavenly salvation. "The vision is this," she explained, "we are working for 'a new heaven and a new *earth,* wherein justice dwelleth.' We are trying to say with action, 'Thy will be done on *earth* as it is in heaven.' We are working for a Christian social order."[15]

But if Day called for a closer "correlation between the material and the spiritual," she also insisted—using a phrase that would become an important Catholic Worker slogan—on the "primacy of the spiritual." On this basis, she insisted that Workers participate in the life of the church, while simultaneously stressing that Christ could be found in every person. "Food for the body is not enough. There must be food for the soul. Hence the leaders of the work, and as many as we can induce to join us, must go daily to Mass, to receive food for the soul. And as our perceptions are quickened, and as we pray that our faith be increased, we will see Christ in each other, and we will not lose faith in those around us, no matter how stumbling their progress is."[16]

Day also balanced her idealistic demands with an acknowledgment of human limits, this time drawing heavily on biblical themes to make her point: "What we do is very little. But it is like the little boy with a few loaves and fishes. Christ took that little and increased it. He will do the rest. What we do is so little we may seem to be constantly failing. But so did He fail. He met with apparent failure on the Cross. But unless the seed fall into the earth and die, there is no harvest."[17]

In some ways, this version of "Aims and Purposes" seems to draw a sharp boundary around the movement—implying, for example, that house leaders must not only be faithful Catholics but must attend daily Mass. Taken in isolation, it provides a certain amount of support for those who believe that the contemporary diversity of the Worker does not fit with Day's original vision. Taken in context, though, it represents one particular stage in Day's intellectual and spiritual development. In this piece—which was, after all, originally intended as just one in a series—Day was working especially hard to fit the concrete elements of Maurin's program, which meshed well with her earlier socialist commitments, with a relatively new aspect of Catholic theology. When she referred to the Mystical Body, she was thinking particularly of the work of the liturgical reformer Virgil Michel, O.S.B., who was then trying to recover the ancient idea that all Christians, lay and ordained, participate fully in the body of Christ that is present in the Eucharist. Michel's position challenged both the clericalism and the devotional individualism of Tridentine Catholicism, and in 1940 the hierarchy was only beginning to take notice. Pius XII cautiously endorsed Mystical

Body theology in his 1943 encyclical *Mystici Corporis Christi,* but it was not until Vatican II that the church affirmed in no uncertain terms that it was, first and foremost, the whole people of God. What appears conservative today was thus quite progressive in its own time.

Moreover, Day made clear that "Aims and Purposes" was not a rule in the sense of a document that sets a distinct group of people apart. The Catholic Worker vision, Day concluded, was intended not only for "members" of the movement but for all people. "When we write in these terms, we are writing not only for our fellow workers in thirty other Houses, to other groups of Catholic Workers who are meeting for discussion, but to every reader of the paper. We hold with the motto of the National Maritime Union, that every member is an organizer. We are upholding the ideal of personal responsibility."[18] Clearly, this emphasis on personal responsibility qualifies Day's position on daily Communion: perhaps one might be required to commune daily in order to be the house manager of a Catholic Worker house, but that was just one of countless ways of connecting to the spirit of the movement.

Day's project of rearticulating Catholic Worker ideals in every issue was dropped shortly thereafter, perhaps because the onset of World War II shifted her energies toward the articulation of a Catholic pacifist vision. But requests for guidance from new houses kept coming in, and again and again Day offered quite specific directives only to retract them in favor of a call to personal responsibility. In 1948, for example, she wrote that during her trip west many people asked her about the possibility of opening new houses of hospitality around the country. "I repeat," she said, "such centers must be opened by a local group who know what poverty and suffering mean, and who are willing to live in the houses with those they serve. It can never be operated from the outside." Such advice might have upset the many Catholic Workers who were, in fact, involved only on a part-time basis, but she went on to offer a more inclusive vision: "The important thing is that hospices, under Catholic auspices, be started no matter by whom, whether by Third Orders, Knights of Columbus, or oblates of St. Benedict. They do not have to be Catholic Worker Houses of Hospitality." And she followed this with a criticism directed squarely at the New York house of hospitality: "We are always being accused of biting off more than we can chew, and indeed we always have more to feed, and to house, and to clothe than we can humanly handle. Breadlines are a disgrace."[19]

Several years later, the New York community turned once again to the task of articulating a unifying philosophy for the movement. Though Day was very much at the center of the community at the time, she and the others decided to entrust three Catholic Workers—Robert Ludlow, Ammon Hennacy, and Tom Cain—with the task of putting the "Catholic Worker Positions" into writing. According to an editorial introduction to Cain's piece, this decision reflected a principle Peter Maurin had borrowed from Ibsen: "The truth must be restated every twenty years." Accordingly, the editors promised, "other statements will follow from time to time."[20] What actually followed were a great many reprintings of the initial three statements, with a wide range of revisions introduced as the years passed.

Robert Ludlow's "Catholic Worker Positions," first published in February 1954, was by far the most frequently reprinted, and it would ultimately serve as the basis for the 1987 "Aims and Means" described above. In its original form, it is much less explicitly Catholic than the later version—perhaps because Catholic Workers of the 1950s could take their Catholicism for granted. Ludlow begins by declaring that "the general aim of the Catholic Worker Movement is to realize in the individual and in society the expressed and implied teaching of Christ," but he does not identify either the Scriptures or the Catholic magisterium as sources of authority for the movement. The only specifically Catholic element in the essay is a quote from Saint Gertrude: "Property, the more common it is, the more holy it is." The body of the piece does reflect the strong influence of both Peter Maurin and American radicalism, with its strong condemnation of "capitalist and bourgeois society."[21]

Ammon Hennacy's version, titled "Our Positions," begins similarly but is much more explicit about the diverse sources of Catholic Worker philosophy. Hennacy either quotes or praises Saint Paul, Saint Francis, Gandhi, Vinoba Bhave, and Henry David Thoreau. Hennacy also alludes to the sacramental dimension of Catholic life, writing that "as Catholics we should and do believe that the Sacraments of our Church which Christ gave to us are more real than the H Bomb." But he gives much more weight to the authority of Scripture and more specifically the Sermon on the Mount. In this, he seems dependent on such nineteenth-century "nonresistant" pacifists as William Lloyd Garrison and Adin Ballou, activists who ascribed high authority to the ethical teachings of Jesus while neglecting both Saint Paul's theology and the subsequent teachings of the church. "The spiritual basis of the Catholic Worker stems from the Sermon on the Mount," declares Hennacy, while "the economic basis of the Catholic Worker is that of the early Christians where 'From each according to his ability and to each according to his need' was the custom." Hennacy also strikes a note of withdrawal from mainstream society that might seem more sectarian than Catholic: "We should withdraw as much as we can do so from participation in our non-Christian society."[22]

Tom Cain, for his part, seems a bit more Catholic when he writes: "Prayer and the Sacraments are in fact our arsenal, whence each one of us is urged to draw the spiritual weapons and energies required for the pursuit of our ends." Even he is cautious, however, about drawing the boundaries of the movement too narrowly: though he invites supporters to join the movement through prayer as well as material support, he speaks simply of "joining to each one's proper degree in the common prayer of the Church." Cain is also as inclined as his predecessors to use strong "revolutionary" language, writing of "the multitude of discrete personal revolutions constituting the general revolution," and of "the one man revolutions, which are the essential components of a peaceful world revolution."[23]

These documents may have taken a lot out of their authors, for both Robert Ludlow and Tom Cain left the Catholic Worker within a few months of the first publication of their essays. Ammon Hennacy, for his part, left New York City to establish a series of hospitality houses in Salt Lake City, where he eventually broke with the Catholic Church, though never with Dorothy Day or the Worker. Their statements of Catholic Worker philosophy, however, lived on in the pages of the *Catholic Worker.* After a hiatus of several years, Cain's reappeared in the May 1961 issue, while Ludlow's showed up in May 1965. (Because the paper had been launched on May Day 1933, May issues usually served to mark anniversaries.) Ludlow's "Positions" then became an annual feature throughout the 1970s.

The 1970s, of course, were a period of dramatic expansion for the movement, and "Catholic Worker Positions" proved to be a valuable tool for fledgling houses of hospitality. It served easily as a ready-made "mission statement" for them to share with local churches and potential volunteers or donors. The founders of the Des Moines Catholic Worker, for example, repeatedly printed it on the reverse side of flyers announcing events or describing their own community projects. Once their newspaper was up and running, moreover, they published a series of articles that elaborated on the "Positions" and, in particular, placed greater emphasis on the scriptural roots of the Catholic Worker program. Ultimately, one Des Moines Worker, Richard Cleaver, was able to expand his essays on the "Positions" into a full-fledged book.[24] The Des Moines Workers seem to have been aware that Day had encouraged the ongoing revision of the "Positions," and by 1979 the community had twice revised the principles, adding a condemnation of "heterosexism" as a "blasphemy against God whose image is incarnate in us all and whose death has redeemed us all."[25]

The New York community did not embrace the position on homosexuality espoused by the Des Moines community, but they seem to have been convinced that the scriptural basis of the "Positions" needed to be more explicit. The first major revision of Ludlow's essay to appear in the New York paper was in 1979, very shortly before Day's death. The preamble underscores the biblical basis of the movement by explaining that "we see the Sermon on the Mount (Matthew 5:38-48) and the call to solidarity with the poor (Matthew 25:31-46) as the heart of the Gospel message." It adds a quote from Vatican II and one from Paul VI, though these have to do with the arms race and private property, not with Catholic doctrine. It also includes a clearer description of the contours of the Catholic Worker movement: "We, as a lay movement, seek our strength and direction in the beauty of regular prayer and liturgy, in studying and applying the traditions of Scripture and the teachings of the Church to the modern condition. Thus directed, our efforts to perform our duty as Christians range widely—from visiting the sick to occupying nuclear plant sites." Curiously, all of this appeared under a quote from Peter Maurin, rather than a title as such.[26]

This version was republished through the early 1980s, but eventually the community in New York seems to have judged that further clarification was needed, particularly with regard to the relationship between the two key texts from Matthew, the Bible as a whole, and the teaching authority of the Catholic Church. A 1986 revision added quotes from Peter Maurin and Dorothy Day (after her death, Day would be quoted with the same deference she had always accorded Maurin) and from the Old Testament book of Deuteronomy, along with an explanation that "as with [Maurin and Day], our sources are Hebrew and Greek Scripture, and the teachings of the Roman Catholic Church; our theoretical basis is found in St. Thomas Aquinas' doctrine of the Common Good, with our inspiration taken from the lives of the saints, 'men and women outstanding in holiness, living witnesses to Your unchanging love' (Eucharistic Prayer)."[27] These changes are refined in the 1987 version, which is accompanied by an explanatory essay written by Katherine Temple, one of the New York Workers who had participated in the revision.

Though her essay is titled "Our Manifesto: The Sermon on the Mount," Temple's real purpose is to warn against understandings of Catholic Worker identity that pit a narrowly defined gospel core against biblical or ecclesial authority. "Whenever we try to write down our 'Aims and Means,'" she begins, in a rare allusion to the writing process behind the document, "they smite us with our inadequacy and our complicity in the very forces we decry the loudest." The most striking "inadequacy," she suggests, had been highlighted by Dietrich Bonhoeffer when he wrote, "What is this Christianity we always hear mentioned? Is it essentially the content of the Sermon on the Mount, or is it the message of reconciliation in the Cross and the Resurrection of our Lord?" Bonhoeffer was asking, in other words, if the nonviolent ethic of the Sermon on the Mount could be separated from the theological belief that salvation comes from the death and resurrection of Jesus. By 1987 a great many people in the Catholic Worker movement thought it could, and without pointing fingers or naming names, Temple was calling them to account. She was also worrying that too much emphasis on the Gospel might mask a creeping anti-Judaism. Thus, she cleverly praised a book on the *Sermon on the Mount* by an Orthodox Jew, Pinchas Lapide, for showing "how St. Matthew Chapter 5 can be read within the Bible as a whole, without a disastrous split between the Testaments." Obviously, the quote from Deuteronomy that had just been added to the "Positions" served the same purpose. But Temple's rebuke was quite gentle: following Lapide, she concludes that the Sermon on the Mount is indeed a "Christian manifesto," presenting a "realistic utopianism" that is well worth following.[28]

Clearly, something interesting was happening in the Catholic Worker movement in the early 1980s. But, as I suggested in the previous chapters, that "something" was most certainly *not* a drift away from the unambiguous sense of Catholic identity that had prevailed during Dorothy Day's lifetime. Rather, communities across the ideological spectrum were struggling valiantly to sort out the spiritual ambiguities that Dorothy Day had tolerated. They reached a wide range of conclusions: New York vested more authority in the hierarchy than had been the case previously;

Des Moines broadened the "Positions" to include sexual orientation; Haley House redefined itself as "in the Catholic Worker tradition." Since Day never specifically addressed these versions of the "Positions," none can claim her authority in an exclusive way. Yet, as thoughtful local expressions by persons who took personal responsibility for their words, all might well have merited her blessing.

Today, most Catholic Worker communities use their own mission statements, rather than relying on any of the variants of the "Catholic Worker Positions." Though these statements vary widely in their implicit understandings of both Catholicism and radicalism, virtually all underscore the movement's centered commitment to the works of mercy. The Los Angeles Catholic Worker, for example, begins with the works of mercy, explaining that "the lay Catholic Worker movement [was] founded over seventy years ago . . . to 'feed the hungry, shelter the homeless, care for the sick, clothe the naked, visit the prisoner' and offer a gospel-based critique of the dominant culture within the Catholic tradition but outside the institutionalized structures of the church." This last phrase could be interpreted either as a critique of the institutional church or merely as an affirmation of the lay character of the community. In any case, the statement goes on to underscore the theological basis of the works of mercy, explaining that "we believe that the Incarnation is the basis of the Christian message. We are called to make the Word of God flesh by responding to the suffering Christ incarnate among our poor and marginalized sisters and brothers."[29] Casa Maria in Milwaukee, similarly, suggests that it has theological roots but no ecclesial boundaries: "We are a community dedicated to living out the Gospel values of loving our enemies and doing good to those who do all manner of evil against us and attempting to take responsibility for the needy sister and brothers in our society."[30] And the Winona (Minnesota) Catholic Worker places special emphasis on the transformative power of the works of mercy, noting: "We pray that through our life and work here, God will transform us into more loving, compassionate persons, and that this house will help create a just and peaceful world—'a society where it is easier for people to be good.'"[31]

Indeed, the works of mercy have transformed the Catholic Worker movement into a kaleidoscopic web of communities. Whether traditionalist Catholics or punk anarchists, Catholic Workers do not hesitate to write their own rules. But in that diversity they are also faithful—to the vision of their founders, to their own capacity to grow in holiness, and to the spirit of community that at least some of them identify as the Mystical Body of Christ.

[1] Rosalie Riegle Troester, *Voices from the Catholic Worker* (Philadelphia: Temple University Press, 1993), xvii.

[2] Day's first formulation of Maurin's program is "Maurin's Program," *Catholic Worker* 1, no. 2 (June–July 1933): 4.

[3] Dorothy Day with Francis J. Sicius, *Peter Maurin: Apostle to the World* (Maryknoll, NY: Orbis, 2004), 4.

[4] Ibid., 3.

[5] Ibid., 46–48.

[6] Dorothy Day, *Therese* (Springfield, IL: Templegate, 1960), v–viii.

[7] Day, *The Long Loneliness* (New York: Harper, 1952), 191, 195, 223.

[8] Interview with Tom Cornell, 23 May 2000.

[9] "The Aims and Means of the Catholic Worker," at http://www.catholicworker.org/aimsandmeanstext.cfm?Number=5.

[10] "Aims and Means of the Catholic Worker Movement," *Catholic Worker* 54, no. 3 (May 1987): 2; "Catholic Worker Positions," *Catholic Worker* 20, no. 7 (February 1954): 2.

[11] "Catholic Worker Celebrates 3rd Birthday; A Restatement of C. W. Aims and Ideals," *Catholic Worker* 4, no. 1 (May 1936): 1.

[12] "Aims and Purposes," *Catholic Worker* 6, no. 7 (January 1939): 7.

[13] "Aims and Purposes," *Catholic Worker* 6, no. 8 (February 1939): 7; "Aims and Purposes," *Catholic Worker* 6, no. 10 (May 1939): 5; "Aims and Purposes," *Catholic Worker* 10, no. 6 (May 1943): 4.

[14] "The Aims and Means of the Catholic Worker," at http://www.catholicworker.org/aimsandmeanstext.cfm?Number=5.

[15] Ibid.

[16] Ibid.

[17] Ibid.

[18] Ibid.

[19] Dorothy Day, "Letter on Hospices," *Catholic Worker* 14, no. 10 (January 1948): 2, 8.

[20] "Aims, Purposes, Positions," *Catholic Worker* 22, no. 4 (November 1955): 8.

[21] "Catholic Worker Positions," *Catholic Worker* 20, no. 7 (February 1954): 2.

[22] "Our Positions," *Catholic Worker* 21, no. 10 (May 1955): 5, 7.

[23] "Aims, Purposes, Positions," *Catholic Worker* 22, no. 4 (November 1955): 8.

[24] Frank Cordaro, "Why the Catholic Worker?" *Via Pacis* 1, no. 1 (November 1976); Frank Cordaro, "A Midrash of the Catholic Worker Positions, part 1," *Via Pacis* 1, no. 2 (November 1976); Frank Cordaro, "A Midrash of the Catholic Worker Positions, part 2," *Via Pacis* 1, no. 3 (January 1977); Richard Cleaver, "Catholic Worker Positions," *Via Pacis* 10, no. 3 (June–July 1986): 6; Richard Cleaver, *New Heaven, New Earth: Practical Essays on the Catholic Worker Program* (Marion, SD: Rose Hill Books, 1993).

[25] "The Catholic Worker Positions/ D. M., IA," circa 1979, in DD/CWC, series W-21, box 1, folder 2.

[26] "'Making a path from things as they are to things as they should be'— Peter Maurin," *Catholic Worker* 45, no. 4 (May 1979): 4–5.

[27] "Aims and Means of the Catholic Worker," *Catholic Worker* 53, no. 3 (May 1986): 3, 6.

[28] Katherine Temple, "Our Manifesto: The Sermon on the Mount," *Catholic Worker* 54, no. 3 (May 1987): 2.

[29] "Who We Are," http://lacatholicworker.org/who-we-are/.

[30] "Our Views," http://www.geocities.com/casa_maria_worker/gen.html.

[31] "Winona Catholic Worker Mission," http://www.catholicworker.org/winona/#mission.

Chapter 6

Inventing the Catholic Worker Family

Another contemporary phenomenon that would merit Day's blessing is the proliferation of families in the Worker movement. Yet many of today's Catholic Worker families seem unsure of that blessing. In my research visits to Catholic Worker families, I encountered many parents who were alternately angry at Day's intolerance for family life and apologetic about the compromises they had made in combining the two vocations of parenting and hospitality. "In my readings of and about Dorothy Day, it seems she was not very 'family friendly,'" reflected Larry Purcell in a newsletter published for Catholic Worker houses in the 1990s. "Perhaps her early, awful experiences with families on the farm or her lack of a husband/father, or her own decision to ship her child out are part of her position; but she really does not seem to verbally (or in writing) strongly support families among the staff of the Catholic Worker houses. I would love to be wrong about this perception."[1] Purcell's perception was echoed in the articles prepared for a 1999 gathering of Catholic Worker families and published in what was intended as the first issue of a newsletter on *Family Life in the Catholic Worker Movement.*[2] A number of scholarly studies have echoed the judgment that Day's influence has given the movement a significant "anti-family bias."[3]

Such judgments are not so much wrong as one-sided, failing to recognize the unsystematic and often contradictory character of her advice on a wide range of topics. "Dorothy did swing back and forth on this issue. . . . She did have an arbitrary streak to her," explained her longtime associate Tom Cornell, himself the father of a Catholic Worker family. "It's dangerous," he added, "quoting Dorothy."[4] Whatever the reason, few Workers or scholars today recognize that, as early as 1936, Day had affirmed that the "reconstruction of social order" relied less on trade unions, cooperatives, and communes than on "the re-creation of the Catholic family, that microcosm of society and type of the Mystical Body."[5] Though she did not encourage families to live full-time at the New York house of hospitality, she consistently invited them to participate in the Worker's "lay apostolate" in other places and in other ways. Particularly in the decades after World War II, a wide variety of families responded to that invitation by inventing their own ways of combining family life with the vocation of the Worker. These models in turn inspired a new generation of Catholic Worker families who, since the 1960s, have argued that the Catholic Worker offers a compelling solution to the contemporary crisis of American family life.

This is not to suggest that Day's legacy for Catholic Worker families is unambiguous. Part of the ambiguity reflects Day's personality, and part reflects her historical context. The Catholic Worker movement was born at a paradoxical moment for American Catholic families. Immigration from southern and eastern Europe had been largely cut off a generation earlier, and the children of immigrants were beginning to move from the working to the middle class when the Great Depression hit. This shared experience of deprivation helped break down the barriers between Catholics and their Protestant and Jewish neighbors, and lent new relevance to the church's advocacy for social justice. Catholic social teaching encouraged lay Catholics to take an active role in promoting social justice, and non-Catholic politicians like Franklin Delano Roosevelt were more than eager to incorporate Catholic ideas like the "living wage" and the "industrial council" into their economic programs. During these years, moreover, a rising divorce rate and declining birth rate fueled widespread concern about family values among both Catholics and Protestants, leading to the formation of a wide range of initiatives and organizations on both sides of the denominational divide.[6]

All of these factors invited Catholic families to reach beyond the parochial ghetto. Yet when it came to the specifics of family policy, official church teachings drew a sharp dividing line. In an era when Protestant ministers were in the forefront of calls for family planning and even eugenics, Pius XI's encyclical *Casti Connubii* reaffirmed the traditional view that "the child holds the first place" among the blessings of marriage and strictly forbade all forms of artificial birth control.[7] In the years following *Casti Connubii,* a new circle of "Catholic sociologists" challenged lenient divorce laws, government intervention in family life, and the mainstream sociological emphasis on personal fulfillment as the purpose of marriage. Between 1920 and 1962, Paul Hanly Furfey (a close friend of Dorothy Day), Edgar Schmiedeler, Jacques Leclercq, John Kane, John Thomas, and Alphonse Clemens all produced major studies of the Catholic family, and most presented traditional Catholic teaching as the antidote to a family crisis caused by liberalism and industrialism.[8] All of this created a delicate challenge for ordinary Catholic families: they were invited to participate fully in an urban, industrial society without sacrificing patterns of family life rooted in the church's rural past.[9]

For Dorothy Day and Peter Maurin, the solution to the dilemma was clear: Catholics could break out of the ghetto not by acquiescing to industrial culture but by joining in a radical struggle to transform it. One did not need to join a religious order or renounce married life to participate in this struggle, for all Catholics were part of the "Mystical Body of Christ." The work of social reconstruction was a "lay apostolate" in which lay people (both single and married) were to take the leading role, with priests and religious providing support. If it was difficult to raise a large family in the city, the solution was not to practice birth control, but to move to a farm. The agronomic universities that constituted the third point of Maurin's program were thus also a way of responding to the challenge of *Casti Connubii*.

Families, in short, were close to the center of Catholic Worker theory. But the way Day and Maurin translated this theory into practice was shaped by another paradox. Neither was involved in conventional family life: Maurin was an ex-seminarian who never married, while Day was a single mother who had abandoned her common-law marriage at the time of her conversion to Catholicism. They stood outside the typical lay Catholic experience in other ways as well: in an era when most American Catholics were children or grandchildren of immigrants and thus products of the immigrant ghetto, Day was a convert from a bourgeois Protestant background and Maurin was himself an immigrant who had been raised in the French countryside. Much as Day valued the agrarian ideal of self-sufficient family farms, moreover, she could not fully envision a place for herself within agrarian society: by vocation, she was a journalist who thrived on the grit and energy of the big city. All of these tensions contributed to the ambivalent messages Day gave to families in the Worker.

This ambivalence is especially evident in two early documents that often provide the starting point for discussions of Day's attitude toward families.[10] In the first of these, a circular letter sent to all Worker houses on 10 August 1940, Day declared: "Our workers have taken it upon themselves to try to follow the counsels of perfection. . . . Many can only go part of the way, what with family obligations, health consideration, even a different point of view. If they wish to work with us, we are glad and thankful to have them, but they cannot be said to be representing The Catholic Worker position." The second document, written in 1948 but apparently never distributed, is even more strident, implying that families are the primary cause of conflict within the movement: "Ever since the work started, the single people have gone along with it and all was peace and quiet until the problem of marriage and family has come up."[11]

Clearly, such inflammatory quotations demand a contextual analysis. The first comes from Day's notorious "encyclical" responding to the refusal of several houses to distribute the *Catholic Worker* during World War II. Though her message to the dissidents was strong, it was also ambiguous. She began by urging readers to "register with us their position as conscientious objectors," then acknowledged the "members of Catholic Worker groups throughout the country who do not stand with us on this issue." Next she drew a crucial distinction between those who "wish still to be associated with us" and are thus willing to distribute the newspaper from those who "take it upon themselves to suppress the paper and hinder its circulation." The latter group, she insisted, must "dissociate themselves from the Catholic Worker movement and not use the name of a movement with which they now are in such fundamental disagreement."[12]

Day's comment about persons who "cannot be said to be representing The Catholic Worker position" comes immediately after this ultimatum. Seen in this light, her inclusion of Workers who can "only go part of the way" because of "family obligations" may be an offhand attempt to soften a hard message. Her intent, Day seems to be saying, is not to excommunicate anti-pacifist dissidents but to identify a variety of reasons why some people or groups might *choose* not to affiliate with the Worker movement. She thus concludes this section with a tone of suggestion rather than command: "Perhaps it would be better in these cases for the House to disassociate themselves from the Catholic Worker movement. They can continue as settlements for the works of mercy, but not as Catholic Worker units." She even added that it would be to their advantage to do so, since official Catholic Workers were likely to face "hindrance from the Government" as long as the war lasted.[13]

It is not clear that Day had seriously contemplated the possibility that families were unwelcome in the movement prior to writing this letter, but the effect was to make their status—as well as the status of individuals who were not pacifist but were willing to distribute the paper—uncertain. Were they expected to withdraw voluntarily or simply to consider doing so? When Day wrote later in the letter, "There is no reason why we should not be associated together as friends and fellow workers, but there is every reason for not continuing to use The Catholic Worker name," was she thinking specifically of the houses that had suppressed the paper or more generally of all the people who "can only go part of the way"?

At least one Worker understood her to mean the latter and concluded that a movement that shunned families was destined to become just another religious order. "I am convinced," wrote Jimmy Flannery of the Pittsburgh house, "that there are many who, because of obligations to that first unit of a Christian society, the family, cannot possibly follow the counsels of perfection, have done as much or more toward spreading and aiding the Catholic Worker movement as have any who live in the Houses. . . . Your ideals will stop with the exclusive few, living in Poverty at the Hospices, [becoming] a 'lay-Franciscan' order, and eventually a clerical order, with the members performing the works of mercy solely for their own spiritual edification." Being a Catholic Worker, Flannery added, should not be understood as a vocation, "except in the sense that one would say being Catholic is a vocation."[14]

Flannery failed to realize that this was precisely the sense in which Day understood the vocation of the Catholic Worker. His misunderstanding was understandable, for in 1940 the overwhelming majority of American Catholics assumed that a vocation was a call to the priesthood or a religious order and identified the "counsels of perfection" with the vows of poverty, chastity, and obedience that were binding on members of religious orders but not on laypeople. Day's usage, however, was shaped by the ideas of liturgical reformer Virgil Michel, O.S.B., who appealed to the ancient doctrine of the "Mystical Body of Christ" to support a more ambitious understanding of the "lay apostolate."[15] In a series of circular letters that preceded that of August 1940, Day repeatedly suggested that the Catholic Worker was not merely a response to the problem of homelessness, but an attempt to revitalize the lay apostolate by asking laypeople to take the counsels of perfection as seriously as those in religious orders. When she mentioned the counsels of perfection, she cited Scriptures rather than the standard formula of poverty, chastity, and obedience, and chastised those who are too quick to "distinguish between counsel and precept." "The counsels of perfection," she quoted Thomas Aquinas, "are . . . expedient for everybody."[16] Peter Maurin cited a recent papal encyclical to even more pointed effect: "'We cannot accept the belief / that this command of Christ / concerns only/ a select and privileged group. . . . The law of holiness /embraces everyone / and admits / of no exception.'"[17]

Given this history, Day's reference to the counsels of perfection cannot be seen as an attempt to remake her movement into a religious order. It was just the opposite: a reminder—for those who understood—of the vital importance of building up the lay apostolate. In this light, Day's suggestion that families "can only go part of the way" is puzzling, but not entirely incomprehensible. It was, I believe, an awkward attempt to reiterate another theme that Day had sounded previously: that while the counsels of perfection are addressed to all, the specific way in which they are to be lived out may vary greatly from person to person. Anyone, and any family, could practice the works of mercy without forsaking his or her vocation or other commitments.

Day's intent in August 1940, thus, was surely not to force families out of the movement entirely. Instead, she may have hoped to liberate families from the sort of either-or thinking that assumes one is either entirely within the movement or entirely outside it. Family responsibilities might prevent someone from living at a house of hospitality, just as ideological differences might prevent someone from distributing the *Catholic Worker* newspaper. But nothing should get in the way of the lay apostolate—of taking personal responsibility for responding to the call of the gospel. This flexible approach was confirmed in a letter sent just a few days later, inviting Catholic Workers to participate in the movement's annual retreat. That letter clearly assumed that people not living in hospitality houses might choose to participate, but it also stressed that they might need to take more financial responsibility by staying in nearby hotels if the farm was overcrowded. "Those who are living in the houses," Day wrote, "have first call on us for hospitality."[18]

Day's understanding of the lay apostolate also provides the general context for interpreting the memorandum of 1948. The more specific context for that document was a crisis at the farming commune in Easton, Pennsylvania—the first of several farms sponsored by the New York Catholic Worker community. This farm was home to several families, each of which had been allotted a certain portion of the common land. But from the perspective of the families, who had been deeply influenced by the "distributist" ideas of Peter Maurin and Eric Gill, they had first claim on all the farm's resources, because the family is the natural "unit" of society and because farming families are the only antidote to the evils of modern technology. This extreme belief was coupled with an idiosyncratic ritualism and a harshly patriarchal attitude toward women (who were, according to William Miller, "forbidden to speak unless spoken to" and "compelled to knock on the doors of even their own kitchens if men were present"). Such attitudes clashed sharply with Day's belief, articulated with increasing clarity after 1944, that the farm's primary role was as a place of respite for the urban poor and of retreat for Catholic Workers from across the nation. Soon the dissident families took to disrupting the retreats, confiscating furniture and food while assuring the retreatants that Day had betrayed the vision of Peter Maurin. Eventually, she simply handed part of the farm over to the dissidents (who remained there for several decades), sold the rest, and purchased a new farm and retreat center at Newburgh, New York.[19]

The 1948 memorandum, written near the opening of the Newburgh farm, was Day's attempt to clarify her vision for the new farm and prevent a recurrence of the unfortunate events at Easton. Given the troubling idiosyncrasies of some of the Easton families, she might have treated the situation there as an aberration, but instead she generalized, writing that in a number of situations (including that of her daughter's growing family) "the problem of the family and farm came up, and who was to have control, where the authority lay, what money was coming to them, and always the family pointed out that they came first, that the family was the unit of society, that their temporal welfare had to be considered, that we are supposed to be making a place for the families on the land, the family community." Day responded to such attitudes by appealing to Peter Maurin's legacy, in much the same way that subsequent Workers would eventually appeal to her: "If people would go over the back issues of the *Catholic Worker,* they would find again and again that Peter was talking of workers and scholars on the land. He never went into the issue of families."[20]

In fact, a review of back issues of the *Worker* reveals that Day had proposed at the founding of the Easton farm that families would "have small houses built for them," while another writer suggested that each family be given two or three acres so that "the man and his wife will be lords on their own little domain."[21] But the underlying problem was more financial than ideological. Day knew, far better than the Easton families, that contributions to the Worker came primarily from people who wanted to help the poor, and she felt responsible for honoring those intentions. Since it cost more to maintain a family than a single volunteer, a predominance of families on the farm threatened the apostolate to the poor. "The literal fact," she wrote, "is that there is not enough money to support families [on the farms] and finance Mott Street [the urban house of hospitality]." Her proposed compromise was, not to exclude families from the Newburgh farm, but to give them small plots of land so long as they committed to building their own houses and supporting themselves financially, through outside work if necessary. (This principle was accompanied with bitter recriminations against Easton families that allowed Peter Maurin and other single men to do their work while they "lay on the couch and listened to the radio.") The retreat house itself, she insisted, "must be managed by the single, and the deed to the farm as a whole should be in the hands of the unmarried."[22]

This privileging of the unmarried might suggest that the Worker movement was evolving into a celibate religious order, were it not for the fact that the memorandum began with a ringing reaffirmation of Day's commitment to the ideal of the lay apostolate. Before making any specific recommendations about families and their place in the movement, Day cited a letter from a cloistered nun who had said that "you are blazing a trail, indeed, in this work for God's poor," then added that "we are blazing a trail in the work of the lay apostolate, and not in just the care of the poor." The church had always cared for the poor, she noted; what was new with the Worker was Peter Maurin's emphasis on "personal responsibility" and the obligation of every person to directly meet the needs of others. She also took pains to "reassur[e] all of you who read this once and for all here in writing: that neither Peter Maurin or I have had any intention of turning the work into a religious order."[23] These words echoed her assertion, in one of her newspaper columns of the same year: "When people talk of our work turning into a religious community, I am impatient at this lack of understanding. This is work for *lay people to initiate and to manage.*"[24]

Far from intending to transform the Worker into a religious order, Day feared that the Easton families, with their willingness to subsist on the donations of others, might turn the movement into a religious order minus the celibacy. This fear led her to place a strong emphasis on the distinct responsibilities of the "married apostolate," noting that the majority of young couples who have met through the Worker "have recognized that in taking a wife and bringing forth children their status in the lay apostolate has changed, that their first obligation has to be to take care of their own and not to ask others to support them, no matter how hard they might have to work, but to go out and to earn the cash that ought to enable them to live as a private unit." Similarly, in the concluding paragraph of the memorandum she warned against the self-righteous tendency to draw too sharp a line between those who practice the lay apostolate at a Worker house or farm and those who contribute to such ventures: "We are in the lay apostolate, and we are supposed to be apostles *to the world.* . . . We can never get away from the fact that we are supported by the money of people living in the world, so we cannot be too self-satisfied about having left the world and industry or industrial capitalism."[25]

Given Day's vision of the Worker as a lay apostolate, William Miller was not quite right to conclude that "the message [of the memorandum] was clear: if you marry within the framework of the Catholic Worker, then you had better leave because your primary obligation is to your family."[26] Worker families, for Day, had no right to live on donations intended for the poor, but that did not mean they had to remain outside a lay movement committed to the corporal works of mercy. It simply meant that they were to take personal responsibility for being in it in a manner appropriate to their family situation. Unfortunately, Day's bitterness toward the Easton families—and toward previous families that had seen the poor as "rotting lumber" and "freeloaders"—prevented her from including positive examples of Worker families, apart from one reference to a "family in our midst" who "by means of such self-discipline and thrift, recognizing the needs of the family, have bought themselves a farm."[27]

These two documents, in short, reveal some bitterness but no systematic hostility toward families in the Worker. The bottom line, implied but never fully expressed in the two memos, was that while families had a limited role in houses of hospitality and on farms that rely on donations, they had a vital role in the larger movement to revitalize the lay apostolate (and to connect that apostolate more fully with the counsels of perfection). It might not be too much to say that in pushing families out of the houses and farms, Day was pushing them into the vanguard of a movement that aspired not to institution building but to the cultivation of smallness. This desire to see families at the heart of the movement, if not at the heart of the New York community, perhaps explains why, just weeks after writing the 1948 memorandum, Day was exulting in the family-friendly atmosphere of the Newburgh retreats. "We are the only Catholic retreat house in the United States," she wrote in a journal entry that was published in her book *On Pilgrimage,* "where mother and father and all the children can come and camp out with us for a few days to partake of refreshment for body and soul. Over the Labor Day retreat there were twenty-two children and eleven couples."[28]

If this message of welcome is not clearly remembered by today's Worker families, this is in part because her words about the role of married people in the lay apostolate were so often laced with ambivalence or frustration at the loss of once-industrious single volunteers. Many contemporary Workers have speculated that the root of this ambivalence may lie in Day's personal experience of family life. "Neither Dorothy nor Peter have much to say to me about the intimacy of family life with children," wrote Larry Purcell, a father and founder of a small Catholic Worker house. "Peter left his family in France and may never have married. As far as we know he had no children. Dorothy was raised in a highly dysfunctional family and made the decision to let others raise her daughter."[29] "While she was undoubtedly a saint," added Larry Holben in his contribution to the Catholic Worker family newsletter, "Dorothy does not appear to have been a very good mother. . . . Tamar appears to have been shunted off repeatedly to this craft school, that farm or community, these friends, while Dorothy pursued the harsh and dreadful love that was her calling. And even when Tamar remained at home, the cost for the young child appears to have been at times significant."[30]

Such judgments have struck other Catholic Workers as presumptuous, especially in light of the fact that Tamar has refused to confirm them. Though her sense of privacy prevented her from giving details about her experiences, Tamar Hennessy told oral historian Rosalie Riegle that "it was wonderful to grow up [at the Catholic Worker]. So much enthusiasm! And everybody had found something they really wanted to do, so it was just so . . . so hopeful. I loved the spirit of that first ten years. But

Dorothy would be away a lot, and I had a hard time with that. I even nick-named her 'Be-going.' I wanted Dorothy so bad! When she came home, she lit up my room, she lit up my life."[31] This account is revealing, because it suggests that Day was not so much a bad mother as a mother who genuinely struggled to balance the demands of parenting with those of being a movement founder.[32] Given this experience, it is understandable that she would encourage other Workers to count the costs before becoming parents, though she may have failed to recognize the differences between her experience as a single parent and movement *founder* and the different possibilities for married parents who were simply *participants* in the movement. (Apart from those who have done significant prison time for civil disobedience, most contemporary Worker parents would say that being part of the Worker allows them to spend more, not less, time with their children.)

Day's seemingly harsh words of 1940 and 1948, coupled with the ambiguous record of her own parenting, do not exhaust her legacy for Worker families. As she traveled the country to raise money and encourage local groups to start their own houses of hospitality, Day often connected with people who were already combining hospitality with family responsibilities, and she rarely failed to offer an encouraging word. Her very first published account of a speaking tour, for example, began by praising a Rochester mother named Teresa Weider as "an outstanding example of personal responsibility and hospitality. . . . She has always gone on the principle that what one had, one must share. She has six children, and a few grandchildren, and she has recently adopted another child. She has gone in for hospitality in a big way, and she hereby invites any and all of the Catholic Workers to stay with her whenever they are in Rochester or passing through."[33]

Such accounts became increasingly common in the pages of the *Catholic Worker* in the years after World War II, as the movement adapted to some dramatic changes in its social context. Before the war, the movement consisted primarily of urban houses of hospitality that both served and were staffed by single men unable to find paid employment. With the onset of war, unemployment declined dramatically, male Workers were either drafted or sent to conscientious objector camps, and most of the Worker houses closed. But the Worker's larger vision of a lay apostolate committed to social reconstruction remained salient for an increasingly broad array of American Catholics. The theology of the Mystical Body of Christ, which Day had learned from Virgil Michel and other liturgical reformers, was partly endorsed by Pius XII in his 1943 encyclical *Mystici Corporis Christi*. A series of World Congresses on the Lay Apostolate were held in 1951, 1957, and 1967, while in the United States an array of new Catholic movements articulated models of lay action in a variety of social arenas.[34] Prominent among these were the Young Christian Workers, Young Christian Students, the Grail, the National Catholic Rural Life Movement, and the Christian Family Movement, which invited married couples to gather in small groups to discuss the connections between their faith, their families, and the larger society.[35] Like the Catholic Worker, these new groups hoped to have a transformative effect on the larger culture precisely by adhering to the best Catholic values, and as a result there was a great deal of cooperation and mutual influence. During these years, the *Catholic Worker* served simultaneously as a chronicle of urban hospitality in New York (where families were not prominent) and as a forum for a nationwide network of activists, most of them committed to family life.

From the 1940s to the 1970s, Day's "On Pilgrimage" column gave constant testimony to the family orientation of this network. Traveling across the country, she stayed with families as often as at houses of hospitality and typically praised her hosts for finding unique ways of combining the ideals of the Catholic Worker with the responsibilities of family life. In Saint Joseph, Minnesota, Don and Mary Humphrey, once members of the Milwaukee Catholic Worker house, were developing various craft projects while Don taught at the College of Saint Benedict. Al Reser, one of the founders of the Chicago house, was now working to support his four children but was also very interested in a "family Apostolate" that would help rebuild homes in Hiroshima and Nagasaki. Yet another family, the Gallaghers, was buying a quaint brick farmhouse where they planned to host "Catholic Worker parties" and "family conferences."[36]

In a similar column written five years later, Day characterized the movement as "the houses of hospitality, the farms, the homes of young married couples whose lives have been given direction and meaning by the teaching of Peter Maurin," then devoted most of her space to describing various models of family life. She described Saint Benedict's farming commune in Upton, Massachusetts, where four families with a total of twenty-eight children were in the process of carving out autonomous family farms—a change that Day supported, for the sake of avoiding legal tangles. After an idyllic description of evening storytelling, she wrote that "I am hoping that these farms, these families around the country will keep their own log books, their own journals telling of their life and struggles, for the comfort and solace of other families in the fields, factories and work shops. So much beauty has sprung up in this synthesis of Peter Maurin of cult, culture and cultivation!" In describing a visit to Rochester, she scarcely mentioned the hospitality house, while dwelling on the work of the ever-faithful Teresa Weider: "I esteem and love Teresa Weider because of her unfailing love for the poor. Her house has always had a Christ room and many were the men who went from our St. Joseph's house on Front Street to convalesce at her home. She has performed the works of mercy all through her married life, and her husband has aided her. She has six children of her own, now all happily married and in the family apostolate. To further this apostolate, Mother Weider has helped in paying hospital bills and buying layettes for innumerable mothers." The column ended with accounts of two families, the Gauchats in Cleveland and the Murphys in Detroit, who were associated with more conventional houses of hospitality; there was virtually no mention of singles-dominated houses akin to the New York Catholic Worker.[37]

Day took a more theoretical tone in her next column. In her public speaking engagements, she mused, she always spoke of the "works of mercy" enjoined in Matthew 25, and of how "our salvation indeed depends on them." This led many people to think she wanted them to start up houses of hospitality and to feel guilty if they failed to do so. "But I try always to explain that it is not just in terms of Peter Maurin's program of Round Table Discussions, Houses of Hospitality and Farming Communes that I am speaking. He said at the very beginning that the way to reach the masses of people, the poor and the destitute who did not know Christ (if they did they would be rich) was through the works of mercy. . . . Since it all does depend on each one of us, that means that we must each try to have a Christ room in our homes where we can shelter others."[38] By maintaining Christ rooms, she implied, families could be at the center of the Catholic Worker movement (and of the lay apostolate), even if they were not at the center of every hospitality house.

"It is not presumption," she added in a later article, "to say that [God] meant most men to marry and bring up a family and our work as laymen is to try to work for that kind of social order where it is easier for men to be good, where it is easier for the family, which is man's natural community, to live."[39] A decade later she repeated the point that "the normal life in this world today and always is that of the family. The majority of us are called to marriage and not to celibacy."[40] She was also emphatic that families were as much a part of the movement as anyone: "When I speak of Catholic Worker families, I mean all those who have worked with us and who married, and are raising children and are encountering all the difficulties of supporting large families."[41]

Unfolding experience also led Day to soften some of the principles articulated in the 1948 memorandum. Though she had insisted that single people should control houses of hospitality, she could not ignore the fact that the Detroit and Cleveland houses, both anchored by families, outlasted most singles-oriented houses. At the same time, her awareness of the genuine struggles of many farming families led her to reconsider her view that families should subsist on wages rather than donations. Writing shortly after the death of Larry Heaney, a Catholic Worker farmer revered by many in the movement as a saint, she initially praised Heaney's fellow farmer Martin Paul for recognizing "the fact that houses of hospitality had to be financed by appeals. . . . A vocation for this work, and it was definitely a vocation, was something else again than a vocation for marriage. When a man got married, then it was up to him to be on his own, support his own wife and children, and go on performing the works of mercy, according to his ability, with a Christ room in the house, the meal set out for the needy guest, the clothes passed on." Thus, the Pauls and Heaneys had used their own resources to buy their farm in Missouri. But, she hinted, they might have taken the principle too far. The lot of the farm families, she suggested, was "indeed harder" than that of the houses of hospitality that had such ready access to donations. Even with hard work, a Catholic Worker farm "is not self-sustaining, it has to be helped. And this is the bitterness which eats into the souls of those Catholic Workers who are married, who are raising families, who are trying to live either on a wage or on the land. In their suffering they reject the idea of almsgiving. And to protest this, is the point of this entire article."[42]

In keeping with the new principle that families should sometimes be "helped," Day occasionally used her column to solicit contributions for Worker families that were struggling to make ends meet. After describing a family that wanted to build: a farmhouse at Upton but lacked the resources, she reflected: "If anyone has any money to invest in a family, to draw dividends in heaven, here is an opportunity."[43] Several years later, she visited the family farm of Jack and Mary Thornton, who had previously lived both at Easton and with the Gauchats in Cleveland, and then challenged her readers: "Why don't people invest in families? There certainly should be some of our readers who can and I wonder if some of our readers can help out here. When we put in an urgent appeal for money for a house for a family in community, relatives and friends came forward with the needed cash. Here are our brothers in need of help."[44] Such appeals often appeared alongside reports on family life among the Bruderhof, or at Koinonia, Taena, or Marycrest, and Day's awareness of these communities may have suggested to her that the conflicts at Easton were not as inevitable as she had supposed. Reflecting on all of these communities, as well as on the Worker farms at Upton, Massachusetts, and South Lyons, Michigan, Day wrote in 1963 that "I am overcome with admiration at the hard work, the endurance, the continuing vision of these families."[45]

Meanwhile, some of the early "agronomic universities" were evolving into clusters of traditional family farms. Throughout the 1950s and 1960s, the *Catholic Worker* consistently promoted both its own agrarian ideals and the "back-to-the-land" theories of Gandhi, E. F. Schumacher, and Helen and Scott Nearing. Day's account of one Labor Day retreat suggests that families were the heart of the movement from the end of World War II until young peace activists began creating a new generation of hospitality houses in the 1960s and 1970s. "Since going to press last month," she wrote in 1957, "we have had a very interesting Labor Day conference, at Peter Maurin farm, our sixth annual discussion of pacifism, with conferences in the grove, many families attending with all their children, two- and three-year-olds. Having no baby sitters, parents had to alternate in the care of the children so that they could listen in on the conferences. In some cases, the children came and played quietly in the dirt, made fortresses of twigs and stones, while we discussed peace."[46]

Those who see the Worker movement as a predominantly urban phenomenon may be struck by the rural character of these examples. Day's enthusiasm for farming families may explain the widely held belief of contemporary Workers that Day was open to families on farms but not at houses of hospitality. The closing of many urban hospitality houses also shifted the movement toward rural life in the postwar years. But families also participated in the Worker's urban apostolate. Two of the houses of hospitality that survived the war, in Detroit and

Cleveland, were able to do so because they were anchored by stable families.

When families did choose to participate in urban hospitality, Day's attitude was often positive. She was consistently supportive of Lou and Justine Murphy, who raised a large family while dividing their time between two houses of hospitality in Detroit and a farm in nearby South Lyons, Michigan. Their work, she wrote, was "evidence that a family can undertake works of mercy and raise their own children in a slum, not only without their being contaminated, but on the contrary demonstrating an ability to lift the level of intelligence and awareness of the other children in the neighborhood."[47] In Memphis, Day's friend Helen Riley ran a house of hospitality and day nursery with her husband and a son from a previous marriage. Day reported on Riley's decision to scale back after having a new baby, bemoaning "how little the married apostolate is accepted in the world even in this day of the lay apostolate," and stressing that even without a "house of hospitality in the formal sense" the Riley family would be "continuing the work."[48] And shortly after visiting a new house of hospitality in Oakland, Day reported that the Callagy family was "another example of how a family, given the temperament, the health and the energy necessary, can take care of work, family duties and such an apostolate as this at the same time. There are five children and enough other young families in the movement so that they babysit and exchange hospitality."[49]

This is not to suggest that Day was always encouraging to Worker families outside New York. When Brendan Walsh and Willa Bickham had a baby shortly after starting Viva House Catholic Worker in Baltimore, Dorothy Day sent them a letter suggesting that they might consider moving on. But even that message had a positive effect, in that it helped them commit to valuing their family as much as their work of hospitality. "The tone I got" from the letter, Walsh recalled, "was make sure you do everything you can to raise your own family, because if you don't do that well nothing else will be done well. . . . She was clear to make some time for a family within a family."[50] In the early years of Viva House, Walsh and Bickham were able to adopt "a flowing attitude toward our Catholic Worker work" that in turn made it possible for them to sustain their commitment for their daughter's entire childhood and beyond.[51]

Is it possible to reconcile the "two faces" of Day's attitude to families? It might be too simple, though not entirely false, to say that Day liked families best at a distance. So long as the demands of family life did not interfere with her personal vision for the New York houses and farms, she was supportive, but when tensions emerged she defended that personal vision with tenacity. A more generous interpretation might be that she was consistently faithful to the principle of "personal responsibility" that figured so prominently in Worker ideology. She took the responsibilities of family seriously and could be quite sharp in warning Workers not to jeopardize their families for the sake of the work. When families took responsibility for blending family and Worker life, she responded positively, even encouraging compromises that seemed to run counter to her ideals. But she rebuffed any explicit or implicit suggestion that she was responsible for creating a model of Worker life that would automatically work for families. In this sense, Julia Occhiogrosso was certainly correct to say that "Dorothy didn't give us models for families." The real work of "inventing the Catholic Worker family" was done not by Day herself, but by the families that figured so prominently in her columns.

Early Catholic Worker Families: A Spectrum of Possibilities

The early Catholic Worker families cannot fit into a single mold. In keeping with the principle of personal responsibility, each family found its own way of embodying such values as hospitality, poverty, and nonviolence in the context of family life. But it is possible to place these families on a rough spectrum stretching from those families that sponsored houses of hospitality similar to the New York houses, through families that devoted themselves to the agrarian ideals of the movement, to families that incorporated elements of hospitality or agrarianism into outwardly conventional lifestyles.

At one end of the spectrum were Lou and Justine Murphy, bulwarks of the Detroit Catholic Worker for several decades. Both came to the movement in the 1930s: Lou was part of the group that started Saint Francis House (for men) in 1937, while Justine became manager of Saint Martha House (for women) after a stint at the New York Catholic Worker. Lou served as an ambulance driver for American Field Service during World War II, after which he returned to marry Justine and resume Catholic Worker activities. They raised their six children in part at Saint Martha House and in part at a farmhouse at the South Lyons farm, which was for a time home to several other families as well. Since they were not always able to attract short-term volunteers, they often "count[ed] on the very men we have sought to help" to make the work manageable. The scale of their hospitality ebbed and flowed as economic needs changed, but they were still at the work when a new generation of Catholic Worker families began turning to them as mentors. Like Dorothy Day, they were quick to caution these younger folks that full-time hospitality was not right for every family. "As far as a family life in the Worker movement," Lou told Mike Cullen of Milwaukee's new Casa Maria community in 1968, "I think it's a very natural thing for some, not for all." A suburban family that volunteered at the house, he added, was "as much a part of the Worker as we are."[52]

In Cleveland, the Gauchat family began much like the Murphys. As a young college graduate unable to find suitable work during the Depression, Bill Gauchat had written to Dorothy Day and Peter Maurin. They encouraged him to "do something in your own locality" rather than coming to New York, so he joined with some local Jesuit high school teachers to found Blessed Martin House. Dorothy Schmitt began volunteering there as a high school student and soon distressed her parents by falling in love with Gauchat. Dorothy Day then intervened by arranging for her to do an apprenticeship with Catholic Worker artist Ade

Bethune in Newport, Rhode Island. By the time they married—
with some help from the local priest in Newport—friends of the
Worker had donated a seventy-six acre farm in Avon, Ohio, just
outside Cleveland. The newly married Gauchats began their
family life at the farmhouse, where they performed small-scale
hospitality while Bill continued to commute to the urban hospitality house.[53]

Though the urban house stayed open until 1954, the flavor
of their work gradually changed. Early on, one of the homeless
men who lived at the farm briefly kidnapped one of their children. Since Dorothy Day treated Dorothy Gauchat as a sort of
second daughter (she was similar in age and personality to
Tamar), it was natural for the younger woman to turn to the
older for advice. "I remember going to Dorothy with it and praying," Gauchat told an audience in 1977, "and she said, 'Never
do anything that you don't want to do,' and at that time I did
not want to have the men in my house; I wanted to keep our
family separate. But Bill and I still clung to this idea of personalism, and we believed and still believe that that personalism has
to be in our lives, not just in one period but lifetime."[54]

A new avenue for personalist commitment emerged when
nuns at a local hospital asked them to take in a young hydroce-
phalic boy. This baby made such a powerful impression on the
family that, several years later, they made foster care for children
with disabilities their apostolate, always keeping "in mind that
our primary vocation was our marriage and our children—our
family." This work in turn evolved into Our Lady of the Wayside,
a nonprofit agency which today has a $14 million budget and
serves 182 residents in 41 distinct households. Before things
reached that scale, however, the widowed Dorothy Gauchat had
withdrawn to start over with foster care for AIDS babies, resolv-
ing to remain unincorporated as a way of preserving Catholic
Worker-style personalism.[55]

Though Our Lady of the Wayside did not publicly identify itself as a Catholic Worker, the Gauchats retained their personal
sense of Catholic Worker identity throughout their lifetimes. "I

still am [sold on the Catholic Worker]," Dorothy Gauchat told historian William Miller in 1976, "even though I think that it means different things to different people. We're doing it in a much different way than Dorothy [Day] ever conceived of, but . . . Dorothy made this point so many times, that every house is different. . . . Each house will have its own character, because it's going to have different characters running it, each one has a different vocation, different weaknesses, and different strengths." Through all the changes, Day was quick to reassure her that "your vocation is to be where you are and doing the work that you are doing right now," and indeed, the Gauchats figure as prominently in Day's columns as any house of hospitality outside of New York. When Bill Gauchat died in 1975, moreover, Dorothy Day summed up the family's ministry by invoking the works of mercy: "But the work Bill Gauchat spent his life for, the work of his wife and his children, now many of them married and with children of their own, still goes on. He has fed the hungry, clothed the naked. They continue feeding the hungry, clothing the naked, caring for the most helpless. In fact they performed all the works of mercy in one way or another."[56]

The Gauchats were certainly not the only Catholic Worker family whose center of gravity shifted from urban hospitality to rural life. Of the farming families who were part of the movement in the 1940s and 1950s, perhaps none were closer to Dorothy Day's heart than the Heaneys and Pauls. Larry and Ruth Heaney met at Holy Family Catholic Worker in Milwaukee, where Larry was a live-in Worker and Ruth was on the staff of the local St. Vincent de Paul Society. Early on, Larry developed a reputation as a Catholic Worker "saint" because of his transformative effect on the homeless guests and his ability to "forgive seventy times seven."[57] They spent the war years at Maryfarm in Easton, then returned to Milwaukee to raise money for a farm of their own. Soon they connected with Marty Paul, who had converted to Catholicism as a result of his association with one of the Chicago houses, and his wife Gertrude. In 1947 the two families purchased a twenty-five acre farm in Starkenburg, Missouri, which they named Holy Family Farm. At the time, the Heaneys had four children, while the Pauls' first child was still a baby. They soon confronted the harsh poverty of farm life, which was exacerbated by tragedy: Larry Heaney died of pneumonia in 1949, while Ruth was in the hospital bearing their sixth child. Marty Paul continued to manage the farm for the next eight years, but his wife's worsening illness eventually forced their family to move closer to her parents. Ruth Heaney then rented out the farmland but continued to raise her children there because "I just felt it was easier to be poor on the farm." Some of the Heaney children were still there as late as 1992![58]

Given the difficulties they confronted, both Ruth Heaney and Marty Paul remembered their experience with some sadness. "We were never," Marty Paul told Rosalie Riegle, "a real community in the sense of what we wanted—you know, a Catholic Worker community, a communal farm. Because we had to make a living. I drove a school bus for a while, and I got some assistance through the GI Bill of Rights. . . . But we managed to survive, I guess."[59] "I think my kids suffered from these ideas," added Ruth Heaney, "because there were so few of us. . . . I know my oldest daughter really suffered over being different, but when she was about thirteen, she said, 'Oh Mom! I used to wish you were like everybody else, and now I'm glad you're not. But I do wish we could have had a community.'"[60] At the same time, they were regularly visited by other families drawn to the Worker's agrarian ideal, and at least one of those families, that of Jack and Fran Woltjen, spent many years on a nearby farm.[61] So if the Heaneys and Pauls never had a full-scale communal farm, they were certainly an anchor for families seeking to integrate rural and community life.

A similar pattern, without such a large element of tragedy, emerged at Saint Benedict's Farm in Upton, Massachusetts. This farm, which grew out of the original house of hospitality in Boston, was the shared home of the Paulson, Roche, O'Donnell, and Ericson families until the mid-1950s. At that point, the families divided the land but continued to share life more informally. "It is again the world in microcosm as any community is," wrote Day after a visit in 1954. "To me, whenever I visit Upton, it seems family life at its most beautiful. . . . Cult, culture and cultivation! There is certainly more than a suggestion of Peter Maurin's synthesis here." Carl Paulson's work as a stained glass artist appealed to the many Workers who wished to restore the craft ethos of the Middle Ages, as well as providing his family with a somewhat more secure economic basis than farming alone. Like the Heaneys, the Roches and Paulsons were able to remain on site into the next decade, with at least some of the children finding ways to remain connected to the Catholic Worker movement.[62]

Throughout the 1950s and 1960s, the pages of the *Catholic Worker* were filled with reports from families seeking, with varied success, to sustain themselves, and the ideal of community, on the land. In Nova Scotia in 1960, two families established Saint Joseph's Farm on two hundred fifty acres, dividing the farmhouse so as to combine cooperation with respect for the integrity of each family.[63] A year later, Pat and Mary Murray wrote that they had moved to a farm after ten years of thinking about it, adding, "We are still talking about the idea of community, but have never been able to interest anyone in this phase of the Catholic Worker. . . . Have a 3 room apartment over the garage which anyone interested in community life on the land could have, or come build here, there is plenty of land for a few more."[64] Among the most faithful correspondents were Jack and Mary Thornton, who had lived at both the Easton and Cleveland farms before attempting life as an independent farm family. "We surely count our blessings," wrote Mary Thornton after more than a decade of this lifestyle. "Nine lovely children, eighty-three acres of land to let them run on and twenty-five head of cows and calves who make a lively schedule for us to keep." They even found a neighboring family who had been reading the *Worker* for more than five years, suggesting that the network of families inspired by the *Worker* included many who never publicized their efforts. Three years later, however, economic pressures forced them to move to California, where they hoped that "your younger, single idealists will . . . take over where we must leave off."[65]

The economic challenges of farming led many Catholic Worker families to combine part-time farming with more conventional careers. Julian Pleasants, a professor at Notre Dame whose family shared an eighty-acre farm with up to seven other families, was among the most articulate of this group, publishing widely on the Catholic Worker movement and the ideals of the lay apostolate. "As we got more into the idea that our farming would be part time," Pleasants recalled, "we saw this as a much more universal pattern. Only so many people could manage to be economically independent, but if you were going to use this kind of life to create a good neighborhood for rearing children and to have opportunities for meaningful work for the whole family, you didn't need lots of land and you didn't need to be an expert in innumerable things. And it sort of freed you to focus on things that you felt you wanted to get the most out of."[66] From Day's perspective, this approach was one way to achieve Peter Maurin's ideal of uniting the scholar and the Worker, and in 1961 she wrote that "Julian is the only scholar I know who has built his own home, to shelter his own family, a job which is never finished, so that as he said, his sons can boast that they helped build the house they were born in."[67]

Other couples felt little vocation to rural life but were also unwilling to be as intimately involved in a house of hospitality as Lou and Justine Murphy. For these families, the ideal of the Christ room had powerful appeal. Dorothy Day reported regularly on people like Paul Moore, an Anglican priest in Jersey City who lived with his family "in a colored section and have their doors open always to all the young folk of the neighborhood. Where love is, there God is."[68] In New York City itself, there were many volunteers like Bob Rambush, who moved out of Saint Joseph's House at the time of his marriage but kept such an "open house" in his new apartment that the house manager "threatened to make it an annex to our house of hospitality."[69]

This was the experience also of Tom and Monica Cornell, who met and married at the New York Catholic Worker in the early 1960s.Though their wedding was held at the Worker, they immediately sought out a new apartment. "I didn't want to be so closely involved in the Catholic Worker community after I married," Tom Cornell explained to interviewer Deane Mowrer. "A family is a community of its own." The Worker house, Tom told me, "had nothing but a storefront and a bunch of unheated apartments that didn't have showers, that didn't have toilets. The toilets were shared by everybody on the floor out in the hall. And I thought that the mother of my children deserved more than that."[70] Still, Tom continued to work as an editor of the newspaper, and the Cornells shared their new apartment's dinner table and shower with friends from the Worker almost every night. Through subsequent moves to Brooklyn, Newburgh, New York, and Waterbury, Connecticut, the Cornells continued to find ways to "work as Catholic Workers," even though it was only in Waterbury, when their children were nearly grown, that they "officially" declared their home a Catholic Worker house. By that time, theirs was just one of a new generation of flourishing, family-oriented Worker houses and farms.

The Legacy of the Early Families

By the time Dorothy Day's movement was a generation old, her vision of the lay apostolate had received significant vindication from both church and society. At the Second Vatican Council, the gathered bishops issued an emphatic "Decree on the Apostolate of the Laity" that called special attention to the apostolic work of families. As "the primary vital cell of society," each family was urged not only to function as a domestic church but also to "offer active hospitality, practice justice and other good works for the benefit of all its brothers suffering from want."[71] Meanwhile, the ferment generated by the civil rights and antiwar movements inspired dozens of young idealists to start new Catholic Worker communities across the country.

As was the case during the founding years, these developments had mixed implications for families. The first generation of Catholic Worker families, like leaders of other lay Catholic movements, assumed that their fidelity to the church's official teaching—including its teaching on family life—would enhance their work for social reconstruction. For Dorothy Day and others, the large size of Catholic Worker families was a countercultural sign of resistance to industrial efficiency, and Day rarely missed an opportunity to point out that a particular family had six, or eight, or ten children. But the notion that family life was itself a religious apostolate led many families to reflect critically on their experience, and out of this reflection emerged significant resistance to the Catholic Church's position on contraception. As more and more Catholics limited the size of their families, leaders in the lay apostolate stopped portraying birth control as a symptom of social injustice, and some even called for a change in the church's policy. The Worker-inspired Marycrest Community, which had been founded to provide Catholic couples the space to have large families, began tentatively speaking out for birth control in 1955.[72] And when Pope Paul VI reaffirmed the prohibition in his 1967 encyclical *Humanae Vitae,* Christian Family Movement founders Pat and Patty Crowley were among the loudest voices in protest.[73]

Catholic Worker families were not vocal on this issue, choosing to maintain their traditional focus on issues of war and poverty. But they were changing along with their cohort: while the first generation of Catholic Worker families often had close to ten children, those who started their families after Vatican II typically had four or fewer. This trend may have made it easier for these families to commit to the urban hospitality that has reemerged as a hallmark of the Worker movement since the 1960s. The overall expansion of the movement has created a wider range of choices for Worker families: those families that do urban hospitality are often in middle-sized cities rather than giant metropolises like New York, and many have moved back and forth between urban and rural settings in response to their families' changing needs.

Both the shift to smaller families and to more involvement in urban houses of hospitality occurred during Dorothy Day's lifetime, and neither seems to have troubled her much. "It is interesting to see young families in charge of houses of hospitality," she wrote in 1967. "David and Catherine Miller are looking around for a house in Washington, D.C. The Cullens [in Milwaukee], the McKennas [in Boston] and the Millers are the youngest in the field. But the Murphy family in Detroit, the Gauchat family in Avon, Ohio, have been operating for more than twenty years and Karl Meyer's house in Chicago has been going five years. At Tivoli the Corbin family are in charge. It is a harder and more realistic approach, this family leadership, and there is less room for pride and dissipation of energy. But it is a most particular vocation, and certainly none should undertake it without a vocation."[74]

Her words were prescient: though not all the houses she mentioned have endured, the presence of families as a central part of the movement is now widely recognized. Families like the Walsh-Bickhams in Baltimore, the Schaeffer-Duffys in Worcester, Massachusetts, and the Purcells in Redwood City, California, have raised children to adulthood within the context of a steady commitment to the work of hospitality. Vastly more families have taken to heart Day's hint that being a full-time Worker is not everyone's vocation; these families have sustained houses of hospitality as "extended community," spent brief periods of time as live-in Workers, or established Christ rooms, in most cases without calling anyone's attention to their efforts. There is, in short, a remarkable spectrum of Catholic Worker families today, though in many respects the spectrum is not that different from that which existed in the 1950s.

What is different is the number of families involved, and the consciousness they bring to the Work. While Dorothy Day was quick to stress the value of the Worker vocation and the family vocation, today's Workers are more inclined to claim that the two vocations are interdependent. Many say that they would not have chosen to become parents were it not for the support of the Catholic Worker community and the inspiration of Catholic Worker ideals. "It is only," declared Julia Occhiogrosso at one conference on families at the Worker, "because of my years of testing out this faith in divine love in souplines and hospitality houses that I gleaned courage and desire to become a mother."[75] Many also suggest that the Worker's integrity as a lay movement depends on the inclusion of families. "So many people in the world are in families," Claire Schaeffer-Duffy told me. "That's their reality. So for the Catholic Worker to embrace so many families, it's a very powerful witness."[76] Such ideas are new and challenging for both the Worker movement and the Catholic Church as a whole. Yet they also build, in a way that should be acknowledged, on the efforts of seven decades of Catholic Worker families.

[1] Larry Purcell, *Catholic Worker Grapevine,* 11 July 1993, in DD/CWC, series W-54, box 1, folder 6.

[2] *Family Life in the Catholic Worker Movement* 1 (May 2001). Perhaps as a reflection of the multiple demands placed on Catholic Worker parents, no additional issues of this newsletter were published.

[3] Marilyn L. Klein, "Families in the Catholic Worker Movement," M.A. thesis, Graduate Theological Union, 1991, 4, at DD/CWC, series W-7.1, box 4, folder 2; see also Elizabeth Flynn, "Catholic Worker Spirituality: A Sect within a Church," M.A. thesis, Graduate Theological Union, 1974, 84, at DD/CWC, series W-7.1, box 3, folder 9; and Frederick George Boehrer III, "Christian Anarchism and the Catholic Worker Movement: Roman Catholic Authority and Identity in the United States," Ph.D. dissertation, Syracuse University, 2001, 163.

[4] Interview with Tom Cornell, 3 October 2004.

[5] Day, "The Family vs. Capitalism," *Catholic Worker* 3, no. 8 (January 1936): 4.

[6] Jeffrey M. Burns, *American Catholics and the Family Crisis 1930–1962* (New York: Garland Publishing, 1988), 1–9.

[7] Pius XI, *Casti Connubii,* par. 11.

[8] Burns, *American Catholics,* 10–105.

[9] For general treatments of American Catholic families in the twentieth century, see Christine Firer Hinze, "Catholic: Family Unity and Diversity within the Body of Christ," in Phyllis D. Airhart and Margaret Lamberts Bendroth, eds., *Faith Traditions and the Family* (Louisville, KY: Westminster John Knox, 1996), 53–72; and Sally Cunneen, "The American Catholic Family: Reality or Misnomer?" in John Deedy, ed., *The Catholic Church in the Twentieth Century: Renewing and Reimagining the City of God* (Collegeville, MN: The Liturgical Press, 2000), 57–71.

[10] These memos, for example, are central to Marilyn Klein's excellent thesis, which rightly cautions "that both of these writings are in response to specific situations that arose in the community; caution should be used toward interpreting Day's responses as absolutely paradigmatic of her views." Unfortunately, in my view, Klein does not dig deep enough in searching for countervailing tendencies in Day's writings. See Klein, "Families in the Catholic Worker Movement," 51–52.

[11] Dorothy Day to "Fellow Worker," 10 August 1940, DD/CWC, series W-1, box 1; Dorothy Day, Memorandum, Feast of the Nativity of the Blessed Virgin Mary, 1948, DD/CWC, series W-4.2, box 1.

[12] Dorothy Day to "Fellow Worker," 10 August 1940, DD/CWC, series W-1, box 1.

[13] Ibid.

[14] Jimmy Flannery, Pittsburgh, to Dorothy Day, circa August 1940, DD/CWC, series W-4, box 4, folder 1, cited in Klein, "Families in the Catholic Worker Movement," 53. Flannery's letter is one of about twenty in the Catholic Worker Collection responding to the circular letter; all the others focus on the question of pacifism and make no response to Day's comments about families.

[15] For an overview of the theology of the lay apostolate in the twentieth century, see David O'Shea, "The Lay Movement in Roman Catholicism—Developments in the Lay Apostolate," *Religion in Life* 31, no. 1 (Winter 1961–62): 56–67. On Virgil Michel's influence on Dorothy Day, see Mark and Louise Zwick, *The Catholic Worker Movement: Intellectual and Spiritual Origins* (Mahwah, NJ: Paulist Press, 2005), 58–74.

[16] Dorothy Day, *House of Hospitality* (New York: Sheed & Ward, 1939), 109–11.

[17] Peter Maurin, "The Law of Holiness," in *Easy Essays* (Chicago: Franciscan Herald Press, 1977), 137–38. This quote also appears in an editorial,

"Pacifism Is Dangerous So Is Christianity," *Catholic Worker* 8, no. 3 (January 1941): 4.

[18] Dorothy Day to "Fellow Workers," 15 August 1940, DD/CWC, series W-1, box 1.

[19] William Miller, *A Harsh and Dreadful Love: Dorothy Day and the Catholic Worker Movement* (New York: Liveright, 1973), 202–4, 209–10.

[20] Dorothy Day, Memorandum, Feast of the Nativity of the Blessed Virgin Mary, 1948, DD/CWC, series W-4.2, box 1.

[21] Dorothy Day, "To Christ—To the Land!" *Catholic Worker* 3, no. 8 (January 1936): 1; and Cyril Echele, "An Idea of a Farming Commune," *Catholic Worker* 3, no. 8 (January 1936): 2.

[22] Dorothy Day, Memorandum, Feast of the Nativity of the Blessed Virgin Mary, 1948, DD/CWC, series W-4.2, box 1.

[23] Ibid.

[24] Dorothy Day, "On Pilgrimage," *Catholic Worker* 13, no. 5 (June 1946): 8. She had not always been quite so clear. In a 1938 editorial, for example, she commented: "For a long time, Peter Maurin has talked about the need for an order of lay people, married and unmarried to live a life pledged to prayer, poverty and labor who will have the strength which comes from banding together." "Jesus the Worker," *Catholic Worker* 6, no. 6 (December 1938): 4.

[25] Dorothy Day, Memorandum, Feast of the Nativity of the Blessed Virgin Mary, 1948, DD/CWC, series W-4.2, box 1.

[26] William D. Miller, *Dorothy Day: A Biography* (New York: Harper & Row, 1982), 394.

[27] Dorothy Day, Memorandum, Feast of the Nativity of the Blessed Virgin Mary, 1948, DD/CWC, series W-4.2, box 1.

[28] Day, *On Pilgrimage* (New York: Catholic Worker Books, 1948), 229.

[29] Larry Purcell, "Reflections of a Catholic Worker Dad," *Family Life,* 18.

[30] Larry Holben, "Family Life and the Catholic Worker," *Family Life,* 11–12.

[31] Tamar Hennessy, in Rosalie G. Riegle, *Dorothy Day: Portraits by Those Who Knew Her* (Maryknoll, NY: Orbis, 2003), 109.

[32] Katherine M. Yohe's insightful analysis of Day's relationship with Tamar, "Dorothy Day: Love for One's Daughter and Love for the Poor," *Horizons* 31, no. 2 (2004): 272–301, suggests that this struggle continued from Tamar's birth all the way to Day's death, with Tamar at her side. Interestingly, Day's regret at her neglect of Tamar during her childhood seems to have led her to invest a great deal of energy into Tamar's own family in later years.

[33] "Day by Day Account of Editor's Travels Thru West and North," *Catholic Worker* 3, no.7 (December 1935): 1.

[34] O'Shea, "Lay Movement," 56–67. As James T. Fisher has suggested, the release of *Mystici Corporis Christi* was only a partial vindication of Day's position, for that document expressed an understanding of the Mystical Body that was significantly more triumphalist and hierarchical than Day's own. See James T. Fisher, *The Catholic Counterculture in America, 1933–1962* (Chapel Hill: University of North Carolina Press, 1989), 47–53.

[35] For an overview of the last movement, see Jeffrey M. Burns, *Disturbing the Peace: A History of the Christian Family Movement, 1949–1974* (Notre Dame: University of Notre Dame Press, 1999). Leo Richard Ward, C.S.C., *The American Apostolate: American Catholics in the Twentieth Century* (Westminster, Maryland: The Newman Press, 1952), is a postwar publication that gives a vivid sense of the interrelations among these movements.

[36] Dorothy Day, "On Pilgrimage," *Catholic Worker* 13, no. 9 (November 1946): 1, 7, 8.

[37] Day, "On Pilgrimage," *Catholic Worker* 18, no. 3 (October 1951): 1, 2, 6.

[38] Day, "On Pilgrimage," *Catholic Worker* 18, no. 4 (November 1951): 1, 2, 6.

[39] Day, "Have We Failed Peter Maurin's Program?" *Catholic Worker* 20, no. 6 (January 1954): 6.

[40] Day, "On Pilgrimage," *Catholic Worker* 29, no. 6 (January 1963): 2.

[41] Day, "On Pilgrimage," *Catholic Worker* 30, no. 2 (September 1963): 2.

[42] Day, "Poverty Is the Face of Christ," *Catholic Worker* 18, no. 16 (December 1952): 3.

[43] Day, "On Pilgrimage," *Catholic Worker* 18, no. 3 (October 1951): 2.

[44] Day, "On Pilgrimage," *Catholic Worker* 24, no. 4 (November 1957): 4.

[45] Day, "On Pilgrimage," *Catholic Worker* 30, no. 4 (November 1963): 1, 6.

[46] Day, "On Pilgrimage," *Catholic Worker* 24, no. 3 (October 1957): 8.

[47] Day, *Loaves and Fishes* (New York: Harper and Row, 1963), 197.

[48] Day, "On Pilgrimage," *Catholic Worker* 23, no. 4 (November 1956): 6.

[49] Day, "On Pilgrimage," *Catholic Worker* 31, no. 9 (April 1965): 5, in *On Pilgrimage: The Sixties* (New York: Curtiss Books, 1972), 220.

[50] Interview with Brendan Walsh and Willa Bickham, 25 May 2000.

[51] Willa Bickham, interviewed by Rosalie Troester, 7 November 1987, DD/CWC, series W-9, box 3.

[52] Louis Murphy, interviewed by Michael Cullen, 23 January 1968, DD/CWC, series W-9, box 2, folder 9; Justine Murphy, in Rosalie Riegle Troester, *Voices from the Catholic Worker* (Philadelphia: Temple University Press, 1993), 296–98.

[53] Dorothy Gauchat, interviewed by William Miller, 29 July 1976, DD/CWC, series W-9, box 1, folder 30; Rosalie Riegle Troester interview with Dorothy Gauchat, 20 January 1988, series W-9, box 4, folder 17.

[54] Roundtable Discussion of the Catholic Worker Movement, Marquette University, 9 November 1977, DD/CWC, series W-9, box 1, folder 19.

[55] Dorothy Gauchat, interviewed by Rosalie Riegle Troester, series W-9, box 4, folder 17; Dorothy Gauchat, *All God's Children* (New York: Hawthorn Books, 1976); and www.thewayside.org.

[56] Dorothy Gauchat, interviewed by William Miller, 29 July 1976, DD/CWC, series W-9, box 1, folder 30; Dorothy Gauchat, interviewed by Rosalie Riegle Troester, series W-9, box 4, folder 17; and Dorothy Day, "Bill Gauchat: The Way of Peace," *Catholic Worker* 41, no. 4 (May 1975): 3. Also see Day, *Loaves and Fishes,* 197–98; Day, "On Pilgrimage," *Catholic Worker* 18, no. 3 (October 1951): 6; Day, "On Pilgrimage," *Catholic Worker* 22, no. 2 (September 1955): 8; and Stanley Vishnewski, "Gauchats Practice Hospitality," *Catholic Worker* 27, no. 6 (January 1961): 1.

[57] Dorothy Day, "Death of an Apostle," *Catholic Worker* (June 1949): 1, 6.

[58] Ruth Heaney, in Troester, *Voices,* 17–19, 23–26; Ruth Heaney, interviewed by Rosalie Riegle Troester, 14 July 1989, DD/CWC, series W-9, box 4, folder 25; Marty and Gertrude Paul, interviewed by Rosalie Riegle Troester, 18 July 1988, DD/CWC, series W-9, box 7.

[59] Marty and Gertrude Paul, interviewed by Rosalie Riegle Troester, 18 July 1988, DD/CWC, series W-9, box 7, folder 4.

[60] Ruth Heaney, in Troester, *Voices,* 26.

[61] Jack Woltjen, "Mo. And Penn. Farms Write," *Catholic Worker* 24, no. 3 (October 1957): 8; Jack Woltjen, "On The Land," *Catholic Worker* 26, no. 10 (May 1960): 3. The latter article reports that they had been farming for nearly nine years and were expecting their sixth child.

[62] Day, "On Pilgrimage," *Catholic Worker* 21, no. 5 (December 1954): 2; "C.W. Weddings," *Catholic Worker* 31, no. 1 (July–August 1964): 5.

[63] Dick and Louis LeBlanc, "Community in Nova Scotia Tries 'Back to the Land,'" *Catholic Worker* 26, no. 10 (May 1960): 3.

[64] Pat and Mary Murray, "Letters from Two Families," *Catholic Worker* 27, no. 6 (January 1961): 8. Four years later they were still on the land and still hoping for a sustained community to break their isolation: Murrays, "Appalachian Spring," *Catholic Worker* 31, no. 10 (May 1965): 8.

[65] Mary Thornton, "Monica Farm," *Catholic Worker* 27, no. 3 (October 1960): 8; and Jack and Mary Thornton, "The Thorntons," *Catholic Worker* 30, no. 1 (July–August 1963): 5.

[66] Julian Pleasants, interviewed by Rosalie Riegle Troester, 1 December 1987, DD/CWC, series W-9, box 7, folder 8.

[67] Day, "On Pilgrimage," *Catholic Worker* 27, no. 6 (January 1961): 2.

[68] Day, "On Pilgrimage," *Catholic Worker* 21, no. 7 (February 1955): 4.

[69] Day, "On Pilgrimage," *Catholic Worker* 21, no. 7 (February 1955): 1, 4, 6.

[70] Tom Cornell, interviewed by Deane Mowrer, 5 June 68, DD/CWC, series W-9, box 1, folder 10, 31; and interview with Tom Cornell, 23 May 2000.

[71] *Apostolicam Actuositatem,* par. 11.

[72] Fisher, *Catholic Counterculture,* 101–29.

[73] Burns, *Disturbing the Peace,* 174–83; and Leslie Woodcock Tentler, *Catholics and Contraception: An American History* (Ithaca, NY: Cornell University Press, 2004), 221–27.

[74] Day, "On Pilgrimage," *Catholic Worker* 33, no. 5 (February 1967): 6.

[75] Julia Occhiogrosso, "Reflections of a Catholic Worker Mom," *Family Life,* 24.

[76] Interview with Claire Schaeffer-Duffy, 5 January 2002.

Chapter 7

Wrestling with the Church

If the role of families in the Catholic Worker movement has often provoked anxious soul-searching in the years since Dorothy Day's death, the Worker's relationship to the Catholic Church has occasionally sparked fireworks. "The Catholic Worker is today in crisis," wrote Peter King and Ann O'Connor in the mid-1990s. "Many houses and individual Catholic Workers have abandoned the faith," they went on, adding that "Catholic Workers who claim adherence to the church . . . are a small minority." Though this allegation presupposes an understanding of Catholic adherence that many would question, King and O'Connor were on firmer ground when they described the "confusion and dissent" in the Worker movement as "a microcosm of the Catholic Church in America."[1]

This assessment was borne out, for example, at a workshop on "Forging Community in Spiritual Diversity" at the 2006 national gathering of Catholic Workers. Asked to describe their spiritual identities, perhaps eight of the fifty participants identified themselves unambiguously as Catholic, a roughly equal number said such things as "photosynthesis is my God" or "Jerry Garcia was my first prophet," and a larger number described themselves by appealing to the Sermon on the Mount or Jesus' path of nonviolence. After listening to this startling rendition, Karl Meyer aptly observed that the diversity in the Catholic Worker simply reflected the transformation of American religion in the fifty years since he had joined the movement.[2]

This observation raises two pointed questions. Should the Catholic Worker mirror religious trends in the larger society? And has it always done so? Many people, both admirers of the Catholic Worker and more dispassionate observers, would say no to both questions. For them, the key to the Catholic Worker's significance is its articulation of a radical alternative to mainstream America that is rooted in orthodox Catholicism. The Catholic Worker, wrote Mel Piehl, was "a true original," and its "religious orthodoxy [was] crucial to its identity and social outlook." "The Catholic Worker movement was radical only in so far as it was radically Catholic," echoed James T. Fisher.[3] If such assessments are correct, then the contemporary Catholic Worker movement has indeed betrayed the vision of its founders.

From my perspective, though, such accounts of the originality of the Worker do not take into account the catholicity of Roman Catholicism. When Dorothy Day became a Catholic in 1927, she was attracted not by the church's orthodoxy but by the fact that it was the religion of the masses. In the doctrine of the Mystical Body of Christ she glimpsed something that she had also seen in the socialist movement: a faith in the heroic and holy potential of all human beings. She sought to radicalize the church not by narrowing its boundaries, but by calling all its members to a transformative practice of the works of mercy. Neither she nor her movement was, in David O'Brien's evocative image, "running along [beside the mainstream church] and saying, 'Stop! Stop! You're making a mistake!'" What Catholic Workers have done instead, today as in the 1930s, has been to invite the whole church to be transformed by the works of mercy.[4]

Apart from the transformative practice of the works of mercy, then, Catholic Workers have always been a microcosm of the larger church in the United States. In the years prior to the Second Vatican Council, this meant that they took the doctrinal authority of the church for granted but were eager to explore a more active participation in the liturgy, a more searching engagement with Scripture, and a more meaningful approach to social problems. Just after Vatican II, it meant that they were confused, searching, and a bit overwhelmed by new possibilities. And in the years since the election of Pope John Paul II—perhaps a more relevant turning point than Dorothy Day's death—Catholic Workers have been almost as polarized as other American Catholics. Most dissent from official church teaching on such issues as sexual orientation and women's ordination, while a significant minority quite vocally promotes a more aggressive orthodoxy as the antidote to the secular confusions of the age.

These divisions are mirrored in the distinctions drawn by two especially thoughtful participant-observers of the Catholic Worker. In a meticulously researched doctoral dissertation, Fred Boehrer—himself the cofounder of a Catholic Worker house of hospitality—noted that the Catholic Worker has always challenged church authorities but then drew a distinction between criticisms of the church that are "done in a spirit of Church renewal" and those that express "a progressive-radical view of the Church." The first sort of criticisms simply "call on the church to better fulfill explicit biblical or church teachings," while the latter call for a change in teachings and for the replacement of the ecclesial hierarchy with "a new way of being 'church' for and with one another." Both sorts of criticisms can be traced to the Catholic Worker's anarchist ideology, Boehrer argued, but the second emerged within the movement only after Day's death.[5] Similarly, in a 1968 article, former Catholic Worker John Cogley drew a distinction between "radical Catholics" who criticize state and society on the basis of Christian principles and "radicalized Catholics" who "look upon the institutional church as a reflection of the secular society, and therefore a fit target for the same kind of disruption, harassment and critical analysis." Cogley clearly assumed that "radicalized Catholicism" existed only outside or—as the article's subtitle suggested—"after the Catholic Worker."[6]

Boehrer and Cogley rightly perceived a tension between two different ways of combining radicalism and Catholicism, but this tension does not mark a sharp boundary between those inside and outside the Worker movement (as Cogley suggested) or between Workers before and after 1980 (as Boehrer argued). Rather, the tension has existed *within* many Catholic Worker communities, both during and after Day's lifetime, and even within the hearts and minds of many individual Catholic Workers. For this reason it is very difficult, as I discovered during the course of a series of interviews, to get most Catholic Workers to take unambiguous sides in the current culture wars dividing the Catholic Church. Catholic Workers aren't shy about expressing their opinions, but when it comes to ecclesial politics most place first priority on creating spaces for dialogue. Most believe, moreover, that the issues that divide the church can be fully resolved only from the distinctive perspective offered by the Catholic Worker's nonviolence and solidarity with the poor.

Active Catholic Workers have thus been quick to challenge facile distinctions between different kinds of Catholic radicalism. After Cogley's article appeared in the *National Catholic Reporter,* for example, the *Catholic Worker* published a thoughtful reply by associate editor Jack Cook, in which he challenged the distinction on many levels. Cogley's picture of the "radicalizing Catholics" was wrong, Cook wrote, both because it assumed that contemporary critics of the hierarchy shared the Worker's pacifism and economic radicalism, and because it defined "disruption, harassment, and critical analysis" as the hallmarks of a radical stance. True radicals, he countered, insisted on "living a life style which is itself reflective of one's critical analysis." Cook then challenged Cogley's assumption that the Catholic Worker was monolithic in its doctrinal orthodoxy. Criticism of such defined dogmas as the perpetual virginity of Mary was not "unthinkable" in the Worker, as Cogley had suggested, but rather "irrelevant in the face of war, poverty, starvation, oppression, and nuclear holocaust." Since the Worker community included people "holding different and opposing beliefs" about Catholic doctrine, it would be "unnecessarily cruel" to dwell on them. But such silence, Cook went on, went hand in hand with the more fundamental challenge to the hierarchy that was implicit in the Catholic Worker's alternative way of expressing the Catholic faith. It was no accident that Dorothy Day and Peter Maurin had neither joined the hierarchy nor waited for its approval to begin practicing the works of mercy. "The most profound criticism of the ecclesial establishment," Cook insisted, "is the very existence of the Catholic Worker—in words and acts, past and present."[7]

More than three decades later, another Catholic Worker echoed Cook's insistence that the movement's relationship to the church was more subtle than conventional depictions of Day's orthodoxy might suggest. Brian Terrell was an associate editor of the *Catholic Worker* during Day's last years, and he went on to spend years at the Worker house in Davenport, Iowa, and the Worker farm in Maloy, Iowa, where he continues to live. In an article published first in a local Worker newspaper and then in a collection of essays, Terrell argued that the heart of Dorothy Day's spirituality was her sense of "permanent dissatisfaction with the church." Contemporary Workers, he suggested, were faithful to Day's legacy only when they challenged the church in this same spirit. "If we come to the Church in a spirit of docility and subservience," he wrote, "then we do not love the Church as much as Dorothy did. If we are not scandalized, but are blind and silent to the Church when it takes the part of wealth and power, then we are not obedient to the Church as Dorothy was."[8]

"Permanent dissatisfaction" is, of course, a much subtler emotion than either categorical rejection or unquestioning obedience. One way to delve deeper into the subtlety of Day's Catholicism—and its influence on the movement as a whole—is to consider two memorable quotations that are often used to epitomize her spirituality. Those who wish to remember Day as a Catholic rebel who rejected the entire hierarchical logic of Catholicism often recall that she told her followers, "Don't make me a saint. I don't want to be dismissed that easily." Others counter that Day's respect for the hierarchy led her to comment that she would stop publishing the *Catholic Worker* if her bishop asked her to. Both quotations must be interpreted with care, for when Day spoke, she was generally more interested in getting her listeners to think than in maintaining a strictly logical consistency. Taken together, the two comments demonstrate a subtle, if somewhat unsettled, understanding of the Catholic Church and her place in it.[9]

Day's reluctance to be canonized, many point out, says more about her humility than her attitude toward the hierarchy. After all, what saint would openly say that he or she *ought* to be canonized? Certainly, devotion to the saints was an integral part of her spirituality, and she repeatedly lifted up Francis of Assisi and Thérèse of Lisieux as models for Catholic Workers. On the other hand, she did not restrict her devotion to saints officially recognized by the church. Both Peter Maurin and Mohandas Gandhi were, for her, modern Saint Francises; indeed, the *Catholic Worker* virtually canonized Gandhi in an obituary that declared, "There is no public figure who has more conformed his life to the life of Jesus Christ than Gandhi, there is no man who has carried about him more consistently the aura of divinized humanity, who has added his sacrifice to the sacrifice of Christ. . . . In him we have a new intercessor with Christ."[10] Day also used hagiographical language to describe the more obscure guests and volunteers who frequented Catholic Worker houses. It may not be entirely far-fetched to suggest that she thought the official canonization process was an unnecessary (and expensive) distraction from the popular process of saint making. But for the most part, she simply was not preoccupied with the pros and cons of official canonization. Her more fundamental concern was to promote the idea that a life of holiness should be the goal of every Christian. The saints, for her, were always examples, never supernatural exceptions to be placed on pedestals.

While Day was understandably reluctant to elaborate on her views about her own sainthood, she made several attempts to explain her comment about obedience to the bishops. During the height of the Vietnam War, when she was regularly criticizing Cardinal Spellman for his pro-war statements, she explained that her position was entirely consistent with the Catholic principle of primacy of conscience, according to which a Catholic must obey her conscience even if it conflicts with the teachings of the church. Though she could not "conceive of Cardinal Spellman making such a request of me, considering the respect he has always shown for freedom of conscience and freedom of speech," her conscience would require her to obey such an order as an expression of her "faith that God will right all mistakes, mine as well as [Cardinal Spellman's]."[11] A few years later, she made the same point more provocatively, noting that other Catholic Workers would make equally conscientious decisions to continue the work: "My conscientious reasoning, if asked to cease publishing, would be this: I may be held responsible for what goes in the paper, but I am a member of an unincorporated association of the Catholic Worker, made up of a very active group of young people. . . . Whatever happened to me, I could count on them to carry on Peter [Maurin]'s program. . . . Yes, I can well see myself obeying—and under the cloak of obedience sit in a rocking chair on a porch and watch the majestic Hudson and its ships pass by; and read, and write more. What kind of obedience would that be? A joy indeed."[12] What Day seems to have advocated is the same sort of rebellious obedience that Jesus had recommended in the Sermon on the Mount: "Should anyone press you into service for one mile, go with him for two miles" (Matt 5:41).[13]

Day's understanding of obedience thus did not prevent her from supporting and participating in direct protests against the hierarchy. In the late 1940s, she picketed Cardinal Spellman's offices because he had tried to break a gravediggers' strike by calling in seminarians as scabs. Two decades later she denounced his call for "total victory" in Vietnam and refused to condemn a group of protesters who had picketed the cathedral itself. "I would not myself have chosen such a place for a demonstration," she wrote, "but I have permitted my name to be used by the group in their effort to raise funds to defend themselves."[14] More gently, she joined a 1963 "pilgrimage" of fifty women, including non-Catholics and nonbelievers, who traveled to Rome to ask John XXIII for "a more radical condemnation of the instruments of modern warfare." She returned during the last session of Vatican II and participated in a ten-day "penitential fast" with twenty other women.[15] None of these actions, of course, directly challenged the official teaching of the church; they simply challenged the hierarchy to live up to the ideals it already professed. At the same time, Day clearly believed that, in the social arena, the Catholic laity had both a right and a duty to take the leading role. Recalling a bishop who had told Peter Maurin, if "[y]ou lead the way—we will follow," Day wrote that "it was up to the laity to plough ahead, to be the vanguard, to be the shock troops, to fight these battles without fear or favor. And to make the mistakes."[16]

This style of wrestling with the church has remained alive and well in the Worker movement. In Los Angeles, the Worker community protested against the archdiocese's plan to spend $100 million dollars on a new cathedral; in Washington, D.C., they challenged the $26 million headquarters for the National Conference of Catholic Bishops and the $50 million Pope John Paul II Cultural Center. Other Workers protested the closing of a soup kitchen in Hartford and inner city parish schools in Philadelphia. Most Workers appreciated the message of the 1985 pastoral on economic justice from the United States bishops, but when the bishops met at Saint John's Abbey that year a nearby Worker community still chose to protest their failure to go further. "We will be outside of the Abbey church on Sunday morning," declared the Workers in a flyer, "symbolizing that even though we support the steps the Bishops have taken, we do not feel the church has moved close enough to the church of the poor for us to enter the building." At the time of this writing, the Viva House community is adamantly opposing an archdiocesan restoration project that will move a soup kitchen "from its current site next to the Basilica . . . [to one] adjacent to Maryland's execution chamber."[17]

Even the most conservative champions of Day's orthodoxy acknowledge the legitimacy of this sort of critique but then distinguish challenges to the church's economic policies from direct attacks on church teachings. Yet for many Workers, challenges to the very idea of a church hierarchy flow directly from opposition to the hierarchy's stance on economic or military issues. Mike Sersch, who attended daily Mass at the Winona Cathedral during his time at the Catholic Worker, told me that "it's really uncomfortable to be sitting in a cathedral for daily mass, because you're sitting there and you're looking at this big monster chair, the *cathedra,* and I really hate the fact that there's that chair there." Mike was particularly scandalized by the bishops' support for the war in Afghanistan, which helped him clarify the principle that the Catholic Worker's first loyalty is to the gospel rather than the church. "I think the Catholic Worker movement is striving to choose the gospel. And I think that can be different than the church, and it's sad that that can be different. . . . But when the two are in conflict we hope to go with the gospel."[18]

At the Des Moines Catholic Worker, Claire Quiner took the same logic a step further, telling me that she no longer identified as a Catholic because of the church's failure to embody the gospel principles of love and nonviolent resistance. Her childhood parish, she noted, has had "a big United States flag hanging up, ever since the September 11 attacks." "Churches," Claire explained, "are not to be identified with countries. That bothers me. I don't like that we bless a country that terrorizes the world." For Claire, such institutional failures justify her refusal to identify her personal beliefs with any institution.[19] Larry Ray-Keil of Seattle's Family Kitchen expressed a similar sensibility when he told Rosalie Riegle Troester, "Personally, I think the only reason for an institution as horrible as the church, in terms of the structure, is to be able to do things like [feeding the hungry]. . . . That's the only reason I can see to have institutions."[20]

Dorothy Day might have been distressed by Claire's and Larry's willingness to abandon the institutional church because of its failure to live up to its own ideals. But this move is consistent with the Worker's longstanding tendency to appeal to the gospel (or even more narrowly, to the Sermon on the Mount) rather than to the entire body of Catholic doctrine in articulating its identity. In 1952, for example, Day herself wrote that "it is a few simple points which *The Catholic Worker,* as a paper, is trying to make. The Fatherhood of God. The Brotherhood of man. 'Love is the measure by which we shall be judged.' 'My little children, love one another.' . . . We have no party line, neither Communist nor Catholic."[21] It also reflects the real differences between the organizational structure of Catholic Worker communities and the institutional church. If one has actually seen decentralized decision-making work, it is hard to keep believing in the God-given character of church hierarchy. Thus, for Mike Sersch, a Worker community can be a "loving" challenge to the assumptions underlying the institutional church. "We're trying to say, we [the Worker] don't have hierarchy, the gospel doesn't have hierarchy, why do we [the Church] have to have hierarchy?"[22]

Similarly, Catholic Workers who dissent from church teaching on such controversial issues as women's ordination or homosexuality typically see their criticisms as deeply rooted in the Catholic Worker tradition. "I would say that the logical conclusion to the last fifty-odd years of the Catholic Worker movement," Gary Donatelli told Rosalie Riegle Troester, "is a position that is . . . somewhere real close to heresy, if not deeply embedded in heresy. If you look at the history of the Catholic Worker, I would say it leaves you with the outsider. Not just the outsider of an economic community, but also the outsider of an ecclesiastical community."[23] More specifically, the Catholic Worker commitment to "outsiders" has led many beyond a solidarity with the poor that is consistent with church teaching to a form of solidarity with women, gays, and lesbians that challenges that teaching. The Catholic Worker movement has been one of the most important centers for advocacy on these issues within Catholicism, even as the movement has remained open to more traditional Catholics who share its solidarity with the poor.

Catholic Workers and Women's Ordination

A substantial number of Catholic Worker communities, for example, sponsor services at which laypeople, including women, preside at Eucharist. One early inspiration for this practice was Jonah House. The temporary excommunication of founders Phil Berrigan and Liz McAlister (for their unsanctioned marriage) provided an early incentive for the community to explore alternative liturgies. For decades, the practice at Jonah House's weekly liturgy has been for community members to take turns preparing a reflection on the gospel, and then celebrating the Eucharist. "[My parents] definitely had a sense that we were the church too, and that we are all priests," Jerry Berrigan told me. "And that certainly women should be able to celebrate the Eucharist. Laypeople should be able to. That God doesn't come through the pope, that God doesn't come through the priest, that God isn't found only in the church, that God is in all of us."[24]

To my knowledge, the New York Catholic Worker houses have never sponsored such Eucharists. But even during Dorothy Day's lifetime, the *Catholic Worker* published several articles challenging the church's sexism, and at least implicitly calling for women's ordination. Perhaps the first was by a Benedictine monk, Anthony Mullaney, who wrote provocatively: "There are women who proclaim loudly the violence done them at every Eucharistic liturgy which announces via the priesthood that they are less than persons. If once we argued that the segregated southern church had no right to celebrate the Eucharist because segregation was an affront to the sign of unity, why does not the same argument apply to the sexist church?" Day's close friend Eileen Egan recalled that "Jesus, who entrusted the good news that He was the redeemer of humankind to a woman, and who entrusted women with the news of his Resurrection, may yet use women to be witness to His message of peace. Will any Church structure oppose such a witness?" And Marj Humphrey and Jane Sammon, reporting on the Latin American bishops meeting at Puebla, Mexico, praised their work but complained that "the ecumenical dimension is absent from the Document and the language is sexist."[25]

Such commentary has actually been *less* common in the pages of the New York *Catholic Worker* since Day's death, but it is ubiquitous in the movement as a whole. The Casa Maria community of Milwaukee probably generated the most controversy for its celebration of priest-less Eucharists, which began around 1983. When this practice came to the attention of Gordon Zahn, a Catholic pacifist and "fellow traveler" of the Worker, he wrote an open letter in protest, sending it for some reason to *Commonweal* rather than to the *Catholic Worker*. A revised version of the letter was published along with a response by Casa Maria's Don Timmerman and an essay by liturgical theologian John Baldovin, and the issue was also covered in the local press.[26]

In his piece, Timmerman placed this liturgical innovation within the Catholic Worker tradition of protest, noting that Casa Maria "is and has been . . . controversial" ever since founder Mike Cullen was expelled from the United States for antiwar activities. He defended the practice on both ecumenical and feminist grounds, then suggested that the Worker had an obligation to challenge injustice wherever it appeared: "Since our community is composed of people of various religious beliefs and denominations, we try to allow these people to take part in our liturgies. . . . We feel that it is wrong to forbid women the opportunity to preside at Mass, and since it is wrong, we refuse to follow the church mandate which states that only men may preside at Mass. If we accuse our society of being unjust and, thus, refuse to cooperate with it, then we also have an obligation to see the injustice in the church and refuse to cooperate with it also." Timmerman also defended Casa Maria's place within the Catholic Worker movement in terms that made no reference to the institutional church. "We still claim to be Catholic Workers since we believe strongly in the philosophy of the Catholic Worker movement. We try to practice the spiritual and corporal works of mercy. . . . And, of course, we realize that God is the source and reason for our work."[27]

Zahn, for his part, proposed a dramatically different understanding of Catholic Worker identity. The Worker, he claimed, "has been a unique force in the history of American Catholicism" because of its "almost perfect fusion between the commitment to service and its no less binding commitment to the Catholic church." He dismissed Day's and Maurin's claim that the Catholic Worker has "no party line" by saying that it was intended only in a narrowly political sense, then suggested that just as the Catholic Worker would expel an advocate of Ronald Reagan's military policies, so it should exclude "those who would reject or disregard generally recognized and accepted norms of Catholic belief and practice." Women-officiated liturgies, according to Zahn "cannot be considered Catholic," and while they may be compatible with "some aspects of 'the philosophy of the Catholic Worker' . . . they are not true to the most essential aspect of that philosophy," which was the liturgy's place as "the indispensable heart of the movement and its work."[28]

Perhaps the most interesting feature of this debate is the fact that it did not provoke a single letter of response from any active Catholic Worker. (John Cort's challenge to Catholic Worker agrarianism in the 1940s, by contrast, provoked a series of responses and counterresponses that filled the pages of *Commonweal* for months.) In part, this may be because Catholic Workers of the 1980s, especially those with "progressive-radical" views of the church, were less inclined than their predecessors to read *Commonweal*. More fundamentally, Zahn simply missed the anarchist thread of the Catholic Worker philosophy. Many, perhaps most, Catholic Workers would have agreed with his understanding of the liturgy's central place in the movement. But very few could support formal expulsions as a strategy for preserving Catholic Worker identity. Many would say that part of the Worker's "catholicity" is precisely its ability to bring people with very different ecclesial views together, forcing them to do their wrestling with the church in one another's company.

In keeping with this anarchist sense of catholicity, many Worker houses have found subtler ways of speaking out on behalf of women's ordination. The members of Saints Francis and Thérèse Catholic Worker in Worcester are members of a local parish and would never sponsor a priest-less Eucharist. But from their founding they have made their feminist commitments clear. In the second issue of their paper, cofounder Scott Schaeffer-Duffy published an article titled "Is God a Woman?" in which he cited feminine images of God from the Bible and concluded: "We are listening for more perfect language, but we can no longer pray to a god who is only male." Five years later, he espoused a fairly traditional understanding of magisterial authority: "Our community has sought the counsel and prayer of our bishops. . . . We believe the teaching authority of the Church can be helpful in the difficult task of discerning God's will for us." But this allowed him to address the ordination issue from the unique perspective of Marian devotion: "Ironically one of our most traditional beliefs also is the basis of our strongest disagreements with current Church practice. We revere Mary as the extraordinarily brave and faithful woman without whom salvation could not have come to us. . . . We believe that Mary was quite literally the first priest and it makes no sense for us to believe that God associated so intimately with her and no longer wishes to do so with other women on the altar at Mass. We hope and pray that the Holy Spirit, described for us in the Book of Wisdom as a woman, will inspire the Church to embrace women's ordination soon." The Worcester community also repeatedly used the April Fools edition of its paper for lighthearted advocacy, running headlines like "Pope ordains women: Priesthood rebounds" alongside stories about Ronald and Nancy Reagan converting to Buddhism.[29]

Advocacy for Gays and Lesbians

Catholic Worker advocacy on behalf of gays and lesbians also covers a broad spectrum from confrontational to irenic and has been shaped by the personal experiences of many Workers. Many believe that gays and lesbians are better represented in the movement than in the general public; one Worker told me that he knew of several houses dominated by people who were openly gay or lesbian, and an equal number dominated by closeted folks. During the last years of Day's life, the New York paper regularly featured articles from Sandy Adams and Chuck Smith, a gay couple whose West Virginia farm was one of the brightest examples of Catholic Worker agrarianism. (It was not until after Day's death that Adams and Smith began publicly "storming heaven for more recognition of gay, lesbian, and women's rights in the C.W. movement and the Church," but their relationship was an open secret much earlier.[30]) Day was well aware that many volunteers in the New York house were gay, and by most accounts she "loved them very well," occasionally challenging others to remember that "*Someone* has to minister to gay people."[31] But she hesitated to speak publicly on the issue.

Other Workers were occasionally more vocal, even during Day's lifetime. In 1952, Robert Ludlow praised a book on *Psychiatry and Catholicism* for saying that society has been unfair to homosexuals and faulted the same book for supporting antisodomy laws and thus "perpetuat[ing] the idea that homosexuals should be treated as criminals."[32] When the organized gay rights movement emerged in the 1970s, Workers were among the first Catholics to rally to the cause. The Seattle community came out in support of gay rights in the middle of the decade, though apparently someone at the New York house hid their article "underneath a heap of old mail in one of the drawers in the desk" to preclude open discussion. Richard Cleaver, a gay Worker who found the article nevertheless, subsequently moved to Des Moines, where the Worker community revised the "Catholic Worker Positions" to include a clear condemnation of heterosexism as expressed in church and society. (At least one supporter asked to have his name removed from the mailing list in protest.) In 1980 Catholic Worker Frank Cordaro spoke at Des Moines's second annual gay pride parade, where he read a statement from the

Catholic Coalition for Gay Civil Rights. The Worker house also served as the local contact for that organization.[33] Boston's Haley House, likewise, included a presentation by Dignity (the Catholic organization for gays and lesbians) on their Clarification of Thought schedule as early as 1985.[34]

St. Joseph's House in Minneapolis began speaking out on gay and lesbian rights in its very first newsletter, apparently in solidarity with a nearby Catholic parish, St. Stephen's, that had taken a public stand on the issue. "Maybe you have heard of St. Stephen's recently because of a controversy about homosexuality," wrote founder Char Madigan in 1978. "Now comes the societal message! Gay people are brothers and sisters some still call enemy. Whether Chinese, mentally handicapped, Indian or black, alcoholic or gay, Catholic Workers must insist and work for a reconciliation, an ending to discrimination toward these whole groups of strangers some call enemy." The community's steadfast allegiance to this position led some supporters to withhold their contributions, while others gave extra to make up the difference. Eventually the community hired an openly lesbian woman as house director; in one newsletter article she wrote about having left her Roman Catholic roots to join a United Church of Christ congregation that celebrated gay and lesbian sexuality.[35]

In 1983, the issue was openly discussed at a national gathering of Catholic Workers, where Chris Montesano challenged the others to reach out to gays and lesbians "in keeping with the love and forgiveness which are at the heart of the Catholic Worker movement." A year later, the New York Catholic Worker community sponsored a roundtable discussion on the "Church's Ministry to the Gay Community," despite the fears of some that Dorothy Day would not have approved. This was followed by a series of articles: Jennifer Imhoff wrote on the mounting AIDS crisis in terms that were at least implicitly pro-gay, while Ernesto de la Vega offered a personal testimony about his experience as a gay Catholic. The issue was "a matter of life and death," he wrote, because so many "fine young men and women" were "driven to emotional disturbances and even suicide" because of the dichotomy between church teaching and their desire for intimacy. Still, he said, "In my own love for the Church, I chose not to leave it but to enter ever more deeply into its mystery." Longtime editor Peggy Scherer, likewise, began by describing silence about homosexuality as a form of violence but stopped short of directly rejecting church teaching. "Some among us," she reported, "are struggling to reconcile our deep love for the Church and our desire to accept its wisdom, with questions raised by our consciences, informed by theological insights based on new developments in Scriptural research as well as traditional understandings, and by the insights as well as the anguish of various men and women." Her article was illustrated with a drawing of Gandhi, a significant choice because Gandhi was revered by virtually everyone in the Worker movement, yet also highlighted the Worker's long tradition of pluralism and inclusion.[36]

These articles sparked what was probably the bitterest conflict within the Worker movement since the dispute over pacifism that nearly shattered the movement during the Second World War. Even prior to the publication of Scherer's article, other editors pressed her to incorporate a strong affirmation of the Catholic Worker's fidelity to official Catholic teaching. The editorial board then articulated two new policies: (1) "no article on any topic (economics, politics, etc. as well as religious matters) can include any 'deviation' from what is understood as the Catholic Worker view," (2) "no one who disagrees with any Church teaching (by implication, on women's ordination, whatever) publicly—no matter if they do so as an individual, in conscience, sensitively and nonviolently—can be an editor of the *C.W.*"[37] These policies led to the removal of two gay editors, Ernesto de la Vega and Gary Donatelli, and the resignation of Geoffrey Gneuhs and Peggy Scherer. In his letter, Gneuhs complained that "a kind of autocracy and individualism became the norm with one or a few arrogating to themselves power and authority," noting that the problem was a long-standing one and that individuals on both sides of the homosexuality debate had exercised power in arbitrary ways. Scherer, for her part, described her departure as "a very messy divorce." Still, the episode had some unintended beneficial effects: Scherer, Donatelli, and others were able to bring some of the Worker ethos to their new jobs at Bailey House, an AIDS hospice sponsored by the city of New York.[38]

Unlike the pacifism conflict, the events of 1985 had almost no impact on the movement as a whole. Catholic Worker houses from coast to coast continued to challenge church teaching on sexuality, with such houses as Friends of Dorothy in Syracuse and Temenos in San Francisco placing such advocacy at the heart of their missions. In 1997, longtime Worker Michael Harank sponsored a national gathering for gays and lesbians in the Worker, and in 2000 he called upon Workers "to articulate and mourn the spiritual violence and debilitating silence that is embedded in the Catholic tradition by its paradoxical, confusing and contemptible teachings on the matter of 'homosexuality.' The Catholic Worker movement has its own legacy of grave silence, conscious censure and spiritual violence committed against people in the movement which needs to be addressed in the present and in the future."[39] At most of the Catholic Worker communities I have visited, support for gay and lesbian rights is so widespread that it is virtually taken for granted; two lesbians with whom I spoke were quite startled to learn that gays and lesbians were not affirmed everywhere in the movement.[40]

Wrestling with Abortion

Though dissent from the official Catholic position on homosexuality is probably the majority position in the Worker, support for abortion rights is rarer. But the distinctive contribution of the Worker is especially apparent with regard to this issue. By placing the abortion issue within the context of solidarity with the poor, the Catholic Worker has consistently challenged both the church and the larger society to think beyond the usual terms of the abortion debate. In the early years, to be sure, the distinctive Catholic Worker perspective was sometimes veiled by the inflammatory rhetoric Catholic Workers used to condemn both abortion and birth control. Peter Maurin described the use of birth control within marriage as a form of prostitution and asserted that "no woman can admire a man who tries to induce her to practice birth control." He also published an Eric Gill essay that suggested that birth control would lead to matriarchy, "a very appropriate arrangement for a society which has reduced all its workers to a subhuman condition of intellectual irresponsibility." Even Michael Harrington, prior to his break with the Worker and the Church, wrote that "it is precisely because I am a Catholic and believe in the Church's philosophy of the family and condemnation of birth control that I must adopt a revolutionary attitude toward society."[41] But the practical implication of such principles, Catholic Workers insisted, was not preaching or legislation, but direct support for large families and single mothers. Donald Powell thus faulted the Catholic Church for offending non-Catholics with its anti-birth control advocacy. The real focus, he wrote, should be replacing industrial capitalism with "a society where Catholics can live as Catholics."[42]

By the 1960s, the tone of discussion had softened but the underlying principles remained. The *Catholic Worker* published a book review by John Hugo reaffirming the Catholic Church's teaching on birth control, but it also published a rejoinder by Canon F. H. Drinkwater, who called for a change of teaching. The debate extended over the better part of a year, until the editors intervened to say that since the parties "have now had two opportunities apiece" to express their views, "we are terminating this particular exchange." Evidently Dorothy Day realized that, in the age of *Humanae Vitae,* discussion of the church's sexual teaching could easily absorb all of a Catholic publication's energies. In the wake of *Roe v. Wade,* she refused to open the newspaper's pages to a discussion of abortion.[43] She occasionally violated this rule herself, but only to suggest personalist solutions to the problem. In a 1972 column, for example, she referred to abortion and birth control as "genocide," but then challenged religious orders to use their land to raise food for the hungry and thus eliminate the motivation for abortion.[44]

With the increased fervor of the abortion debate in the late 1970s and early 1980s, most Catholic Workers responded by tracing the roots of abortion to militarism and economic inequality. The New York houses hosted a roundtable session with Juli Loesch of Prolifers for Survival, a group that promoted reconciliation between pro-lifers and pacifists.[45] The paper also responded enthusiastically to Cardinal Joseph Bernardin's call for a "seamless garment" of Catholic opposition to abortion, war, and the death penalty, and published an article by Jane Sammon, who recalled the way pregnant girls in her Catholic high school were expelled, with "no talk about respect and mercy for a young girl"—a practice she compared to abortion.[46] The Des Moines newspaper published a handful of articles on the topic. One described the "technological abortions" brought about by nuclear radiation; another argued that abortion was "another method devised to maintain the patriarchal system" by absolving the larger community of its responsibility for poor children; and a third, by cofounder Frank Cordaro, affirmed a pro-life position even as it sought to understand the underlying values of the pro-choice movement.[47]

This last article, written in response to the peace movement schism that resulted when the Mobilization for Survival refused to accept Prolifers for Survival as a member organization, also exposed some of the divisions within the Worker movement. The community published two lengthy pro-choice responses (neither, I believe, written by live-in members of Worker communities), which in turn provoked former Worker Jim Forest to write to Frank Cordaro: "It has caught me very much by surprise to realize there is such deep disagreement over this issue within the Catholic Worker. . . . I have always thought that, since the great fray within the CW over pacifism during World War II, that a very solid pacifism had been generally accepted by CW folk, and that it was a sort that would include the unborn as fully as those of us more on view."[48] Around the same time, Saint Joseph's House in Minneapolis published an article in which they "came out . . .

not so much pro-choice as anti-pro-life. . . . Because they end up condemning the women."[49]

Catholic Workers also took notice when pro-life movements like Operation Rescue began using Catholic Worker-style direct action in their protests against abortion clinics. On at least a few occasions, Catholic Workers found themselves protesting against other Catholic Workers, leading to charges and counter-charges about the use of violent tactics and inappropriate slogans.[50] Haley House responded to the resulting debate by inviting Boston College ethicist Lisa Sowle Cahill to do a "clarification of thought" presentation on abortion in 1985. Reporting on that event in the community's newsletter, Vickie Combs expressed sharp opposition to hierarchical authority, coupled with a more nuanced position on abortion itself. "It was heartening," Combs wrote, "to see that the moral credibility of the Roman hierarchy on this issue was widely suspect" as a result of the bishops' reluctance to condemn the arms race, their "absurd teaching on birth control," and "the exclusion of women from their sacred tree-house." But just because the bishops were wrong didn't make abortion right: Combs went on to describe it as a "final, tragic choice" that could be avoided through a "non-violent revolution" and a reorientation of public priorities toward support for mothers.

Evidently even this mildly pro-choice position was controversial at Haley House, as the same newsletter featured a statement titled "No Party Line" which explained, "In these pages you may read some things with which you agree, some which interest you, and some that may enrage you. We are a diverse community and so our ways of perceiving and understanding the Truth and God's call to us are different. . . . We approach the issue of abortion and all the myriad complex issues of our day with humility—acutely aware of our own fallibility. . . . We conclude with Dorothy Day's observations over thirty years ago that we will join with any who affirm life, regardless of ideology, and we will lovingly but firmly resist those who do not. 'We have no party line.'" (This statement was reprinted in community newsletters for years, although the specific reference to abortion was eventually dropped.) The disclaimer did not satisfy Ann O'Connor of Unity Kitchen Community, who wrote back that Combs's "negative remarks . . . indicate a rejection of the magisterium and a separation from the Catholic Church," then challenged Haley House as a whole: "Are you a Catholic Community? . . . Perhaps you have never identified yourselves as Catholic. Have you, or do you, identify yourselves as Catholic Worker?"[51]

More constructively, Haley House held a gathering on September 21, 1985, to sort out the issues raised by Combs's article and the aftermath. The discussion began with a Buddhist compassion meditation, then individual sharing of "experiences and feelings about abortion." The participants identified several areas of consensus: that abortion should not be criminalized to the extent that mothers would be imprisoned; that everyone should cultivate "compassion for *both* babies in utero and their mothers who are often trapped and afraid"; and that a deeper discussion of sexuality, "especially on the part of the Church," was needed to resolve the issue. Participants described the tone as one of genuine searching, with "complexity" and "ambiguities" seeming "to increase geometrically as each person joins the discussion."[52]

Among those who participated in this event were Scott and Claire Schaeffer-Duffy, who were in the process of founding Saints Francis and Thérèse Catholic Worker in Worcester, Massachusetts. They identified themselves as a "seamless garment community" (that is, one opposed equally to war, abortion, and capital punishment), participated occasionally in protests at abortion clinics, and urged other communities to follow suit. But they also nuanced their position on abortion through frequent articles in their newspaper, *The Catholic Radical*. In keeping with Catholic Worker anarchism, most of these articles *opposed* the criminalization of abortion, arguing (in the words of Marcia Timmel) "that if we are to begin saving lives that are currently being lost to abortion, we must start by giving [women] control over their own lives."[53] Timmel's argument wasn't that different from that found in a contemporary article in the Haley

House Newsletter, where Brayton Shanley (of Agape House) traced abortion to a "broken covenant between men and women. . . . The real 'cause' in abortion is not just saving the unborn child but saving the biological parents considering abortion and who are lost in a sea of domination and self-concern."[54] Other articles in *The Catholic Radical* featured calls for "humility and openness to dialogue" and the testimony of a woman who regretted her choice to have an abortion but still described it as "an aspect of Catholic sexism that women who have had an abortion are treated considerably different than men who have taken hundreds of lives in the military."[55] Around the same time, a roundtable discussion in New York City led to a clear embrace of the seamless garment principle and an almost equally clear rejection of criminalization. "From the beginning," wrote the editors, "the CW has not seen governmental or legal processes as the way to right wrongs, or to bring about fundamental change. . . . Above all, we do not accept the authority of the state to define life and death." What was needed were not laws against abortion, but "personal and communal responsibility for the works of mercy to care for mothers and children, to build a society where a decision such as *Roe v. Wade* would not be asked for or considered, a society where such laws would wither away."[56]

In keeping with its commitment to dialogue, the Worcester community also shared the responses of those who rejected their suggestion that all Worker communities embrace the "seamless garment" philosophy. Brendan Walsh of Viva House, for example, wrote that they responded to the request "by telling about a friend. She was brutally raped. She believes, as we do, that rape is an act of violence. Our friend's conscience told her that the resultant pregnancy was a continuation of violence in her body. . . . We believe there is a difference between nuclear weapons and abortion. We can be 'absolute' in condemning the nukes, but not abortion." Walsh's point was not that he personally approved of abortion, but that Catholic Worker communities could make room for those with conscientious differences on the issue.[57] And his long-standing commitment to the movement allowed him to be heard even by those who disagreed. Though Polly Mahoney was sure that abortion was not justified even in cases of rape, she responded by "affirm[ing Viva House] and all others in the Catholic Worker Movement for their good conscience efforts to live the Gospels in a world milieu which consistently devalues Christ's great teachings and the way of true love."[58]

Refusing to Divide

The Catholic Worker debate on abortion, in short, revealed a broad consensus on the importance of dialogue, of honoring individual consciences, of wrestling with the official teaching of the church, of supporting and empowering women, of tracing the connections between abortion and other forms of violence, and even of resisting the coercive power of the state. This consensus was strained at the 1991 national Catholic Worker gathering hosted by Haley House, which may stand as the high point of ecclesial controversy within the Worker movement. Troubled by a conference program that promised Buddhist meditation, a Quaker meeting, and a feminist liturgy (as well as a Catholic Mass), members of Syracuse's Unity Kitchen Community chose to boycott, sending in their place an "Open Letter" that blasted Haley House for having "given up its Catholic identity. This is evident in their newsletters which have become a pro-abortion forum, belittling the teaching authority of the Church and endorsing various forms of paganism, particularly the goddess-witchery type. Their stated communal and editorial neutrality towards all kinds of religions and even deathmaking does not conceal their sympathy for these dangerous anti-life, anti-Church directions." From Unity Kitchen's perspective, "the Catholic identity of the Catholic Worker" was at stake, and they "admonish[ed] those who are not submitted to the teaching authority and discipline of the Church nor convinced that the Catholic Mass and Sacraments are the ultimate form of worship, to forgo the name Catholic."[59]

One member of Haley House responded with her own open letter, which mirrored the Unity Kitchen Community letter in its reluctance to participate fully in dialogue: "I do not wish to engage in dialogue with anyone who is convinced that abortion is murder. . . . The issue that is basic to many of us is solidarity with women who are still brutalized in this culture. . . . If tomorrow I chose to terminate a pregnancy, for whatever reason . . . I would hope that you would accompany and support me in my decision, and help defend me against assault."[60]

Given the sharpness of these opposing positions, what is most remarkable about the 1991 Gathering is the fact that so few people in the larger Catholic Worker movement rallied to either side. The only allusion to the Open Letter in Haley House's newsletter was a cartoon (reprinted from the Quad Cities Catholic Worker newspaper) on "How to Spot Those *Non-Catholic* Catholic Workers," while Worcester's *Catholic Radical* continued to run pro-life articles without any mention of Unity Kitchen Community. The only mention of the gathering in the New York *Catholic Worker* was a brief note that also described an anniversary celebration at Milwaukee's Casa Maria. Though Catholic Workers are not generally known for their fear of conflict (after all, many have gone to jail for their protests), this was clearly not a battle they wished to fight. One of the few who did respond directly to Unity Kitchen, Brian Terrell, made just this point. Rather than directly defending the practices Unity Kitchen had attacked, Terrell noted that "the works of mercy . . . hold an older and deeper place in the Catholic tradition than the doctrines of transubstantiation or papal infallibility" and thus suggested that any community committed to the practice of hospitality deserved a place in the movement.[61]

Through its silence, the movement issued a strong rebuke to anyone who would allow ecclesiastical politics to trump the Catholic Worker's commitment to the poor. Still, the cost (and benefit) of the widely shared commitment to anarchism and dialogue is ongoing tension with a church that has at times valued the preservation of hierarchical authority as much or

more than fidelity to gospel values. Day's orthodoxy notwith-
standing, she founded a movement that was organized very
differently from the Catholic Church. While every Catholic parish
and diocese, bishop, priest, and deacon has a clear place in a
formal hierarchy, the Worker movement has no official structure
to hold it together. Each house is free to practice the works of
mercy in its own way, and each individual member is likewise
encouraged to take "personal responsibility" for caring for the
poor and homeless. So long as the Worker embodies an organizational model that is diametrically opposed to that of the
church, it is likely to remain (as it was even in the beginning) a
thorn in the church's side.

The Catholic Worker also differs from the larger church in
that it offers its members an integrated, holistic path of faith
that can make traditional parish life seem insipid or one-
dimensional. Unity Kitchen Community's contention that "some
Catholics have lost their Faith after coming to a Catholic Worker
house, which is a tragedy and a bad fruit for the Catholic Worker
movement," contains a germ of truth—though few would use
the phrase "lose their faith" to describe their changed sensibility.[62] What many Workers would say, however, is that the integration of faith with daily life that is possible at the Worker has an
authenticity that is lacking in the parish. In joining the Worker,
Kathleen Rumpf told Rosalie Troester, "I went through a conversion into a real church. And that real church was the Catholic
Worker. What I was raised on was not the real church. Everything
was fairy tales—no reality."[63] More tentatively, Ted Walker of Des
Moines described the Worker as "a way of leading your life and
making it one big whole instead of having separate areas for
separate things, like you go to church for religion, go to home
to have your family, go to school to have your education. . . .
In a place like this you can pretty much have everything in one."[64]
Indeed, the presence of Father Frank Cordaro meant (until
Frank's recent laicization) that the Des Moines Workers could
receive the sacraments within their house, while Workers in
other places attend liturgy with neighboring religious orders,

participate in lay Eucharists, or opt out of sacramental observance altogether.

One of the things that surprised me most as I spoke to Catholic Workers was the fact that this discomfort with traditional parish life was not confined to the left end of the theological spectrum. Mike Miles and Barb Kass, for example, described themselves as theologically conservative but allowed their daughter to drop out of what she called "Catholic Children's Detention" at a parish that had given their community the cold shoulder. The loss of formal education, Mike and Barb suggested, was compensated by community living itself. "What they've gotten, they've gotten by osmosis. . . . They see the way we live. . . . They know that God has something to do with it."[65]

If this experience of integration creates tensions with the church, however, it also makes Catholic Workers reluctant to resolve that tension through polarization or division. Some Catholic Workers, to be sure, have left the Catholic Church, but most of these people have found ways to remain in creative fellowship with the faithful Catholics in the movement. Despite the advocacy of Unity Kitchen Community, the Worker movement may actually be less vulnerable to schism than the American Catholic Church as a whole. For many Workers, the daily or weekly practice of breaking bread with people of all races and classes is—even more than the official Eucharist—a foretaste of the eschatological banquet. This common experience, in Dorothy Day's time and in the present, has empowered Catholic Workers to be both creative and persistent wrestlers with the church.

[1] Ann O'Connor and Peter King, "What's Catholic About the Catholic Worker Movement: Then and Now," in William Thorn, Philip Runkel, and

Susan Mountin, eds., *Dorothy Day and the Catholic Worker Movement: Centenary Essays* (Milwaukee: Marquette University Press, 2001), 136–39. See also Richard Becker, "Let's Get Radical: Has the Catholic Worker Movement Betrayed Its Founders?" *Crisis* 8 (September 1990): 25–29; Ann O'Connor, "The Catholic Worker: Is It Still Catholic?" *New Oxford Review* 61 (March 1994): 5–8; and, more recently, Stephen Hand, "Dorothy Day Would Turn Over in Her Grave," Traditional Catholic Reflections and Reports, http://www.tcrnews2.com/anotherday.html.

² "Forging Community in Spiritual Diversity," panel at National Catholic Worker Gathering, October 2006.

³ Mel Piehl, *Breaking Bread: The Catholic Worker and the Origin of Catholic Radicalism in America* (Philadelphia: Temple University Press, 1982), ix, xi; and James T. Fisher, *The Catholic Counterculture in America, 1933–1962* (Chapel Hill: University of North Carolina Press, 1989), 71.

⁴ David J. O'Brien, "The Significance of Dorothy Day and the Catholic Worker Movement in American Catholicism," in Thorn et al., *Dorothy Day,* 42.

⁵ Boehrer, "Diversity, Plurality and Ambiguity," in ibid., 110–27; and Frederick George Boehrer III, "Christian Anarchism and the Catholic Worker Movement: Roman Catholic Authority and Identity in the United States," Ph.D. dissertation, Syracuse University, 2001. Boehrer's distinction builds on a typology proposed by Eugene Kennedy in *Tomorrow's Catholics, Yesterday's Church: The Two Cultures of American Catholicism* (New York: Harper & Row, 1988).

⁶ John Cogley, "Radical Catholics: After the Catholic Worker," *National Catholic Reporter* 5, no. 2 (30 October 1968): 8.

⁷ Jack Cook, "Cogley and the Relevance of Radicalism," *Catholic Worker* 34, no. 9 (November 1968): 2.

⁸ Brian Terrell, "Dorothy Day," in Thorn et al., *Dorothy Day,* 149.

⁹ Day apparently made each comment in a variety of contexts, but rarely in writing. The first is quoted ubiquitously, but does not appear in the searchable collection of Day's writings at the Catholic Worker website, www.catholicworker.org. For an extended analysis of the sainthood question, see Carol J. Jablonski, "The Radical's Paradox: A Reflection on Dorothy Day's 'Legendary' Resistance to Canonization," in Thorn et al., *Dorothy Day,* 323–35. With regard to Day's willingness to obey the hierarchy, she wrote in 1948 that "we do not feel that we need permission from the clergy or Bishops to start a house to practice the works of mercy. If they do not like it, they can tell us to stop and we will gladly do so. But asking them to approve *before* any work is done is like asking them to assume a certain amount of responsibility for us." In later columns, she referred to having said more specifically that she would stop publishing the *Catholic Worker*

if the chancery office asked her to, and that she would stop writing on war if Cardinal Spellman asked her to. See Dorothy Day, "Letter on Hospices," *Catholic Worker* 14, no. 10 (January 1948): 8; Day, "On Pilgrimage," *Catholic Worker* 39, no. 4 (May 1973): 8; and Day, "On Pilgrimage," *Catholic Worker* 32, no. 4 (December 1965): 7.

[10] "We Mourn Death of Gandhi Non Violent Revolutionary," *Catholic Worker* 14, no. 11 (February 1948): 1.

[11] Dorothy Day, "On Pilgrimage," *Catholic Worker* 32, no. 4 (December 1965): 7.

[12] Dorothy Day, "On Pilgrimage," *Catholic Worker* 39, no. 4 (May 1973): 8.

[13] In fact, as Brian Terrell has pointed out, Day's response was not entirely obedient in 1951, when Cardinal Spellman did ask her to change the name of the *Catholic Worker*. She replied that her associate editors had outvoted her, insisting that the name stay the same. Terrell suggests that this was somewhat disingenuous, insofar as the associate editors did not ordinarily have such power. But the underlying consistency, perhaps, was that while Day's conscience might require her to obey personally, it did not allow her to impose what she regarded as an unjust order on other people. See Terrell, "Dorothy Day," in Thorn et al., *Dorothy Day,* 146.

[14] Day, "On Pilgrimage," *Catholic Worker* 15, no. 12 (April 1949): 1–2; Day, "In Peace Is My Bitterness Most Bitter," *Catholic Worker* 33, no. 4 (January 1967): 1–2; and Day, *On Pilgrimage: The Sixties* (New York: Curtiss Books, 1972), 294.

[15] Day, "On Pilgrimage," *Catholic Worker* 29, no. 10 (May 1963): 2; Day, "On Pilgrimage," *Catholic Worker* 32, no. 3 (November 1965): 6; and Stephen Thomas Krupa, "Dorothy Day and the Spirituality of Nonviolence," Ph.D. thesis, Graduate Theological Union, 1997, 179–82.

[16] Dorothy Day, "On the Case of Cardinal McIntire," *Catholic Worker* 31, no. 1 (July–August 1964): 8.

[17] Fred Boehrer, "Diversity, Plurality and Ambiguity," in Thorn et al., *Dorothy Day,* 110–11; Michael Kirwan, "Should Not the Shepherds Pasture Sheep?" *Catholic Worker* 56, no. 6 (September 1989): 1, 8; "Circular 1985," Jean Donovan Catholic Worker, DD/CWC, series W-39, box 1, folder 1; and Viva House Catholic Worker, Christmas letter, December 2006.

[18] Interview with Mike Sersch, 12 April 2002.

[19] Interview with Claire Quiner, 2 February 2002.

[20] Larry Ray-Keil, interviewed by Rosalie Troester, 14 May 1987, in DD/CWC, series W-9, box 7.

[21] Dorothy Day, "No Party Line," *Catholic Worker* 18, no. 9 (April 1952): 1, 7.

[22] Interview with Mike Sersch, 12 April 2002.

[23] Gary Donatelli, interviewed by Rosalie Troester, 9 July 1988, 30–31, in DD/CWC, series W-9, box 4, folder 3.

[24] Interview with Jerry Berrigan, May 2000. As early as 1971, likewise, the Los Angeles Catholic Worker reported that founder Dan Delany, a married laicized priest, "also celebrates during the liturgies we have on the 2nd and 4th Sundays of each month at 11 a.m.," though it is not entirely clear what was meant by "celebrates." Dan and Chris Delany et al., "Los Angeles," *Catholic Worker* 37, no. 6 (July–August 1971): 6.

[25] Anthony Mullaney, O.S.B., "The Women's Movement and Nonviolence," *Catholic Worker* 40, no. 5 (June 1974): 3; "Woman and the Peace Message of Jesus," *Catholic Worker* 42, no. 4 (February 1976): 4–5; Marj Humphrey and Jane Sammon, "Facing Human Anguish," *Catholic Worker* 44, no. 3 (March–April 1979): 8.

[26] Don Timmerman, Gordon C. Zahn, and John F. Baldovin, "The Eucharist: Who May Preside?" *Commonweal* 115, no. 15 (September 9, 1988): 460–63, 466.

[27] Ibid.

[28] Ibid.

[29] Scott Schaeffer-Duffy, "Is God a Woman?" *The Catholic Radical* (October–November 1986): 1–2, DD/CWC, series W-54, box 1, folder 2; Scott Schaeffer-Duffy, "The Catholic Worker and Catholicism," *The Catholic Radical* (October–November 1991): 4; *The Catholic Radical* (April–May 2004); *The Catholic Radical* (April–May 1987).

[30] "Houses of Hospitality," *Catholic Worker* 55, no. 3 (May 1988): 7; cited in Rosalie Riegle Troester, *Voices from the Catholic Worker* (Philadelphia: Temple University Press, 1993), 543.

[31] Chris Montesano, in ibid., 526.

[32] Robert Ludlow, "Book Reviews: The Relationship between Psychiatry and Catholicism," *Catholic Worker* 18, no. 13 (September 1952): 5.

[33] Richard Cleaver, interviewed by Rosalie Troester, 1 November 1989, 9, DD/CWC, series W-9, box 3, folder 13; "Catholic Worker Positions," DD/CWC, series W-21, box 1, folder 2; Jim Murdock to Frank Cordaro, 19 November 1979, DD/CWC, series W-21, box 1, folder 4; "Gay Rally May Become Annual," *Des Moines Register,* 30 June 1980, 7B, DD/CWC, series W-21, box 3, folder 3.

[34] Clarification of Thought flyer, DD/CWC, series W-19, box 1, folder 12.

[35] Char Madigan, "Society Column," *News and Thanksletter* (St. Joseph's House, Minneapolis), January 1978, DD/CWC, series W-4, box 6, folder 15; *St. Joseph's House News,* 4/7-8 (July–August 1990): 2, DD/CWC, series W-4, box 12, folder 23; Deanna Carter, "Reflections of My Spirit," *St. Joseph's House News* 4, no. 6 (June 1990): 5–6, DD/CWC, series W-4, box 12, folder 23.

[36] Peggy Scherer, "National CW Gathering," *Catholic Worker* 50, no. 5 (August 1983): 6; Boehrer, "Christian Anarchism," 206; Michele Teresa Aronica, R.S.M., *Beyond Charismatic Leadership: The New York Catholic Worker Movement* (New Brunswick, NJ: Transaction Books, 1987), 121; Jennifer Imhoff, "AIDS: Trust Not Fear," *Catholic Worker* 52, no. 6 (September 1985): 1, 3; Ernesto de la Vega, "A Personal Testimony," *Catholic Worker* 52, no. 7 (October–November 1985): 3; and Peggy Scherer, "Homosexuality: Searching for Understanding," *Catholic Worker* 52, no. 7 (October–November 1985): 3.

[37] Open letter by Peggy Scherer, January 30, 1987, in DD/CWC, series W-11, box 7. This quotation represents Scherer's understanding of a policy that was, apparently, communicated verbally to her. To my knowledge, the editorial board never published this policy in the paper and mentioned the expulsions and resignations only obliquely, in a house column by Robert Peters, "St. Joseph House," *Catholic Worker* 53, no. 7 (October–November 1986): 2. Deane Mowrer also described the crisis in a letter to Mary Durnin, 11 September 1986, DD/CWC, series W-14, box 1, in which she praised Scherer's article but defended the expulsion of Ernesto de la Vega. "Jane Sammon and Kassie Temple," she wrote, "insisted that Dorothy intended our paper to stay with the teaching authority of the Church. I feel sure they are right."

[38] Geoffrey Gneuhs to Catholic Worker editors, 18 August 1986, DD/CWC, series W-52, box 1; Boehrer, "Diversity, Plurality, and Ambiguity," 122; and Peggy Scherer, cited in Troester, *Voices,* 531.

[39] "Michael Harank's Letter of Endorsement," at http://www.soulforce.org/article/461, cited by Boehrer, "Christian Anarchism," 211.

[40] Interview with Sara Thomsen and Paula Williams, 24 August 2002.

[41] Peter Maurin, "Prostitution," *Catholic Worker* 7, no. 5 (January 1940): 7; Peter Maurin, "Birth Control," *Catholic Worker* 7, no. 7 (March 1940): 1; Eric Gill, "This Is Matriarchy," *Catholic Worker* 11, no. 11 (January 1945): 5; and Michael Harrington, "Birth Control," *Catholic Worker* 18, no. 7 (February 1952): 2.

[42] Donald Powell, "We Can't Afford a Baby," *Catholic Worker* 2, no. 10 (March 1935): 2.

[43] Informal conversation with Brian Terrell, 13 March 2005. Brian was not certain when or why Day initiated this policy.

[44] Dorothy Day, "On Pilgrimage," *Catholic Worker* 38, no. 9 (December 1972): 2. Day's brief comments, in the context of a rambling letter to Daniel Berrigan, were recalled and elaborated on in Jane Sammon, "The Complex Grief of Women," *Catholic Worker* 57, no. 5 (August 1990): 5.

[45] *Catholic Worker* 47, no. 4 (May 1981): 7.

[46] Eileen Egan, "Cardinal Speaks on Life," *Catholic Worker* 51, no. 1 (January–February 1984): 5; Jane Sammon, "All Life Is Blessed, *Catholic Worker* 50, no. 1 (January–February 1983): 1.

[47] Jacquee Dickey, "A New Look at Abortion," *Via Pacis* 3, no. 1 (January–February 1979): 7; Jo McGowan, "A Pacifist on Abortion," *Via Pacis* 2, no. 1 (January 1978): 5–7; and Frank Cordaro, "Abortion: Two Ways to Look at It," *Via Pacis* 6 (March–April 1981): 9.

[48] "Responses to Abortion: Two Ways to Look at It," *Via Pacis* 5, no. 3 (May–June 1981): 10–11; and Jim Forest to Frank Cordaro, 16 August 1981, DD/CWC, series W-21, box 1, folder 7.

[49] Char Madigan, interviewed by Rosalie Troester, 8 July 1989, DD/CWC, series W-9, box 5, folder 21.

[50] Christopher J. Doucot, "The Seamless Garment," *The Catholic Radical* (February–March, 1989): 1–2, DD/CWC, W-54, box 1, folder 2; and Ciaron O'Reilly, "Open Letter to the Catholic Worker," *Catholic Radical* (April–May 1990): 1–2, DD/CWC, series W-54.

[51] Vickie Combs, "Clarification of Thought: A Feminist Reflection," *Haley House Newsletter,* Easter 1985, 11; "No Party Line," *Haley House Newsletter,* Easter 1985, 16; Ann O'Connor, "For the Unity Kitchen Base Community," "Clarification of Thought," *Haley House Newsletter,* Hiroshima-Nagasaki-Feast of the Transfiguration 1985, all at DD/CWC, series W-19, box 1, folder 12, 11–12.

[52] Ilona O'Connor, "Abortion: A Day of Dialogue," *Haley House Newsletter,* Feast of the Holy Innocents 1985, 11–12, DD/CWC, series W-19, box 1, folder 12.

[53] Marcia A. Timmel, "Pro-Life Feminism," *The Catholic Radical* (June–July 1987): 1–2, DD/CWC, series W-54, box 1, folder 2.

[54] Brayton Shanley, "Abortion: A Broken Covenant," *Haley House Newsletter,* Easter 1987, 10–13, DD/CWC, series W-19, box 1, folder 12.

[55] Meg Brodhead, "The Abortion Debate," *The Catholic Radical* (December–January 1989–90): 1, 6, DD/CWC, series W-54, box 1, folder 2; and Cheri Andes, "The Announcement," *The Catholic Radical* (June–July 1991): 1, 3, DD/CWC, series W-54, box 1, folder 3.

[56] The Editors, "Conversion without Courts," *Catholic Worker* 57, no. 5 (August 1990): 3.

[57] Brendan Walsh, "Be of Conscience (a little) more careful than of everything," *Enthusiasm* (March 1993): 8–11; reprinted in *Catholic Worker Grapevine,* April Fools Week 1993, DD/CWC, series W-54, box 1, folder 6; and phone conversation, 23 February 2005.

[58] Polly Mahoney, in *Catholic Worker Grapevine,* 11 July 1993, DD/CWC, series W-54, box 1, folder 6.

[59] "Open Letter to the Gathering of Catholic Workers," 28 June 1991, DD/CWC, series W-19, unboxed folder.

[60] Open Letter from "Deirdre," DD/CWC, series W-19, unboxed folder.

[61] Ilona O'Connor, "Catholic Worker Gathering," *Haley House Newsletter,* Winter 1992, 1, DD/CWC, series W-19, unboxed folder; "How to Spot Those *Non-Catholic* Catholic Workers," *Haley House Newsletter,* Autumn 1992, 3, DD/CWC, series W-19, unboxed folder; Claire Schaeffer-Duffy, "On War and Abortion," *The Catholic Radical* (December–January 1991–92): 4, 7, DD/CWC, series W-54, box 1, folder 3; "News and Appeals from Friends Near and Far," *Catholic Worker* 58, no. 8 (December 1991): 5; and Brian Terrell, "Is there a Catholicism crisis in the C.W.?" *[Quad Cities] Catholic Radical,* Spring 1992, pp. 4–5.

[62] O'Connor and King, "What's Catholic," in Thorn et al., *Dorothy Day,* 137.

[63] Kathleen Rumpf, cited in Troester, *Voices,* 219.

[64] Interview with Ted Walker, 2 February 2002.

[65] Interview with Mike Miles and Barb Kass, 22 August 2000.

Conclusion

The Future of the Works of Mercy

What is the future of the Catholic Worker? Certainly, the present seems bright. There are houses of hospitality and farms in more places than ever before, and many mainstream homeless shelters emulate the Catholic Worker style of face-to-face hospitality. Catholic Workers are at the forefront of the current struggle to end the war in Iraq, even as they remind us of the abiding threat posed by nuclear weapons. In cities from Baltimore to Los Angeles, Catholic Workers lovingly call a wealthy church to practice the preferential option for the poor. Young people flock to Catholic Worker houses for spring break service trips or summer internships, and many stay for a lifetime or at least a life-changing year or two.

Yet the movement is also precarious—indeed, many Workers would say that "precarity" is as much a mark of the Worker as poverty, hospitality, and nonviolence. Most Catholic Worker newspapers and newsletters carry pleas for new Workers, and even some relatively enduring houses of hospitality have spent much of their histories teetering on the brink of closure. As the remarkable generation of Workers who arrived in the 1960s and 1970s nears retirement age, it is not yet clear that the new generation will prove as capable of lifelong commitment. Even more troubling, from my perspective, is the relative invisibility of the Catholic Worker: though the movement is larger than it was in the 1930s, it does not loom as large in the Catholic or the national consciousness. People who volunteer at local Catholic Worker houses are often unaware of the national scope of the movement. Though Catholic Workers are mainstays of many movements for peace and economic justice, those movements are rarely associated in the public mind with the Catholic Worker. Catholic publications such as *Commonweal* and *America,* though they regularly invoke the memory of Dorothy Day, rarely feature contemporary Catholic Worker perspectives on the issues of the day. Many Catholic Worker newspapers devote more space to republishing the writings of Dorothy Day and Peter Maurin than they do to applying those writings to new circumstances.

Just as many observers concluded erroneously in the 1970s that the Catholic Worker movement had had its day, so one might well conclude now that the Worker has had *both* its days. For both the 1930s and the Vietnam era were unusually auspicious times for the movement. The Catholic Worker's moment of birth was auspicious because, just as millions of American Catholics were moving from the immigrant ghetto into the mainstream of American life, and just as the Communist left was being discredited by Stalin's purges, the crisis of the Great Depression forced both policymakers and ordinary Americans to take a closer look at Catholic social teaching. Then, as now, Catholic social teaching offered an intriguing alternative to the extremes of both communism and capitalism. This "third way," as it was articulated in Pius XI's *Quadragesimo Anno,* called for the formation of free associations of workers and employers in each industry or profession. Like the medieval guilds, these associations would mediate between the state and the individual, safeguarding the common good by avoiding the dangers of both individualism and totalitarianism. While most interpreters of Catholic teaching assumed that the state would play a leading role in promoting industrial associations, the Catholic Worker offered a more decentralized variant that fit well with the libertarian and agrarian tradition of the United States. Rather than large industrial guilds, the Worker promoted small-scale farming communities dependent on individual initiative rather than state support. Though mainstream Catholic thinkers doubted that it was possible to "repeal the industrial revolution," they took the Catholic Worker seriously, and intense debates spread out over issue after issue of journals such as *Commonweal*.

Ultimately, this ferment changed America. Though neither mainstream "corporatism" nor the Catholic Worker's "distributism" was embraced wholesale, minimum wage laws and social welfare programs were passed with strong Catholic support because they honored the core principle that it was possible to balance individual economic freedom with respect for the common good. As usually happens to radical social movements, this partial success pushed the Catholic Worker to the margins, and for the next two decades the Catholic Worker continued, on a much smaller scale, to call for more sweeping social transformation and to experience a foretaste of that transformation through the practice of the works of mercy.

The Vietnam era provided the Catholic Worker with a second auspicious moment. The Second Vatican Council sparked widespread interest in the "lay apostolate," even as the rise of the New Left generated a hunger for alternative models of socialism. The Catholic Worker had a fully developed theory to offer both Catholics and Leftists. It had also had a powerful legacy of peacemaking that proved enormously relevant as the Vietnam War heated up. Worker pacifism was no longer a marginal position: the gross evils of Vietnam made it at least a respectable option for both Catholics and Leftists. As a result, the Worker was able to avoid the sort of crisis that had nearly destroyed it during World War II. Instead, the strength the movement achieved during the 1970s made it capable of expanding in response to the crisis of homelessness in the following decade.

Unfortunately, the very success of the Catholic Worker may have muted its core message. Though most long-term Workers have held fast to Dorothy Day and Peter Maurin's conviction that it is possible to "build a new society within the shell of the old" simply by practicing the works of mercy, outsiders typically perceive the Worker either as a merely charitable response to homelessness or as a peace movement that says "No!" to war louder than it says "Yes!" to any specific social vision. The sense of crisis that many Workers feel about the war in Iraq and persistent urban poverty often causes them to reinforce this perception. Despite their best intentions, Catholic Worker newspapers often devote more space to "denouncing" these social evils than to "announcing" an alternative.

The Catholic Worker alternative, I have suggested, is as simple as the works of mercy. Confronted with any social problem—global warming, the war in Iraq, conflict within a parish or diocese—the Catholic Worker's first response is to ask, "How can I take personal responsibility for feeding the hungry and clothing the naked, and for instructing the ignorant and comforting the afflicted?" This simple question still has the potential to revitalize both the church and the Left in America today. Indeed, the specific challenges facing both the church and the Left could make the beginning of the twenty-first century a third auspicious moment for the Catholic Worker.

As a non-Catholic myself, I hesitate to offer a specific agenda for the Catholic Church. But it seems clear that American Catholicism is threatened both by a crisis of leadership, evident in the declining numbers of priests and in the sexual abuse scandal, and by the polarized divisions between liberal Catholics and those who embrace the full vision of Popes John Paul II and Benedict XVI. The two challenges reinforce one another, as liberals interpret the leadership crisis as evidence of the need for democratization in the church while conservatives see it as a symptom of excessive accommodation to secular culture. The polarization in turn exacerbates the leadership crisis insofar as fewer people relish the thought of exercising leadership in a bitterly divided church. Under such circumstances almost everyone is tempted to point fingers, to say (in Peter Maurin's words),

"They don't do this, they don't do that, they ought to do this, they ought to do that. Always 'They' and never 'I.'"[1]

The works of mercy could offer a way forward in several respects. Most immediately, practicing the works of mercy is a way of "being the church" that does not cost much money or require large numbers of priests. The parish consolidations resulting from the leadership crisis are causing a painful loss of community among American Catholics, but Catholic Workers have long known that there is no better way to build community than to break bread with the poor. Perhaps the movement would do well to offer hospitality more explicitly to those made spiritually homeless by parish consolidations. This is not to suggest that serving in a soup kitchen is necessarily a substitute for receiving the Eucharist, or that participation in a Catholic Worker community should supplant involvement in a local parish. There have always been some Catholic Workers who have reached such conclusions, but at least an equal number have found that the works of mercy only enrich their involvement in the sacraments and parish life.

Moreover, the Catholic Worker has the potential to offer a safe meeting space for "liberal" and "traditionalist" Catholics, insofar as both groups can readily affirm the value of the works of mercy. The sort of dialogues promoted by the Catholic Common Ground Initiative would likely be more successful if participants had the opportunity first to share some common labor and a common meal. As I suggested in chapter 7, a number of Catholic Worker communities have sponsored meaningful dialogues for persons divided by the abortion issue. Unfortunately, the divisions present in the Catholic Church are too often reflected in divisions among Catholic Worker houses: some are closely aligned with the Call to Action wing of the church, while others are sharply critical of what they see as accommodations to secular liberalism. The movement might do more to foster dialogue among these houses, as well as to encourage the formation of more communities where both sorts of Catholics may feel at home.

Just as the Catholic Worker approach to the works of mercy has the potential to heal divisions within the church, so it also may be able to revitalize an American Left that has been on the defensive ever since the election of Ronald Reagan. The Catholic Worker is not only an inspiring expression of Catholic faith, but it is also an heir to some of the most distinctively American radical movements, from the nonresistant abolitionists of the nineteenth century to the International Workers of the World at the turn of the twentieth. In particular, it has inherited the strong emphasis on personal freedom and initiative that has always distinguished the American Left from its European counterparts. For Catholic Workers, it is never enough merely to diagnose the problems besetting American society; the important thing is to act, however small or local one's effort may be, in the faith that large social transformations are the fruit of countless individual actions.

In the introduction, I quoted Mike Baxter's contrast between liberals who march on city hall because people are hungry and radicals who feed them. As a definition of the terms "liberal" and "radical," Baxter's distinction falls short. In my experience, self-described "radicals" are as prone to marching on city hall as self-described "liberals." The image of "big-government" liberals looking to city hall for the solution to every problem, moreover, does not do justice either to the complexity of the liberal tradition—itself a major antecedent to anarchism—or to the complex hearts of individual liberals, many of whom do spend time in the soup kitchen as well as on the picket line. Still, Baxter's quote aptly expresses the core Catholic Worker insight. Confronted with hungry people, Catholic Workers say, "Let's feed them!"

The Catholic Worker emphasis on the works of mercy can thus provide an antidote to the temptation of many on the Left to see structural analysis as both the first and last response to any social problem. Structural analysis is, of course, important: problems like poverty, racism, war, and climate change all have complex, systemic roots. Changes in individual attitudes and behaviors are rarely sufficient to resolve such problems. The civil rights movement, for example, radically transformed American attitudes about race and dramatically reduced overt expressions of prejudice. Yet, fifty years later, millions of African American, Hispanic, and Native American children still attend segregated and substandard schools, in part because American racism is perpetuated as much by the economics of homeownership as by individual ill will. Similarly, peaceful sentiments alone are unlikely to dismantle structures of militarism that are thoroughly interwoven with the livelihood of millions of people.

The problem with structural analysis, though, is that it does not provide a starting point for social transformation. If the problem is everywhere, it is also nowhere: no point in the system, it may seem, is sufficiently central to become a focal point of change. As a result, structural analysis readily leads to despair. This despair is especially apparent in the recent American response to global warming. The scientific evidence linking carbon dioxide emissions to potentially cataclysmic climate change is now generally accepted by the public, yet the buying and driving practices of Americans are virtually unchanged, and there is no groundswell of support for the Kyoto accords. And the increasing awareness that the modest emissions caps prescribed by Kyoto would scarcely make a dent in the problem only exacerbates the sense of despair.

For some on the Left, moreover, structural analysis leads to an overly negative approach to social change. The "structure" is identified with a few powerful individuals or institutions, and these institutions are subject to unrelenting attack. This approach has been all too widespread during the George W. Bush administration. George Bush, Dick Cheney, and others are easily demonized for their coziness with large corporations, their eagerness to go to war, and their incompetence in managing that war. Making fun of the powerful is enjoyable, and it sometimes builds esprit de corps among activists. But it has allowed too many Americans to avoid asking the hard questions about how administration policies flow from patterns of overconsumption and addiction to cheap energy that are shared by virtually all of us.

Though Catholic Workers have not been immune to either despair or excessive negativity, at their best they offer an approach that recognizes that if a problem is everywhere its solution can start anywhere. This point can, perhaps, be best illustrated with reference to the enormous challenge of global climate change. Though the Catholic Worker has in recent decades been more associated with issues of war and homelessness, the decentralized economics of Peter Maurin's Green Revolution provide one of the most promising solutions to global warming.

In the 1930s, Maurin's suggestion that the urban poor relocate to self-sustaining agricultural villages was often dismissed as a quixotic attempt to "repeal the Industrial Revolution." But today it is widely accepted that the Industrial Revolution must, in some respects, be repealed, for the fossil fuels that made it possible are simultaneously running dry and destroying the health of the planet. It is also becoming apparent that such a "repeal" would not necessarily result in economic collapse or dramatic population decline: some studies, for example, have found that it is possible to produce more food per acre using small-scale, labor-intensive organic techniques than with conventional methods. As a result of such insights, and despite the failure of the United States government to take meaningful action on global warming, a new ecological society is already taking shape within the shell of the old. This society can be seen in the proliferation of Community Supported farms that sell their produce directly to consumers, in the popularity of farmers markets and natural food cooperatives, and in the creation of "eco-villages" in both rural areas and urban centers.

Catholic Workers have been intimately involved in many of these initiatives. At the same time, the Catholic Worker movement has the potential to shed a bright light on an important shortcoming of the new economy: it has not truly made room for the poor. Because the new economy relies on the good will of consumers, it has focused too much of its energy on producing luxury products for well-educated, professional-class liberals. When Catholic Workers get involved in organic farms or food cooperatives, on the other hand, they do so not only for the sake of their own nutrition but also in order to feed the hungry. And when they invite the poor to participate as well in such ventures, they help to ensure that the new economy will truly work for everyone.

It is possible, in short, to save the world by practicing the works of mercy. But this will happen, I suspect, only if Catholic Workers are more willing to share what has long been an open secret in the movement: practicing the works of mercy is a source of great joy. Ultimately, people come to the Worker not to save the world but to save themselves—from isolation, from aimlessness, from despair. In the movement they find hard work, companionship, purpose, and friendship. Larry Purcell of the Redwood City (California) Catholic Worker made the point provocatively but accurately when he told Rosalie Troester that "Catholic Worker houses are for the Workers who live in them, and I think it's important to be clear about that. . . . You try to set up an environment that makes sense out of everyday life in the Gospels. And it's not making sense out of everyday life in the Gospels if you can't be a good lover. If you can't develop and hold on to dear relationships. If you can't relax. If there isn't a quality of joy."[2]

Dorothy Day is often praised for her self-denial, her willingness to tolerate the extremes of poverty. But she herself said that through the works of mercy "[I] found myself, a barren woman, the joyful mother of children."[3] Countless other Workers have experienced the same transformation simply by feeding the hungry, sheltering the homeless, and comforting the afflicted. It is in these simple yet radical actions that the movement will find its future.

[1] Peter Maurin, "Institutions vs. Corporations," *Easy Essays* (Chicago: Franciscan Herald Press, 1977), 105.

[2] Larry Purcell in Rosalie Riegle Troester, *Voices from the Catholic Worker* (Philadelphia: Temple University Press, 1993), 354.

[3] Dorothy Day, *The Long Loneliness* (New York: Harper & Row, 1952), 285.

Acknowledgments

I began work on this book eight years ago, during my first year of teaching at the College of Saint Benedict and Saint John's University. I was searching for ways to connect my teaching with my personal commitments to nonviolence, anarchism, and intentional community. As I searched, I encountered student after student who had been personally touched by the Catholic Worker movement. Through these students, I soon encountered an extraordinary group of Saint Ben's and Saint John's alums who were living at Catholic Worker houses. My first debt of gratitude is thus to Chris Gamm, Mike Sersch, Christine Munger, Kate Dugan, Rachel Castor, Eric LeCompte, Reba and Scott Mathern-Jacobson, Paul and Sara Freid, Phil Steger, Chuck Berendes, and Gary Brever for teaching me that the ideals of the Catholic Worker mean as much to the millennial generation as they did to the children of the Depression. I also thank Tom Heuser and the rest of the community at Saint Catherine of Genoa Catholic Worker for introducing me to the contemporary Catholic Worker movement during my graduate school years.

Between 1999 and 2006, I visited a number of Catholic Worker communities and interviewed about thirty-five Workers. Though these interviews are described more fully in my previous book, *Touching the World,* this book would not be possible without the insights so generously shared by all the people I interviewed and the hospitality so generously extended by community members at the New York Catholic Worker, Viva House in Baltimore, the Des Moines Catholic Worker, the Winona Catholic Worker, Loaves and Fishes in Duluth, the Anathoth Community Farm, Haley House in Boston, Saints Martin and Thérèse Catholic Worker in Worcester, and Saint Martin de Porres Catholic Worker in Hartford. I am also grateful to Chris Gamm for conducting several interviews on my behalf.

As I translated these experiences into two books, I benefited greatly from a series of research releases provided by the Saint John's School of Theology and from a full-year sabbatical granted by Saint Ben's and Saint John's. I thank the Henry Luce Foundation and the Association of Theological Schools for extending me a Henry Luce III Fellowship during my sabbatical year. I also thank the editors of *Church History* for their help in refining the argument of chapter 6, and for extending permission to include portions of "Inventing the Catholic Worker Family," *Church History* 76 (March 2007): 84–113, in this book. Finally, I thank the editorial staff at Liturgical Press for encouraging me to use the material that did not fit into *Touching the World* as the basis for a separate book on the Catholic Worker movement.

Though this book had a long gestation, it had an unusually rapid birth. I am grateful to my spouse Tammy and my daughter Oriana for many things, but at this moment I especially want to thank them for their forbearance during at least two frenzied holidays. By the time this book makes it into print, they will know whether I have kept my promise to take a real vacation in the summer of 2007.

Index